Praise for
A BRIEF HISTORY OF
KOREA

T0247486

COLOR IMAGES

A BRIEF HISTORY OF
KOREA

**ISOLATION, WAR, DESPOTISM AND REVIVAL:
THE FASCINATING STORY OF A RESILIENT BUT DIVIDED PEOPLE**

MICHAEL J. SETH

TUTTLE Publishing
Tokyo | Rutland, Vermont | Singapore

Published by Tuttle Publishing, an imprint of Periplus Editions (HK) Ltd.

www.tuttlepublishing.com

Copyright © 2019 by Michael J. Seth

Front cover's top image © Robert Koehler Travel Photography

LCCN 2021302266

ISBN 978-0-8048-5102-2

27 26 25 24   8 7 6 5 4   2404VP

Printed in Malaysia

TUTTLE PUBLISHING® is a registered trademark of Tuttle Publishing, a division of Periplus Editions (HK) Ltd.

Distributed by:

North America, Latin America & Europe
Tuttle Publishing
364 Innovation Drive
North Clarendon VT 05759 9436, USA
Tel: 1(802) 773 8930
Fax: 1(802) 773 6993
info@tuttlepublishing.com
www.tuttlepublishing.com

Asia Pacific
Berkeley Books Pte Ltd
3 Kallang Sector #04-01
Singapore 349278
Tel: (65) 6741 2178
Fax: (65) 6741 2179
inquiries@periplus.com.sg
www.tuttlepublishing.com

Japan
Tuttle Publishing
Yaekari Building 3rd Floor
5-4-12 Osaki Shinagawa-ku
Tokyo 141 0032 Japan
Tel: 81 (3) 5437 0171
Fax: 81 (3) 5437 0755
sales@tuttle.co.jp
www.tuttle.co.jp

CONTENTS

Korean Peninsula

CHINA

RUSSIA

Mt Paektu
2,744 m

Tumen River

Yalu River

NORTH KOREA

Taedong River

Pyongyang

Sea of Japan

Kaesong

TAEBAEK MOUNTAINS

Seoul

Incheon

Han River

Yellow Sea

SOUTH KOREA

SOBAEK MOUNTAINS

Nakdong River

Gyeongju

Gwangju

Busan

JEJU ISLAND

JAPAN

126°E

130°E

Introduction

A way from the world's main crossroads, in the shadow of China and Japan, Korea was a land little known outside of East Asia. It was one of the last countries in the world to be visited by Westerners. The first book in English on Korea, William Griffis' *Corea, the Hermit Nation*, published in 1882, was written by an American in Japan who had never been to Korea or met any Westerner who had. Long after it had been "opened" to the outside world, Korea seldom drew much attention. The scarcity of books on Korea testified to the lack of interest held in the West and much of the rest of the world for this peninsular land in Northeast Asia.

In recent years, however, this has changed considerably. South Korea has attracted attention with its breathtakingly fast transformation from poverty to prosperity, its globally popular smartphones and other products, and its vibrant entertainment industry. And who hasn't heard about North Korea, or doesn't recognize the image of its young dictator with a weird haircut?

Yet Korea still is not well understood by most outsiders. The existence today of two very different Koreas only adds to the challenge of comprehending this ancient land. And how different they are! South Korea is a wealthy, high-tech center of international industry and entertainment. Its people are among the world's most diligent travelers—few countries have such a high percentage of the population trotting across the globe each year. It is an open, democratic country; indeed, one of the most democratic countries in Asia. Seoul, its capital, is a dynamic, hyper-modern city. Then there is North Korea, the world's most isolated state, the only one whose ordinary citizens are not allowed access to the World Wide Web. The one place without Coca-Cola. An impoverished society whose people

suffer from high rates of malnutrition, and live under what is arguably the world's least democratic, most repressive government.

How did it happen that one of the world's oldest and most ethnically homogeneous states developed into such two different societies in a couple of generations? How can we explain why they
developed along paths that were not only radically different but both
very unusual? And just who are Koreans, anyway? How are they
different from Chinese and Japanese? How does their story fit into
the larger narrative of the history of humanity?

These are a few of the questions that this book will try to address.
At the same time, it presents the story of Korea, which is interesting
in itself. There are many good tales in the history of this ancient
land; this book will tell some of them.

Shaped Like a Rabbit: The Geography of Korea

Korea looks small sitting next to China and Russia on the world
map, but it's not so small. It has a population of seventy-five million
people—fifty million in South Korea and twenty-five million in
North—making for a total somewhat larger than Britain's and a little
smaller than Germany's. North Korea covers about the same area as
England or New York State, while South Korea is a little smaller; in
its entirety, Korea is roughly equivalent in area to Great Britain. Koreans say their country is shaped like a rabbit, with the northeast
forming the long bunny ears. It also resembles Italy in that it is
mostly a long peninsula anchored to the mainland in the north by
a mountainous region.

The country is some 1,000 kilometers (621 miles) long and aver-
ages about 200 kilometers (124 miles) in width. A great chain of
mountains, the Taebaek Range, covers most of the northeast and
runs like a spine along the eastern part of the country. The Taebaek
Range has spurs; the most important of these, the Sobaek Range,
forms an arc separating the southeast region from the other parts of
the country. The mountains are not high, reaching only 2,000 meters
(6,562 feet) in South Korea and over 2,700 meters (8,858 feet) on
North Korea's border with China, but are rugged enough to hinder
overland travel. Most of the country's rivers flow from this eastern

spine westward into the Yellow Sea. There are no broad plains; in fact, no matter where you go in Korea you are in sight of mountains. Because it is a well-defined peninsula bordered on the north by mountains and on three sides by the sea, Korea forms a distinctive geographical area attached to but not integrated into the mainland of Asia. Its current borders (that is, of North and South Korea together) were formed six centuries ago. Since then, the end of the Korean world has been Paektu (or Baektu) Mountain, a 2,744-meter (9,003 foot) volcano, and the two rivers that flow from it: the Tumen River, which heads northeast and empties into the East Sea (Sea of Japan), and the Yalu River, which flows southwest to the Yellow Sea.

Despite its modest size, there is a considerable temperature range, from long, bitter cold winters in the northeast that would challenge the most rugged New Englander to the milder weather on the southern coast, where it only occasionally becomes cold enough to snow. The weather changes dramatically with the seasons. In the winter, dry cold air from Mongolia and Siberia spreads over the peninsula, often accompanied by frigid winds. In the summer, the great land mass of Asia heats up, sucking in moist air from the Pacific and thus bringing about the summer monsoons; this is when the country receives the better part of its rain. Most of the country becomes a tropical steam bath, with heavy downpours that bring only a brief respite from the heat.

The arable land in Korea is limited, but fertile and well-watered. As a result, for much of its history it has been fairly densely populated. The people are mostly concentrated in four "rice bowls"—the largest pockets of good farmland—consisting of the Naktong basin in the southeast, in an area known as Gyeongsang; the southwest area of Jeolla; the Han basin, near the center of the peninsula where Seoul lies; and the Daedong basin in the north where Pyongyang, North Korea's capital, is situated. As the Naktong basin, Jeolla, and most of the Han basin are in the south, with the Daedong basin and a small part of the Han basin in the North, South Korea has most of the good agricultural land. The seas around Korea are rich in sea life, so fish, squid, and other ocean products have been an important part of the diet. However, Koreans are mountain people, not sea people, and have historically not been much for seafaring. This might be surprising, since few live far from the ocean, but the seas around Korea, except for the south coast, are not friendly to navigation. The east coast has good harbors but is cut off from the populated areas by mountains. The west coast has shifting sandbars, barely immersed reefs, and some of the world's highest tides, making navigation tricky at best.

In premodern times, immigrants came from the forests and plains of the north; high culture from China in the east; and invaders from all directions. Koreans have called themselves a "shrimp among whales," meaning they are a small country surrounded by much bigger ones. These include China, which for the past two thousand years has been the world's most populous country and one of the most territorially massive; Japan, which has historically had about three times Korea's population; and the vast continental empire of Russia. In earlier times, before Russia spread all the way east, the whale to the north was one of various nomad empires such as the Mongols and the Manchus. Furthermore, while China's northeast region of Manchuria shares the Korean border today, for most of its history this region was not Chinese but part of the steppe and forest peopled by some of the world's most formidable warrior groups. However, China was close enough to be the source of most of Korea's ideas about government, society, art, literature, and religion.

The 185-kilometer (115-mile) Korea Strait separates the peninsula from the Japanese archipelago—just wide enough to make these very different lands, but narrow enough to ensure frequent interaction. In fact, Korea has often been a bridge between Japan and the mainland. Sometimes this has meant that Korea acted as an emissary, bringing Chinese-derived culture to Japan; at others it meant that Japan viewed Korea as its avenue to a continental empire.

In any event, this is Korea, a geographically compact peninsula, fertile enough to support a large agricultural population. A land isolated enough by mountains and seas to develop its own culture and society, but also close enough to China to be powerfully influenced by it. Modest in size, it has at all times been under the threat of conquest and absorption by its powerful neighbors. Yet Korea has somehow managed to maintain its political autonomy most of the time, and its distinctive culture and identity always.

A Note on Romanization

The Korean writing system, called Hangul, works well for Korean, but is difficult to convert into the Roman alphabet. Having no tones, the Korean sound system in no way resembles or sounds like Chinese—the two are completely unrelated—but it is radically different from European languages as well. The sounds are tricky: there are three different "k" sounds and three "ch," "p," and "t" sounds, as well as two "s" sounds. Furthermore, the same letter can be pronounced differently depending on the sound that precedes or follows it, so the problems multiply. For many years there was no standard way of romanizing Korean. For example, the common names romanized as Lee, Yi, and Rhee, and the less common ones written Lie and Ri, are all the same name. This author remembers traveling along a highway that led, according to the signs, to Sorak Mountain, but later the road signs began to refer to Seolag Mountain. One provincial government wrote the name of this rocky, beautiful, and popular mountain in one way; the next in another.

American scholars developed the McCune-Reischauer system for writing Korean in the Roman alphabet, and this gradually became the accepted practice in scholarly literature. Then, in 2000, the South Korean government came up with the Revised Romanization system. Now writers on Korea have two systems to choose from, which presents quite a dilemma, since they can be quite different. In this book I have chosen to use the Revised Romanization system, even though I have used McCune-Reischauer in my other books, in the belief that this newer system is likely to become the more common one in the near future. In some cases, when a person or thing is more widely known by a different spelling, I use that one. For example, instead of writing the South Korean president's name as "Pak Jeonghui," I write it as "Park Chung Hee," the way it more commonly appears.

Korea and Its Neighbors

RUSSIA

Khabarovsk

MONGOLIA

CHINA

MANCHURIA

Vladivostok

Sea of Japan

Beijing

Pyongyang

Seoul

KOREA

Ulleungdo

Dokdo

JAPAN

Toky

Busan

Osaka

Yellow Sea

Korea Strait

Fukuoka

Shanghai

Taipei

TAIWAN

CHAPTER 1

ORIGINS

Bears, Gods, and Mountains: Mythical Origins of Korea

A ccording to a popular legend, Korean history began almost five thousand years ago when the deity Hwanung descended from heaven to a high mountain. There he was approached by a tigress and a she-bear who wished to become human. Hwanung gave them each some sacred herbs and cloves of garlic and asked them to stay out of the sun for 100 days. The she-bear climbed into her den as requested and stayed there, but the tigress became restless and ventured out after a few days. Clearly the she-bear was more trustworthy, and in the spring, Hwanung transformed her into a woman and had intercourse with her. As the story goes, on October 3, 2333 BCE, their son Dangun founded the first Korean state, which was called Gojoseon. The date on which Dangun's kingdom was established marks the beginning of Korean history, and is still a national holiday in South Korea. Modern tradition has identified the mountain where Dangun was born as Mount Paektu, which lies on the border of Korea and China. Koreans today are proud of having "five thousand years of history." (This claim is based on the founding of Dangun's kingdom plus a generous rounding off.)

First recorded in the thirteenth century during a time when Korea was being overrun by the Mongols, the Dangun myth has reinforced in Koreans a belief that they are an ancient and distinct people with their own history. The myth identifies what it means to be Korean, starting with their love of mountains. Mountains in Korea are sacred places where shamans still perform rituals. Important Buddhist temples are located in the mountains, so Buddhists as well as shamanists go off to the mountains to pray; furthermore, almost every Buddhist temple has a shrine to Sanshin, the mountain spirit.

Today Koreans celebrate mountains mostly by climbing them. Hiking is a national pastime; Koreans are ardent hikers. No matter where one goes in Korea, there is always a mountain in sight, and a hiking trail up it not far away. The mountain associated with Dangun, Mount Paektu (Whitehead), is Korea's most sacred peak, mentioned in South Korea's national anthem and depicted on North Korea's national emblem. Mount Paektu was regarded as special by the Manchus and other Northeast Asian peoples as well. It towers over the area with a small crater lake called Cheonji (Heaven Lake) at the top. The Dangun myth therefore places the origins of the Korean people at the border with Manchuria. This is not far from the historical truth, since almost all modern Koreans are at least partially descended from Manchurian tribes. The garlic that the god gave the she-bear is significant to the Korean identity as well; Koreans boast the highest per-capita consumption of garlic in the world.

Important as it may be, not every Korean historian began the story of his land with Dangun. Some started with the story of Gija, a relative of the last Shang-dynasty Chinese emperor, who fled to the Korean peninsula when the dynasty fell in 1122 BCE. According to this legend, it was Gija who introduced agriculture, sericulture (silk making), literature, and all the refinements of civilization to the Korean people. He went on to rule the Korean state of Gojoseon. For historians who emphasized this story, Korean history began when Koreans became civilized; furthermore, the Gija story linked their society with that of ancient China, which was regarded as the home of true civilization. From China flowed ideas about religion, ethics, government, law, art, and literature, and it was from China that Koreans acquired literacy.

In modern times, Korean nationalists were uncomfortable with the Gija myth, since it suggested that Korean culture was derivative rather than original, and subservient to outsiders rather than independent. Dangun, by contrast, appealed to nationalists, as it supported their belief in Korea as being home to a unique people with a culture older than China's. Today Dangun is celebrated in both Koreas—as a myth and symbol in the South and as a real historical ruler in the North—while Gija is nearly forgotten. Yet both myths contain important elements for understanding the facts of Korean history. Dangun represents the Korean people's connection to the mountains, forests, and plains of northeast Asia; Gija, the enormous impact China had on shaping their culture.

Cul-de-Sac and Springboard: Early Migrations of Peoples into the Peninsula

Who were the first Koreans? For thousands of years people migrated from Manchuria into the Korean peninsula. For some, the peninsula was a cul-de-sac where they settled permanently. Others took to the sea, using the peninsula as a springboard to the lush Japanese islands. The 185 kilometers (115 miles) that separate the southern part of the peninsula from the nearest of Japan's four main islands was close enough that some people crossed the Korea Strait. DNA analysis, reinforced by archaeological evidence, indicates strong links between the ancient peoples of Korea and Japan. It is possible that some of the migrations went both ways, with people mingling on both sides of the straits. We should not think of early Korea, Japan, and the mainland of Northeast Asia as self-contained areas, but rather as places where people and cultures mixed and overlapped.

The peoples who migrated into what is now Korea discovered a land nearly covered with forests that provided a rich variety of food sources—not only game animals, but also acorns, chestnuts, and edible plants including arrowroot, turnips, onions, and wild millet. The coastal areas teemed with fish, shellfish, and squid. Pottery, which is usually associated with agricultural societies (since hunters and foragers on the move did not carry pots), appeared ten thousand years ago, several thousand years earlier than in the Middle East or Europe. This suggests an environment with a sufficient abundance of wild plants and game to support at least a semi-sedentary population. Village life began in earnest, however, with the domestication of millet and pigs some six or seven thousand years ago, possibly as the result of Chinese influence. These were important additions to the people's diet, but the real transformation to a densely populated agricultural land began with the introduction of rice.

The Reign of Rice: The Introduction of Agriculture and the Rhythms of Korean Life

Korean society as we know it from historical records begins with rice cultivation. Rice is the chief staple of the Korean diet. The word for cooked rice in Korean, *bap*, also means "meal." A Korean lunch or dinner—or even breakfast—consists of rice and *banchan*, dishes eaten with rice. Koreans ate other grains, including barley, millet, and sorghum, but these were considered only poor substitutes for rice. When there was plenty of rice at every meal, life was good; when there was not enough and one had to eat other "coarse" grains or not much at all, life was hard.

The most common form of rice in Korea is the short-grained, sticky *japonica* or *sinica* variety, which was probably introduced from China four thousand years ago. It thrives in the Korean climate. Planted in the spring, it grows rapidly during the hot, humid summer monsoons, and ripens in the sunny, dry weather that follows in the fall. It yields well when planted in dry fields, but yields more when transplanted into wet paddies. Small streams along the mountain and hillsides can be channeled into wet rice paddies, part of the complicated rice-growing techniques that took many generations to perfect. Flat land is limited, but what is available contains nutrient-rich alluvium that rice and other crops thrive in. As yields increased, more people could be fed. This is how Korea, a small, mountainous country, was able to support a fairly large population.

Though the process of converting the forest to rice fields was a slow one, by 1000 BCE agricultural villages dotted the land. Since the cultivation and cooking of rice are so basic to the rhythm of life in Korea, one could say Korean culture began around this time. These early people left no written records. We don't know what they called themselves or what language they spoke, but they did leave behind something to remember them by: megalithic structures called dolmens. These often resembled a table, with legs and a flat top, while others are reminiscent of an upside-down *baduk* (go) set with the pieces on the bottom and the board on the top. Koreans were not the only ones to build these stone structures; dolmens dating from around the same time are also found in nearby parts of Manchuria and northern China, as well as in parts of Europe. No Korean megalith on the scale of Stonehenge has been found, but the numbers are amazing: more than ten thousand dolmens have been found throughout the country, far more than anywhere else in the world.

Around 700 BCE, bronze came into use for making daggers, mirrors, and other objects; by 300 BCE, iron objects were being used. Such artifacts from Korea are similar in style to earlier objects found in China, suggesting both had Chinese origins. Around the same time that iron implements emerged, Chinese sources began referring to a "Joseon kingdom" (now called Gojoseon or Old Joseon by modern historians to distinguish it from the later Joseon dynasty that ended in 1910). This, of course, is the same state that according to much later accounts was founded by Dangun. Some assert that the name Joseon is derived from the Chinese *chaoxian*—written with the character *chao* meaning dawn or morning, and *xian* meaning fresh or calm. This has been translated into English, with some literary license, as "Land of the Morning Calm," a title bestowed upon Korea by earlier authors that still appears in tourist literature. From the Chinese perspective, Korea is to the east, near the dawn or the quiet early morning, so it has long been assumed that the Korean pronunciation of these characters was the origin of the name Joseon—also written as Choson, which is the official name of North Korea. North Koreans call themselves *Joseonsaram* or "Joseon people"; that is, Koreans. (That name is used in South Korea as well, but not officially.) Recent scholarship suggests a less colorful explanation—that the name Chaoxian (Joseon) was simply the Chinese attempt to pronounce the name of an indigenous Korean people.

We know next to nothing about the early Korean state of Gojoseon. We think it was centered in the Liaoning region of southern Manchuria at first, and then moved to northern Korea, with its capital Wanggeom at the site of modern-day Pyongyang. Gojoseon likely had only the most rudimentary structures of a state; in fact, it may have been no more than a confederation of tribes. But it did have a king. The last king of Gojoseon, Ugeo, who is the first historically attested figure in Korean history, appears to have blocked or tried to monopolize trade between Wudi, the Han emperor of China, and the tribal peoples of the area, becoming such an annoyance that in 109 BCE Wudi invaded Gojoseon. The hapless Ugeo, facing one of the mightiest military forces of the day, was murdered by his own ministers, who then submitted to Chinese rule in 108. Thus China entered the Korean peninsula and a new phase of Korean history began.

Enter the Chinese: Early Chinese Involvement and Influence
With the arrival of the Chinese, Korean history took a major turn. From 108 BCE, parts of Korea were incorporated into the Chinese empire. Chinese settlements and administration were located in the northeast, again centered in the vicinity of present-day Pyongyang. This area (called Lelang by the Chinese and Nangnang by Koreans) was part of China for more than four centuries. It was a remote frontier outpost of the empire that had two main purposes: one was to promote trade with the tribal peoples of northeast Asia (Manchuria, Korea, and even distant Japan); the other was to keep an eye on them. In addition to Chinese soldiers and officials there were some Chinese settlers, but the population was mostly a mix of various people. From the "eastern barbarians," as the imperial annals called the Koreans, the Chinese imported wood, fish, salt, iron, and agricultural products in exchange for porcelain, silk, jade, bronze mirrors, and other luxury goods for the tribal elites. Along with Chinese products, the eastern barbarians also acquired artisan skills and ideas about how to organize society.

It was during this period that we can first put a name to the peoples that lived in and around Korea. According to a document from the third century CE, there were nine "eastern barbarian" peoples (meaning non-Chinese) living east of China. Among these were the Wa in the Japanese islands and several peoples who lived mainly in Manchuria, including the Buyeo, a powerful tribal federation. For Korean history, the most important of the "eastern barbarians" were the Goguryeo and the Han. The Goguryeo, a federation of warrior tribes, lived just north of Yalu River. Skilled horsemen and archers, they were culturally related to the nomads of the great Eurasian steppe, from whom they may have been descended. The Goguryeo first appear in Chinese records around 75 BCE as a group engaged in peaceful trade. However, from the first century CE they began to gradually move south, raiding northern Korea and stirring up trouble for the Chinese in the process. Not surprisingly, Chinese records speak negatively of the Goguryeo, describing them as volatile, emotional, difficult, and dangerous folk.

South of the great Han River, where modern Seoul sits, were the Han peoples—the Mahan, the Jinhan, and the Byeonghan. All spoke the same language, which is ancestral to modern Korean. Indeed, Koreans today, especially in the south, see themselves as direct descendants. Han'guk (Han Country), one of the common names for Korea, is the official name of South Korea. South Koreans often call themselves Han'guksaram (Han Country People), whereas North Koreans call themselves Joseonsaram, but both terms, Joseon and Han'guk, are common names for Korea. The three Han groups were farmers who grew barley and rice, raised pigs, plowed with oxen, and lived in small villages. They had earthen homes that were half underground, making them cooler in summer and easier to warm in winter. The Chinese describe them as being fond of drinking and dancing, a reputation that Korean farmers still hold. They were organized into "guo"—the word for kingdom—but were only tiny chiefdoms consisting of a chief who controlled a few villages, not really states.

The Mahan, the most numerous group, lived in the fertile farmlands of the southwest, and were divided into fifty-four guo. The Jinhan occupied the fertile upper and middle parts of the Naktong area in the southeast, and the Byeonghan the lower Naktong basin; both were divided into twelve guo. Thus the Han had settled in the two southernmost of Korea's four "rice baskets," while the Chinese controlled the northern Taedong basin; the Han River basin was a sort of neutral territory. The seminomadic Goguryeo were on the northern fringes of Korea, and a few less numerous tribal peoples lived in the northeast.

This was the situation when the Chinese empire began to disintegrate. Like its contemporary, the Roman Empire, the mighty Han Chinese state went into decline and was overrun by barbarians, and then disintegrated. After 220 CE the empire broke up into three kingdoms. The northernmost of these, the Wei kingdom, reasserted its power in northern Korea in a military campaign that destroyed the Goguryeo capital, lasting from 238 to 245. China was briefly reunited, but after 311, when the imperial capital of Luoyang was captured by barbarians, the empire collapsed. A smaller empire survived in the south, ruled from the capital at Nanjing, but northern China in the area near Korea was taken over by a confusing number of mostly short-lived barbarian-ruled states. Only in 589 was the empire fully restored. Thus, for nearly three centuries the Korean peninsula was without a Chinese presence, Chinese intervention, or the influence of a powerful Chinese state. These three centuries gave Koreans enough space to develop in their own way.

The Three Kingdoms of Korea

CHINA

GOGURYEO

Pyongyang

Hanseong (Seoul)

Gongju (Ungjin)
Sabi

SILLA

Gyeongju

JAPAN

BAEKJE

GAYA

Magic Eggs and Kings: From Mythical Chiefs to Early States

After the Chinese left Korea in the fourth century, the local peoples created three major states: Goguryeo in the north, Baekje in the southwest, and Silla (pronounced "Shilla") in the southeast. The three kingdoms then fought for supremacy for three centuries until Silla won and united the peninsula. Modern Koreans look back to this period as a romantic and exciting time in which the state of Silla, direct ancestor to their own country, emerged.

Goguryeo was the oldest and biggest of the three kingdoms. According to tradition, it was founded in 37 BCE by Jumong. The legend goes that a beautiful woman, Yuhwa, attracted the attention of the king of the Manchurian state of Buyeo, who made her his concubine. One day she was impregnated by a sunbeam and gave birth to an egg. The king, suspicious about what might emerge from this egg, fed it to some animals, but instead of eating it they guarded the egg until it hatched. Out came Jumong, a boy who proved to be a skilled archer (this is, in fact, the meaning of his name). Jumong's half-brothers were jealous of his skills and tried to kill him, but he mounted his horse and fled. When he came to a great river, turtles appeared and formed a footpath that only he could take, and he managed to escape, later founding the kingdom of Goguryeo.

Jumong-mania hit South Korea in 2006 and 2007 when the MBC television network aired its enormously popular eighty-one-part *Jumong* series. The show portrayed the boy as a rather spoiled step-child who gradually matured into a responsible person, becoming a national hero and uniting the Korean people against the oppressive rule of China. However, the public broadcaster KBS in 2010 and 2011 aired another historical drama in which Jumong was depicted as a tyrannical king. The truth is, we know almost nothing about him, or even whether he existed at all. Furthermore, the date the story gives for the founding of the kingdom is misleading—Goguryeo was likely a loose federation of tribal leaders that only gradually coalesced into a state, probably around the early fourth century.

To return to the legend, Jumong had three sons. One, Yuri, was designated heir; the two others by a different wife, Onjo and Biryu, saw no future for themselves and fled south. Each founded a kingdom. Onjo's, founded in 18 BCE according to the story, came to be called Baekje. Biryu's did not work out well, so he merged it with his brother's. Onjo expanded his state until he had conquered all the Mahan and built its capital along the south banks of the Han River, and his descendants ruled Baekje until 660 CE. Here, too, the dates don't correspond historically, since there is no evidence of a Baekje state until the fourth century. The first verifiable king was Geunchogo, who reigned from 346 to 375 and is mentioned in a Chinese document from 372. Some of the story has a grain of truth, though, such as the consolidation of Baekje out of the Mahan chiefdoms. And the location of the first capital, Hanseong, has been recently discovered by archaeologists at a site in southern Seoul in about the same place indicated by tradition. In 474, as a result of pressure from Goguryeo, the capital was moved further south in the Chungcheong region.

The third kingdom, Silla, emerged in the southeast in the Naktong basin in the fourth century. Tradition holds that it is the oldest of the three kingdoms, founded in 57 BCE among the Jinhan peoples by Pak Hyeokgeose. One day the elders of six villages met to discuss forming a kingdom, but could not decide who would be king. While they were pondering this, a strange light shone in the forest, where a white horse was kneeling before a large egg. Out hatched a boy. His body radiated light and birds and animals danced in his presence. Impressed—who wouldn't be?—one of the elders raised him, and at the age of thirteen the boy was selected by all six to be their king. Pak Hyeokgeose chose Lady Aryeong, who had been born from the rib of a dragon, as his queen. Together their little kingdom, Seorabeol, prospered; food was abundant and no one locked their doors at night. From Seorabeol emerged the state of Silla. Here again, modern historical scholarship contradicts tradition, suggesting Silla was probably the youngest kingdom. There are no historical records of its existence until 377, at any rate, when it and its ruler, King Naemul, are first mentioned in Chinese records. Since the legends concerning the founding and early history of these kingdoms come from Silla sources, it is not surprising that they gave themselves seniority. But the tale does reflect the actual historical formation of

Silla from a small city-state to a large one unifying the Jinhan. The capital of Silla became Geumseong, later named Gyeongju.

The three kingdoms were not the only states on the peninsula. The Byeonghan of the lower Naktong basin and the southeast coast never unified, but evolved into six tiny kingdoms referred to collectively as Gaya. The legend of their founding, first recorded in the eleventh century, centered on the sacred Kujisan (Turtle Mountain), where local chieftains were gathered for a festival. A strange voice was heard from the mountain, and then six eggs floated down from the sky and hatched the future rulers of the six Gaya states. They matured in only twelve days, and each one founded his own state. The legend holds that this took place in 42 CE, but as with the other foundation stories, this date is probably too early. The Gaya did, however, form a federation that played an important role by exploiting iron deposits and acting as a conduit for trade between Korea and Japan. Archaeological evidence shows they left impressive tombs with displays of artifacts suggesting fairly sophisticated state structures and a prosperous population. Yet the Gaya states were too small to maintain their independence, and were conquered and absorbed by Silla in the sixth century. They did leave behind one legacy, the *gayageum* or Gaya harp, a kind of zither that is the most popular Korean traditional instrument; it is still played by some Koreans in both the north and the south.

While it is hard to fully unravel the possible meanings that the magical eggs might have had for ancient Koreans, one thing is clear: the royal families were special. Their miraculous births, precociousness, and skills show they were no ordinary humans but had a connection with the supernatural world. Even the animals recognized their awesomeness. Who could question their authority? The detail about the turtles is interesting, because in other parts of East Asia turtles have negative associations. They are bad parents who lay their eggs and then abandon them, totally neglecting their Confucian duties to their offspring. In Korea, though, turtles are viewed positively and are depicted in iconography. This is just one small way in which Korea, while part of the larger Chinese-centered East Asian civilization, is also a separate land with its own traditions.

Besides these early kingdoms, another possible presence in Korea at this time was the Wa, the ancient people of western Japan. Japanese histories from the eighth century claim that the Japanese empress Jingu conquered southern Korea in the fourth century and set up a state called Mimana, administered by a Japanese official. This was later seized upon by Japanese imperialists to justify their annexation of Korea, claiming they were simply reuniting what had once been a single state—Korea and Japan. There is no evidence of Japanese rule in southern Korea, nor of the existence of an Empress Jingu. Nor did Japan yet exist; rather, like Korea, it comprised a number of small states, of which Yamato emerged as the most important.

In any event, since they loom so large in the modern Korean imagination and manifest some of the features that characterized later Korean history, let's take a moment to examine each of the Three Kingdoms in a bit more detail.

Horse Warriors of the North: Goguryeo

Goguryeo was the largest of the three kingdoms; at its peak it covered most of southern Manchuria, almost all of what is now North Korea, and the area around modern-day Seoul. It expanded southward under King Gwanggaeto, who reigned from 391 to 413. Gwanggaeto is best known for the description of his military accomplishments inscribed on a large stone erected by his successor the year after he died. It is the oldest written document authored by a Korean—though it's written in Chinese. Gwanggaeto's successor, Jangsu, whose name appropriately means "long-lived," ruled from 413 to 491. Jangsu further expanded the kingdom southward, going deeper into the Korean peninsula. The capital of Goguryeo was located near modern Ji'an in China, on the Yalu River. It is a beautiful setting; today the ruins are a UNESCO World Heritage site, but being a bit out of the way are not often visited. Jangsu moved the capital to Pyongyang in 427. This shift in location is important to settling the question of whether Goguryeo was a Korean or Manchurian state, as from this point on its center was firmly planted in Korea.

Goguryeo was a warrior-state, with an aristocracy of mounted archers. When not fighting they hunted deer, boar, bears, and tigers. As in ancient Sparta, young men from the elite class of this warrior state lived and trained together separately from their families, constituting an institution known as the Gyeongdang. These young aristocrats were taught to read and write while studying archery and forming bonds of loyalty to one another and to the state. Goguryeo's Central Asian roots are obvious in its customs—the whole mounted-archer tradition originated in the steppe, entered Korea via Manchuria, and then was introduced by Koreans to Japan. Aristocrats were buried in elaborate tombs painted with scenes of hunting, horse riding, and archery, as well as dancers and wrestlers. Women are depicted as mixing freely with men. There are also many animals, both real and mythical—dragons, tigers, snakes, and, of course, turtles. The vivid paintings give us a glimpse of a world that seems much more linked to Manchuria, Siberia, and Central Asia than to East Asia. Even their dress looks more Central Asian than Chinese or later Korean clothes.

For all its rough seminomadic warrior ways, Goguryeo gradually fell under the influence of China, in large part due to Buddhism. In 372, a Buddhist missionary from China named Seondo converted Goguryeo's leadership to Buddhism, and it was adopted as the state religion. Two centuries later, the kingdom was sending Buddhist missionaries to Japan; one of them, Hyeja, was an advisor to the famous Prince Shotoku. Among his other achievements, the prince, whose picture used to adorn Japan's currency, is credited with adopting the name Nippon for the emerging Japanese state. The same year Goguryeo adopted Buddhism, it established a Chinese-style academy in the capital to teach a Chinese curriculum to the elite.

Today there is some controversy over just how Korean Goguryeo was. Chinese textbooks today represent it as a Manchurian state affiliated with China, whereas Korean nationalists believe it was part of Korea. Both claims have important geopolitical implications. If it really was an extension of China, does that mean North Korea, too, is part of historical China? Or if the Korean nationalist interpretation is more accurate, does that suggest that much of Manchuria is really part of the Korean homeland? This disputed interpretation remains unresolved and is currently a source of tension between China and the two Koreas.

Between China and Japan: Baekje

In the rich agricultural lands of southwest Korea, with its milder, more humid climate, Baekje was a more cultured society than its rougher warrior neighbor to the north. Baekje served as an intermediary between China and Japan, supplying the latter with monks, scribes, and artisans. Nonetheless, its ruling family claimed Goguryeo origins and ultimately linked their heritage to the ancient Manchurian state of Buyeo. Like Goguryeo, Baekje was dominated by warrior-aristocrats who wore armor, rode horses, practiced archery, and were buried in tombs. But the art they left behind was more refined and showed greater Chinese influence. The tomb of King Muryeong, discovered in 1971, is the greatest surviving example of Baekje art. It somehow escaped the grave robbers that looted other tombs, and archaeologists found the remains of the king and his queen inside, along with more than 2,900 priceless objects, including their beautiful gold tiaras.

Buddhism was brought to Baekje in 384 by an Indian monk named Marananda. It quickly took hold, at least among the royal family, who were great patrons of the religion and built many temples. They were especially keen on the pagodas that came to dot the countryside, two of which survive today. One king, Beop (r. 599–600), became so devout that he banned the killing of all animals and ordered the release of all domestic animals and the destruction of hunting weapons. Not surprisingly, his reign was short.

As it had in Goguryeo, Buddhism acted as a conduit for Chinese culture, and Baekje gradually adopted Chinese bureaucratic institutions and customs. The greatest patron of Buddhism was King Seong (523–54), whose name literally means "holy king." He famously sent a mission to Japan that is credited with introducing Buddhism and literacy to that land. In fact, there were strong links between Baekje and the emerging state of Yamato. Many of the Baekje elite are believed to have migrated there and intermarried with the Japanese elite; indeed, the Japanese imperial family today is probably of partial Baekje ancestry.

The Bane of Buddhist Missionaries: Silla

The most isolated of the three kingdoms from China and civilization, Silla was the last to adopt Chinese-style bureaucratic institutions and the last to convert to Buddhism. A number of missionaries attempted to introduce the faith, but came to a bad end. The last in this line of martyrs was Ichadon, who in 527 made a number of predictions about what would happen if he were killed. His prophesies came true: when he was beheaded, the earth shook; his head flew off to land on the top of a nearby sacred mountain; and a tall fountain of milk poured out of his decapitated corpse. This was enough to convince the court and the aristocracy of the power of Buddha and they converted—or so the story goes. The Silla king took the name Beopheung ("the rising of the dharma"), built temples, and made Buddhism the state religion. About this time the state issued a code of administrative law roughly based on the Chinese practices, thus bringing Silla into the China-centered world in the sixth century.

Much of the change was superficial, however; underneath some new names and forms it remained a northeast-Asian warrior-aristocratic state with strong Manchurian and Siberian characteristics. Kings wore crowns of deer antlers and used jeweled bear claws as symbols of authority—a common practice in the region that was also used by Japanese emperors. Horse riding and archery were the most prized skills of the aristocracy, and shamanism remained an important part of spiritual life. Another link with the northeast was the bone-rank system, a hierarchy of hereditary castes with the "sacred-bone" lineage of the royal family at the top. The very title, along with the origin myths, suggests the semidivine nature of early kings. There is evidence that they may originally have had some shamanistic role as well; that is, the kings served as spiritual as well as political leaders. In any case, next was the "true-bone" rank of the upper aristocracy, including those that had married into the royal family. Below them were the head ranks, of which the highest, the sixth rank, represented much of the upper aristocracy who served as officials in the state. This rigid system of inherited status would remain a characteristic of Korean society into the twentieth century.

Representatives of the great aristocratic families were sent to the

Hwabaek, a council that met at four sacred spots near the capital Gyeongju. The Hwabaek had the power to decide the succession to the throne and to declare war. It also adjudicated disputes over property among the landowning elite. This, too, would be a longstanding characteristic of Korean society: powerful councils of aristocrats that shared power with the kings. A third institution of Silla worth noting was the Hwarang—literally "flower boys"—a confederation of young unmarried youths much like the elite archers of Goguryeo. Though the exact function of the Hwarang is a bit unclear, perhaps a hint can be found in a peculiar story about their origins that was recorded in the thirteenth century. It relates that the court was looking for talented young people, and finally selected two beautiful women. But they grew jealous of one another (jealous women are a common theme in Korean tales), and one got the other drunk and drowned her in a river. Instead of beautiful women, the court then turned to handsome young men and dressed them in makeup and fine clothes, which worked out so well that the institution of "flower-boys" was established. Most modern scholars believe the Hwarang served as a kind of bonding and training to prepare aristocratic youth for service to the state. They were supposed to be totally dedicated to the kingdom. When General Pumil learned that his only son, a Hwarang, had been killed, he famously proclaimed his regret that he had only one son to sacrifice for his kingdom. In modern times the Hwarang became a symbol of patriotism; South Korea's military academy is named after them. All this reflects another characteristic of society—the pattern of shared monarchical and aristocratic rule in premodern Korea.

Wars and Unification

For two and a half centuries, the three Korean kingdoms fought each other for supremacy. Silla emerged victorious and unified most of the peninsula. But it was a long process, and it succeeded only with help from China.

At first Goguryeo, by far the largest in territory, was the main contender for supremacy. In 433 Baekje and Silla formed an alliance against the northern power, but this did not stop Goguryeo from taking the Baekje capital of Hanseong in 475. Baekje's King Kaero died in battle, and the fertile Han River basin came under Goguryeo control. In the sixth century, Silla went on the offensive. It consolidated its position to the south by conquering the small Gaya states and gaining control over the entire Naktong valley and the southeast coast. Since Gaya had strong links with the emerging Japanese state, this blocked direct Japanese influence in Korea for the next thousand years. At the same time, King Jinheung (r. 540–76), under his general Keolchilbu, wrested control of the Han River basin from Goguryeo in a series of campaigns from 551 to 554. He then turned on Silla's ally of 120 years and inflicted a major military defeat on Baekje at the battle of Gwansan in 554, in which Baekje's King Seong and 30,000 of his troops perished. Jinheung placed stelae boasting of his successes along strategic passes. These have since been moved to secure locations, but hikers in the mountains of Korea can still see the facsimiles that have replaced them along these scenic spots.

For nearly three centuries, China was too weak and divided to pay much attention to Korea. This changed when the Sui dynasty from the north reunified China in 589. Not long afterward, the second Sui ruler, Emperor Yang, began an effort pacify the frontier regions and to emulate the achievements of the Han by expanding the empire. He subdued the formidable Turks to the northwest, then turned his attention to the northeast. The biggest prize was Goguryeo, but it was one that he failed to capture. He sent an army of 1,130,000 men into the region, attacking Pyongyang with a force of 300,000, but they were repulsed. Returning, they had to cross the Cheongcheon River north of the capital, and there Goguryeo general Eulji Mundeok inflicted a serious defeat on the Sui forces, partly by damming the river and releasing the floodwaters. Of the vast army from China, only 2,700 survived. Still, Emperor Yang did not give up; he sent two more armies in 613 and 614, but both were defeated. These setbacks cost him and his dynasty the throne, and the discredited Sui dynasty was replaced by the Tang.

Although undoubtedly exaggerated by Tang chroniclers in order to justify the new dynasty's seizure of power, these were surely huge setbacks for the newly reconstituted empire that the new Tang rulers could not let stand. After once again subduing the Turks, the rulers of the new dynasty turned their attention back to Korea. Tang emperor Taizong launched an attack against Goguryeo in 645, but was defeated by General Yang Manchun; he tried again in 648 with the same result. Taizong's successor, Emperor Gaozong, carried out two more unsuccessful campaigns. Long supply lines, rugged mountain terrain, and the harsh winters all contributed to Chinese defeats; even so, Goguryeo's success in repeatedly defeating the full weight of the largest empire in history up to that time is truly impressive. It is not surprising that modern Koreans look back to this era with pride. General Eulji, in particular, later became a Korean national hero, and one of the main streets in Seoul is named after him.

While Goguryeo was busy holding off the Chinese empire, Baekje and Silla were occupied with fighting each other. Queen Jindeok of Silla (r. 647–54) sent her official, Kim Chunchu, to seek assistance from every direction. Kim went to Japan and to Goguryeo (as if the court at Pyongyang didn't have enough on its hands), and went twice to China. Considering the dangerous nature of travel at that time, let alone the political risks, this was an impressive feat of diplomatic energy. He had some luck with the Tang, who needed an ally against Goguryeo. To curry favor with them, Kim got the Silla court to adopt Tang dress, encouraged his kingdom to adopt Chinese administrative practices, and even wrote Chinese poetry to the emperor. An alliance developed. The Hwabaek were so impressed by his achievements that they selected Kim Chunchu as king in 654 when Queen Jindeok left no direct heirs.

The Tang's plan was to invade Baekje by sea and conquer it with Silla's help. From there, they would launch a two-sided attack against Goguryeo from the north and south. In 660, Admiral Su Dingfang sailed his ships up the Geum River into the heart of Baekje, while Silla forces under General Kim Yushin crossed the Sobaek range dividing the southeast from the southwest. There, at the battle of Hwangsan Plain, the greatly outnumbered Baekje forces under General Gyebaek were defeated. King Uija surrendered at his capital of Ungjin. Some of the elite fled to Japan, and Baekje as a state disappeared from the map. Later Koreans see both Gyebaek and Uija as tragic figures fighting bravely against hopeless odds. The hero in Korean history, however, is Kim Yushin, a former Hwarang who was one of Korea's most famous generals. He went on to further victories, helping to bring about unification, and there are many stories about his resourcefulness. Once, as he led his men into battle, they saw a falling star and refused to march further as they considered it an ill omen. In response, Kim set a kite on fire, launched it into the sky, and announced that the star had returned and all was well in Heaven. Korean history recognizes Kim Yushin and Kim Chunchu as the two heroes who brought about the unification of Korea.

With Baekje out of the way, the Chinese and the Silla forces–the latter under Kim Inmum–together took Pyongyang in 668, and Goguryeo fell. This final assault was well timed, since the king, Gaesomun, had died in 666 and his two sons were busy fighting over the succession. It was a great victory; Silla had eliminated its rivals and could now rule the peninsula. Their Chinese allies, however, had ideas of their own: Baekje and Goguryeo were to be incorporated into the Tang Empire, and Silla was to become an autonomous part of the empire called the Great Commandery of Gyerim, with the Silla king as its head. Silla's king Munmu (r. 661–681) wasted little time rejecting the offer. In 671, he invaded Baekje and drove the Tang forces out, and in 676 he invaded Goguryeo and pushed the Chinese north of the Taedong River. The Chinese troops, which had been fed by Silla, now found their supply lines overstretched and had trouble supporting themselves. With the troublesome Goguryeo gone, the Tang relented, leaving the Silla to rule about two-thirds of the peninsula, including almost all of its good agricultural land and the great bulk of its population. The Tang set up a small puppet Goguryeo state in the Liaodong region of southern Manchuria, which historians refer to by the somewhat insulting name of Lesser Goguryeo. But otherwise they gave up on their efforts to control Korea and made peace with Silla.

Silla's victory was due at least in part to geography and timing. Goguryeo had a vast, sparsely populated northern frontier to defend; further, there were no natural barriers protecting its southern army, and it had to contend with Baekje. For its part, Baekje was vulnerable to invasion from the north as well as from the sea. Silla, however, was too far away to worry about a Chinese naval attack, and its capital region had a natural defense in the Sobaek mountain range, which curves around it. The timing was fortunate, as well: Goguryeo had exhausted itself fending off the Chinese, and by the time of Silla's final invasion of the north in 676, the Tang had largely ended their expansive phase.

At this point it might be fair to say the unification of Korea began. This brings us to the question: how old is Korea? There is no definitive answer to this. Does it begin with Dangun in 2333 BCE? With Gija? With the first historically verified state, Gojoseon, whose existence is supported by evidence that only goes back to the second century BCE? Does it begin in 676 CE, with the unification of most of the peninsula under Silla? That last date may not mark the beginning of Korean history, but it was the start of Korea as a political unit. From this time on, most if not all of what we know of today as Korea was under the rule of a single state—that is, until the partition of the country by the US and the USSR in 1945. There were two other states after Silla, but they were really just the same state given a different name under new dynasties. In fact, one can argue that the state constructed by Silla was in essence the same peninsular state that existed into the twentieth century. Within this state framework, a common culture and identity emerged that can be called Korean.

CHAPTER 2

BUDDHIST KOREA: THE SILLA AND GORYEO KINGDOMS

Unified Silla: Kings and Councils

W hen Kim Yushin and Kim Chunchu unified most of the Korean peninsula, they created one of the longest-lasting states in history. The Korean kingdom established in 676 continued in some form until 1910, and is the basis of the two Koreas today. It fell briefly in the tenth century, but was restored in 935 under the new name of Goryeo, and was renamed Joseon in 1392. Despite these name changes, it was basically the same state governed by many of the same prominent families. There were differences, however. The first two dynasties, Silla and Goryeo, were profoundly Buddhist; the Joseon was more Confucian. Thus, the unified Korean kingdom spent seven centuries in a Buddhist temple and five centuries before a Confucian shrine. This was not the only significant change. During the first two Buddhist dynasties, Korea evolved from a collection of semi-autonomous regional strongmen into a more centralized administrative state, and the aristocracy shifted from a group of warrior-elites to one of scholar-bureaucrats.

Silla was as much a coalition of powerful warrior clans as it was a unified state. The Korean kings were not the all-powerful rulers that are associated with Oriental despotism. They claimed great authority, but in reality, they had to share power with the great noble families of the "true bone" aristocratic rank. In fact, politics consisted of the struggle between the aristocratic clans and the monarchs, each trying to concentrate power in their hands. For a while the kings succeeded in creating a centralized state with themselves at the center, but then real power began to shift back to local nobles.

To counter the threat of the aristocratic clans, Silla kings needed two things: a loyal army directly responsible to them, and a dependable source of revenue. Before unification, Silla armies were headed by aristocrats and organized along clan lines. There was no royal army, so in the seventh and eighth centuries, Silla kings created one with recruits from Goguryeo, Baekje, and the Malgal tribes of Manchuria. Though royal military forces enhanced the power and prestige of the monarch, they were expensive, as was the staff of royal officials who were to govern the greatly enlarged state. Kings tried a number of tax systems to obtain revenue and gain control over the countryside, the most radical of which was the "Able-Bodied Land System." Derived from Chinese models, this was based on the idea that the state owned all the land. Agricultural holdings were periodically redistributed to individual households based on the number of able-bodied adult males each one had, and the households would pay taxes directly to the royal government. This ensured that rich aristocrats who would be able to evade taxes didn't obtain control of the best farmland.

Once historians thought that this was a system that existed only in theory, not practice. It was generally assumed that the state's ability to control society was too limited to make such this work. How could such a weak state, with so few literate officials, implement such a comprehensive and intrusive system? Yet a strange scrap of paper has challenged what historians previously believed. Most existing information about Silla dates from histories written two or more centuries after its fall, with few documents remaining from the dynasty itself. In 1933, however, some people were sorting through the Shosoin, a kind of storage house for possessions of the Japanese imperial family located in Kyoto, and they found an old piece of paper wrapped around an item. Upon close inspection, the paper turned out to be, rather bizarrely, a census record from Silla dating most likely from 755. On it were accounts of all the property in four villages in central Korea.

Following the categories of the able-bodied tax system, each household was classified in one of nine grades based on the number of members capable of public labor duty. Everything about the household was listed: the land; the types of fields—rice paddies, dry fields, fields for growing hemp; the number of mulberry, pine nut, and walnut trees; the number of oxen, horses, and even slaves. Historians had simply never thought that such a level of detail about villages far from the capital could have been known or recorded by the state. Perhaps, at Silla's height, the kings were more successful in creating a centralized state than was previously believed.

Besides creating a loyal army and squeezing more taxes out of the peasantry, the kings also strengthened their rule by promoting Confucianism, borrowed from China. Confucianism was a line of teaching dating back to Confucius (whom the Chinese call Gongzi and the Koreans Gongja), a fifth-century BCE thinker who emphasized filial piety, loyalty to the ruler, and respect for authority. Naturally, this system of thought would have been attractive to a king. Royal officials created a Confucian Academy with a curriculum based on that used in Tang-dynasty China to train scholars to serve the state. Lower-ranked aristocrats found this an opportunity for advancement to higher office. Many attended the academy, and hundreds went to China for advanced studies. Some of these men, proud of their erudition in classical Chinese and their knowledge of ethics, administration, and law, rose to high administrative office. One of them, Choe Chiwon, who served in government in the late ninth century, is still held in high regard for his literary talent. Still, they could never rival the members of the true bone aristocracy, who needed no credentials other than their family background to secure the top posts. Nor did Confucianism supplant Buddhism as the main belief system of the elite—that would come later.

Temples, Poems, and Wine: The Buddhist Aristocratic Society of Silla

The society the kings reigned over was a strictly hierarchical one, in which one's status was determined by the position of one's parents and grandparents. This was the case in Korea into the twentieth century. At the top were the aristocrats, whose status was based on bloodline and wealth—the latter derived from land and slaves. The aristocrats lorded over the great mass of common people, who were mostly farmers. These common people were divided into *pyeongin*, or "good people," and a lower stratum of "mean" or "base" people. The "good people" who made up a majority of the population were mostly independent farmers or tenant farmers working the land of some noble or perhaps royal family, with whom they shared the crops. Some were craftspeople. Commoners, like almost everyone else, inherited their position, and it was extremely difficult to rise above it.

Laws ensured that the social ranks were clear. The few commoners who somehow became wealthy were put in their place by legislation that limited the size of their houses, required their front gates to be modest, and restricted the size of their carts, which could have no more than three horses. They had to wear simple clothing that was clearly distinguished from that of the higher orders. These strictures applied even to their underwear, although it's unclear how this was enforced. Royal decrees prohibited common people from owning luxury goods to avoid "confusion of the ranks." For most commoners, that was not a problem, since they were too poor to possess much beyond the basic necessities. They led humble lives, but could console themselves that at least they were not "mean people"—a miscellaneous category consisting of various hereditary outcasts such as butchers, tanners, and ferrymen, as well as slaves. We don't know how common slavery was at this time, but the four-village register found in the Shosoin indicates that even some "good people" owned a few.

Like almost all premodern societies, Silla was male dominated, but compared to later eras, women seem to have had more opportunities, higher status, and fewer restrictions. Unfortunately, we only know about women at the top of society, who sometimes served as family heads—three became queens—and appeared to socialize freely with men. For aristocratic men and women, life was filled with festivals, pageantry, and parties. The Festival of Wine was celebrated at the palace with a winding water channel that held floating drinks. (This entertaining feature can still be seen in Gyeongju.)

Buddhism was the state protective cult; monks prayed for the kingdom and rulers lavished money on temples. Initially Buddhism was the religion of the aristocracy, who favored the Flower Garland (Hwaeom) sect, with its esoteric teachings and elaborate rituals. Aristocrats used Buddhist worship as a means to display their wealth, to make it known that they had the leisure to learn the rituals and demonstrate good taste. With the introduction of the Pure Land sect, which focused on devotion to Amitabha, the bodhisattva of mercy, Buddhism took hold among the common people. Followers were promised a reward in the Happy Land (also called the Pure Land), comparable to the Christian idea of heaven. It was an accessible form of Buddhism that appealed to the humble. No costly ceremonies, time-consuming rituals, or mastery of sacred texts were needed to achieve this wonderful afterlife that compensated for all the sufferings of this world—only prayers and devotion were required.

Silla Koreans were great builders of temples. One of the most important of these, Bulguksa, still stands today. During restoration work carried out on Bulguksa in 1966, printed prayers were found in the stupa that had been placed there at the time of construction in 751. They are the oldest known printed materials in world. Koreans didn't invent printing—the Chinese did—but they made early use of it to produce multiple copies of Buddhist materials.

Temples also required bells, and the Koreans were the greatest bell-makers of the premodern world, casting the largest ever made up to that time. One, the Bongseok temple bell, is still the world's second largest. The most famous is the Emile Bell, which can be seen in Gyeongju today. According to legend, the bell-maker failed in his first attempts to create it, succeeding only after he cast his daughter into the molten metal. Koreans believe her name can be heard crying out every time the bell is rung.

United Silla and the Wider World

Korea had to deal with the reality of being a small country wedged between China to the west, Japan to the southeast, and Manchuria to the north. An expansionist Yamato (or Nippon, as it renamed itself) posed a threat from the sea: a fleet of Japanese ships attacked Silla in 746. To the north it faced the Manchurian state of Balhae, which was a constant menace during much of the dynasty and had numerous clashes with Silla. Especially troubling for Korea was the fact that Balhae maintained good relations with Japan. The two allied themselves against Silla at times; twice, coordinated planned attacks were aborted. After 800, however, Japan ceased to be a threat, and relations with Balhae became more peaceful. In fact, the ninth century was a time of harmony with all its neighbors. With peace, trade flourished, extending to Southeast Asia and even to the Middle East via Arab merchants in China. Silla exported gold, silver, textiles, and ginseng—the last being one of Korea's most famous exports, prized throughout East Asia.

Silla developed good relations with Tang China; neither was a threat to the other since Tang was longer in expansion mode, and Silla and Tang had a common enemy in Balhae. Regular trade and diplomatic exchanges took place, but in a peculiar manner: trade was disguised as exchanges of gifts. Koreans sent missions to China in which emissaries bearing gifts for the emperor—so-called tribute—acknowledged him as the great celestial emperor who ruled all under heaven. In exchange, the Chinese emperor gave "gifts" to the emissaries and recognized the legitimacy of the Korean ruler. Hence, in theory, the Korean king's authority to rule came from the Chinese emperor, who received his authority from heaven. Thus, Korea was part of the tributary system through which the Middle Kingdom conducted relations with its neighboring states. Korea was often considered a model tributary, with its emissary given a special seat of honor next to the emperor. This tributary status should not be taken too literally, however; it was mostly a fiction to flatter the Chinese ruler and to link the authority of the Silla kings to the celestial emperor. In reality, Korea was a completely independent state, but the fiction served both sides.

Balhae—the Other Korea?

The question of whether Korea was united under Silla or whether there were two Koreas has animated Korean historians for three centuries. The debate centers around Balhae, Silla's northern neighbor. The state was founded in 713, and for two centuries, until its destruction by Central Asian invaders in 926, it was a formidable neighbor to Silla. Based primarily in southern Manchuria, it ruled part of northern Korea and at its peak extended to the Amur River on what is now the Chinese-Russian border. Its warlike rulers drove Tang and Silla together as allies. Silla built a wall across the peninsula—a miniature "Great Wall"—to keep it at bay. Yet over time, Balhae came under Chinese cultural influence, adopting Chinese as an official and literary language and sometimes engaging in peaceful trade with both Tang and Silla.

In the eighteenth century a Korean historian argued that Balhae, which often claimed to be a successor to Goguryeo, was really a Korean state; if this were true, the United Silla period was not actually a period of Korean unification but one of two Korean kingdoms. Ever since, Korean scholars have been asking whether Balhae was Korean. If this were the case, it would require a significant shift in our perspective on Korean history. The period of Korean political unity would be shortened, and Manchuria would also be a part of the historic Korean homeland, not a foreign frontier. Adding to the historical confusion are recent claims from China that Balhae was in fact somehow Chinese. All this adds fuel to the ongoing controversy between the more extreme nationalists in Beijing and their Korean counterparts as to whether northern Korea is historically part of China or whether much of Manchuria was historically part of Korea. Interestingly, if Balhae was a Korean state, the current division of the country into north and south would not be unprecedented.

Most evidence, however, indicates that while Balhae may have had some ethnic groups related to the ancestors of modern Koreans, including elements of the Goguryeo people, it was mainly a Manchurian-based state that was not ethnically Korean, having more in common with the later seminomadic empires of northeast Asia than with Korea. The great majority of ethnically Korean people lived in

Silla. Thus it is not unreasonable to regard Silla, with its institutions and practices that continued on in later dynasties, as the first unified Korean state.

The Good, the Bad, and the Ugly: The Latter Three Kingdoms

In the late 800s Silla went into decline. This is a familiar pattern; premodern history in general tends to be the story of rise and decline. A state or empire emerges and prospers; the population grows; its arts and crafts flourish, and it expands. Then it declines: its borders contract, its population shrinks, the quality of its crafts slips, and its intellectual achievements become less impressive. There are many reasons to explain this. The limits of premodern technology are a major factor—states reach a technological and organizational limit to their capacity to administer and control a large territory or population. Peace and prosperity encourage a growing population that is beyond the ability of their technology to feed and support. The weight of tradition also stifles innovation as new problems arise.

External factors often play a role, creating new pressures or upsetting the larger environment that enabled the society to flourish. All these things seem to have happened to Silla in the ninth and early tenth centuries when it went into decline. It was not alone; China's Tang, and to a lesser extent Heian Japan, also experienced a political and economic downturn at this time. Incidentally, so did Carolingian Europe and the great Abbasid Caliphate that ruled the Middle East. Historians—at least those who pay attention to such things—do not agree on why this happened in so many places at the same time, but something certainly was affecting much of Eurasia. By the later tenth and eleventh centuries most of the area, including Korea, underwent a politically reconstituted revival.

Both a symptom and a cause of Silla's decline was that aristocrats began to win the tug-of-war with the king. While this was happening, revenues to the central government declined, which further weakened the throne's ability to compete with its most powerful subjects and led to a downward spiral in the central government's authority. The state, and the society as a whole, also suffered from shrinking trade with China as that vast empire entered its own political and economic decline. As the Silla state weakened, local bandits plagued the countryside. Provincial aristocrats began forming private armies and calling themselves generals, a sign that much of the country was in the hands of local strongmen, or "castle lords" as Koreans often refer to them.

One famous regional strongman who emerged in the 840s was the maritime commander Jang Bogo (Chang Pogo), a man of humble background. He was in charge of a fortress off the southern coast of Korea built to fight pirates, but converted it into his own fiefdom. He expanded his power outward, controlling the majority of the sea lanes between Korea, Japan, and China, and became known as the "King of the Yellow Sea." Jang made a bid to extend his influence over the court by helping to seat a contender to the throne and then offering his daughter to the new crown prince. He was assassinated, but the fact that a total outsider with a questionable background came close to controlling the throne was unsettling to the established order.

An already weakening monarchy went into further decline during the reign of Queen Jinseong (887–97). During her decade of rule, the peasantry rose up and bandits took over much of the countryside—among them a gang with the interesting moniker of the "Red Pantaloons." While the kingdom was crumbling, Jinseong surrounded herself with handsome young men and "engaged in lewdness" (or so later historians reported). At the end of her reign, the kingdom was on the verge of disintegration, making her an object lesson in the folly of letting women rule. (Koreans took the lesson to heart; the country didn't see another female leader until the twenty-first century.) Soon afterward, in 900, Silla broke up into three kingdoms: Silla, Later Baekje, and Later Goguryeo. This period, which Koreans refer to as the "Later Three Kingdoms," lasted only until 936, when the country was reunified. It was the only period of disunity until 1945.

Three major figures emerged during the Later Three Kingdoms, referred to aptly by the historian C. Cameron Hurst as "the good, the bad, and the ugly." Gyeonhwon, the bad one, was a provincial warlord in the southwest who proclaimed himself king of Baekje in

900. His state, located in the area of the original Baekje, became known as Later Baekje. Gungye, the "ugly" one, was related to the Silla royal family, although sources are contradictory on the nature of the relationship. Exiled to the north, he made alliances with a couple of bandit leaders, turning on them when they no longer were useful to him. After killing the second, Yanggil, in 901, Gungye declared himself ruler of a restored Goguryeo—or Later Goguryeo, as historians have called it. Gungye's avowed aim was to destroy Silla and its capital Gyeongju, which he hated passionately. As being a king was apparently not enough for him, he announced that he was the Maitreya Buddha, the Buddha of the future. He and his sons wore elaborate outfits and staged ostentatious processions to awe his subjects. Claiming that he possessed the power to read minds and see into the future, he murdered officials who were, he claimed, considering acts of disloyalty or would commit them later. In fact, he seems to have been suspicious of almost everyone around him. After murdering a wife, two sons, and several trusted officials, Gungye was killed by his own generals, who then put Wang Geon, the "good one," into power.

Wang Geon's background is a bit murky. Like Jang Bogo, he seems to have had maritime connections, with a base of operations on the islands off the western coast. After succeeding his former boss Gungye, he renamed the state Goryeo, a name derived from Goguryeo. What was left of Silla, now the weakest of the three states, allied itself with Goryeo against Later Baekje, whose leader Gyeonhwon devastated the Silla capital. Then one of Gyeonhwon's sons, Shin'geom, murdered his brother, the designated heir, and imprisoned his father. Gyeonhwon escaped and fled to Wang Geon's camp. Wang Geon, who of course had plenty of blood on his hands, was able to pose as the avenger of Gyeonhwon, whose son had committed a most heinous act of unfilial conduct. In 935, the last Silla king abdicated the throne, recognizing Wang Geon as his successor; the following year Wang defeated Shin'geom and reunified the country.

This whole episode of Korean history—chock-full of murder, betrayal, revenge, and the final triumph of the righteous—is subject to varying interpretations. Did the conjuring up of the old Baekje and Goguryeo kingdoms mean Korea was not so unified? Were the people of Baekje, Silla, and Goguryeo ethnically or linguistically distinct? Historians don't agree on the answers. In any case, the history of this time has been written by the victors—that is, from the Goryeo point of view. Its historians were eager to put Wang Geon, the dynastic founder, in the most favorable light and to make the man he replaced (and perhaps assassinated) appear as villainous as possible. Emphasizing continuity with Silla, they portrayed its last rulers as weak but not bad.

The First "Real" Korea: The Goryeo Kingdom

Wang Geon began a nearly five-century dynasty that ruled the state he called Goryeo (also spelled Koryo). The English name Korea is derived from this name, and Goryeo is still one of the common names used by Koreans for their country, along with Joseon and Han'guk. Was Goryeo a new state or just a new dynasty? Mostly the latter. The name was derived from Goguryeo, and the capital shifted northward to Kaesong, fifty kilometers (thirty-one miles) north of Seoul, just inside the modern North Korean border (it is possible to see it from the South Korean side). It had a good location near the center of the peninsula, in the important Han River basin. Gyeongju and Pyongyang, the old Goguryeo royal center, were secondary capitals.

Wang Geon was careful to establish himself as the successor in Silla. He married into the royal Kim family and appointed Silla aristocrats to key positions in his government, and his chroniclers were careful to point out that the last king of Silla had designated him as successor. He left many of the existing officials and institutions in place. But many of the same problems remained in place, too. Goryeo, like Silla, faced the task of creating a centralized state out of a land of powerful warrior-aristocrat clans rooted in their home bases. The mountainous geography, with its numerous little valleys and ridges, reinforced the autonomy of the local castle lords. In an effort to bind these clans to his new dynasty, Wang Geon married their daughters, eventually winding up with twenty-eight wives. But this only complicated the succession when he died. Each of the great families he had married into had their own private army and aimed to put their son-in-law on the throne. The result was bloody chaos.

Wang Geon made only modest headway in creating a unified, centralized state. Those who came after him were more successful, especially his fourth son, who became King Gwangjong (r. 949–75). Gwangjong, who succeeded to the throne after a brief power struggle, was determined to enhance the authority of the monarchical state, and used several means to do so. He increased the power and prestige of the monarchy by proclaiming himself *hwangje* (emperor). He renamed Kaesong "Hwangdo," meaning "imperial capital." This was a radical step, since Korean kings had always accepted the Chinese emperor as supreme. Only in 1897, during the twilight of the Korean monarchy, did a king proclaim himself emperor again. Gwangjong also tried to weaken the aristocracy by limiting the number of slaves they could own, freeing tenant farmers, and carrying out violent purges of high-ranking officials from powerful families. None of these efforts proved successful in the long run. His successors abandoned the imperial title, avoided bloody purges of aristocrats for the most part, and let them keep their slaves.

Gwangjong did, however, take one measure that not only strengthened the state but truly transformed Korea. In 958, Chinese scholar Shuang Ji assisted the king in setting up a civil examination system to select officials for the state. That year, seven men were selected to serve the kingdom after passing exams testing their mastery of Chinese classics, their literary skills, and their knowledge of geomancy. It was a modest beginning, but gradually the civil-service examination became a path for ambitious aristocrats to achieve higher or lower office in the military or civil service.

The importance of the civil-service exams can hardly be exaggerated. Over time they transformed the Korean aristocracy, turning sword-wielding fighters who were as ready to defend the kingdom as they were their own lands into writing-brush-wielding scholars and bureaucrats who loyally served the state. The change came slowly; in Goryeo times the majority of officials still acquired their positions through family connections, but those who passed the exams gained great prestige and influence. The exams not only bound officials to the state, but also acted as a homogenizing force in two ways. First, aristocrats all studied the same curriculum, so they began to share the same culture. They also developed nationwide teacher-student networks and classmate bonds. A unified, shared culture among the aristocracy emerged, along with a shared identification with the kingdom they served. At the same time, the state benefitted from being governed by an increasingly literate bureaucracy.

As it was consolidating itself internally, Goryeo encountered three major external threats, all from the mounted warrior people of the north: the Khitans, the Jurchens, and the Mongols. The Khitans were the first threat, becoming Goryeo's new neighbors after they destroyed Balhae in 926. Wang Geon hated them, calling them "a nation of savage beasts." When they sent envoys with a gift of fifty camels, he banished the envoys to an island and let the camels starve. But this did not eliminate the Khitan problem. The tribe formed a Manchurian state called Liao and used it as a base to raid parts of northern China and Korea, invading Goryeo three times, in 993, 1010, and 1018. The Goryeo forces, which had the advantage of fighting in heavily forested and mountainous terrain—not the best environment for mounted archers to operate in—were able to score some victories, but still ended up paying tribute to Liao. The troubles with the Khitans ended in 1126, when Liao was conquered by a second group of warriors, the Jurchens. Being the ancestors of the later Manchu, they were even more formidable than the Khitans had been, but directed most of their attention toward China, eventually conquering most of the northern part of that empire. The Goryeo paid tribute to the Jurchen and were spared any major upheaval.

The Khitans and the Jurchens were not just a serious military challenge; they were a serious financial burden due to the costs of defending against them and paying tribute. Furthermore, the suspicious Chinese were reluctant to enter into maritime trade with Goryeo, since the latter had established tributary relations with the Manchurian warrior-states. With the overland trade routes closed off, Korea was separated from China—a loss for Korea, as it was the era of the prosperous Song dynasty, in many ways a high-water mark in China's premodern technological and economic development. Still, there was some trade, giving Goryeo a few opportunities to benefit from the extraordinary achievements and rich culture of Song China.

Meditating Monks, Competitive Aristocrats, and Rebellious Slaves: Goryeo Society

Goryeo, despite its limited contact with China, saw a growing Chinese influence reflected in its art, literature, and government. The elite wrote poetry in classical Chinese, dressed in Chinese fashions, and read Chinese tales. The kingdom also adopted Chinese historical traditions, employing historians to keep records; detailed accounts of each reign were written upon the death of a king, helping move Korean history into a clearer light. These accounts were later compiled into the *Goryeosa*, or history of Korea, a valuable resource for scholars. The history of Korea before Goryeo was also written; one such account, the *Samguk sagi* (History of the Three Kingdoms), is the first great work of historical scholarship to survive in its entirety today. Edited by Korea's most famous historian, Kim Bushik, and completed in 1145, the *Samguk sagi*, which covers Korean history from the founding of the Three Kingdoms to the end of Silla in 935, is our most important source for early Korean history.

In the Goryeo kingdom, society continued to be divided into three major social classes: the aristocracy, commoners, and low-born or "mean" people. The aristocracy for the most part comprised the same elite families that had dominated Silla, with some newer ones emerging and some old lineages disappearing. Each elite family was identified by place of origin. While many shared the family name Kim, they were from different clans: the Gyeongju Kim were descendants of the Silla royal family; the Gangneung Kim hailed from Gangneung province; the Hamchang Kim were descended from the old Gaya Confederation, and so on. Originally only the aristocracy belonged to these clans, but now all Koreans do, which is why so many today share the same few surnames. The many Kims, Lees, and Parks are subdivided into different clans named for their ancestral home.

Among the elite, the two sexes mixed freely. Men and women drank, danced, played cards (the earliest known playing cards are from Korea, but card games probably originated in China), rode horses, and even participated in mixed polo games together. Xu Jing, a twelfth-century Chinese visitor who wrote an account of Korean life, was shocked by the failure of Korean men to restrict the activities of their women. They even bathed together! Women could divorce their husbands and gain custody of the children, and could inherit property; in fact, family property was divided equally among sons and daughters. A woman kept her property even after marriage, and she could pass it on to her children. Women sometimes headed households. They did not serve in government, which was men's work; nonetheless, Korean women, like Japanese women at that time, were among the least restricted in the civilized world.

While Confucian ideas were gaining influence, Buddhism remained central to Korean culture as a state protective cult. Monasteries protected the kingdom not only by praying for it, but by literally fighting for it. Many temples had warrior monks who were skilled in the use of weapons and martial arts. Many were excellent archers. Kings and officials consulted monks for their spiritual assistance and advice. Still, rulers had to keep an eye on the Buddhist establishment. Monasteries owned huge quantities of land and slaves, and could emerge as a rival power to the court and the bureaucracy.

Korean "Samurai" and Korean "Shoguns": The Period of Military Rule

In the 1100s, the aristocratic clans were divided into two groups of lineages: the *munban* or civil officials, and the *muban* or military officers who carried out the older martial traditions of the warrior-aristocracy. Together they were known as the *yangban* (the two sides), since military and civil officials sat on either side of the king. Eventually, *yangban* became the common term for aristocrat. The *munban* were proud of being calligraphers, poets, and men of learning, and they looked down on the military lineages. They came to dominate state and society, while the *muban* declined in status and power and were increasingly left out of major decision-making. Even during times of war, civil officials were put in command of the forces above the generals. In 1170, however, this historical trend reversed itself dramatically when the military officials seized power in a bloody coup led by Jeong Jungbu, a commander of the royal guard.

While Jeong came from a powerful Haeju Jeong clan, he was part of the less prestigious *muban* military lineage. He and other military leaders felt increasingly sidelined from power and disregarded by the court officials. The ultimate humiliation reportedly took place when Kim Donjung, son of Kim Bushik, set fire to Jeong's beard, to the amusement of the court. It was the last straw. When King Uijong and his many courtiers were away visiting a temple, Jeong and his military comrades murdered most of the remaining members of the court. Then they exiled the king to the remote Geoje Island (this island, incidentally, served as an internment center for North Korean and Chinese prisoners during the Korean War). Uijong was later rolled up in a blanket and drowned, a way to avoid shedding royal blood. The crown prince was exiled to another remote island, Jindo; Jeong placed a puppet king, Myeongjeong, on the throne and created a Supreme Military Council to govern the kingdom. Many civil officials were purged, and while those that remained were allowed to continue to function, real power was held by the military rulers, their their retainers, and their slaves.

Jeong's coup unleashed twenty-six years of continual turmoil in the capital as generals plotted and ousted each other. Jeong himself was killed by a rival military commander in 1179. Meanwhile, chaos spread to the countryside, where peasants rose up against landlords and local officials, and slaves rebelled against their masters. The most famous incident occurred when a slave named Manjeok organized a general uprising of his fellow slaves, but was betrayed and killed. Everyone, it seemed, was rebelling or fighting. Buddhist temples proved no refuge from the disorder; rather, the warrior monks contributed to the violence and instability of the time. Unrest only increased when Yi Uimin, an especially cruel and corrupt general from a slave background, came to power.

The turmoil finally came to an end in 1196, when General Choe Chungheon murdered Yi Uimin and seized power. Choe restored order to Korea, putting down the peasant revolts and slave rebellions. He did this in part by appointing some of the rebel leaders to positions in government, meeting some of their demands, and relieving some low-born people of their status. He took control of the Buddhist monasteries, severing their ties to the courts and curbing the power of the armed monks, and exiled many Buddhist leaders who had been active in public affairs from the capital. He also re-structured the military to make it subordinate to him.

Choe's most radical move was to establish a dual government. He maintained the king, the court officials, and the civil bureaucracy with little change from before, but created a parallel "house govern-ment" directly under his control. The monarchs continued to reign, but only at his pleasure—he removed two of them when they be-came unreliable. Real power was in the "house government" staffed by his own retainers or by officials personally loyal to him. At its apex was the Office of Decree Enactment, which he headed. Choe was too clever to let untutored retainers completely run the govern-ment; instead, he appointed distinguished scholars from the civil lineages to serve him as well. So effectively did he maintain control over the country that he smoothly transferred power to his son Choe U, who further elaborated on the house government. Choe U was succeeded by his son Choe Hang.

The parallel military government of the Choe family was remark-ably similar to the Japanese shogunate created by Choe Chungheon's contemporary, Minamoto Yoritomo, in Japan in 1192. Yoritomo's rule marked the start of what is thought of today as "samurai Japan." In both Korea and Japan, effective power passed from the court-centered aristocracy to the military in the late twelfth century. In both, following a period of conflict, a strong, effective ruler created a parallel military clan government that held the real power while maintaining the monarchy and older civil institutions. Yoritomo be-came the first shogun, or paramount military commander, just four years before Choe established a similar military-led house govern-ment in Korea. Both Choe and Yoritomo made use of an elaborate system of military retainers and military leaders who pledged their personal loyalty to them.

How was it that such a curious but similar development took place simultaneously in both countries? Were they influenced by each other? We don't really know, since until fairly recently historians of Japan didn't pay that much attention to what was going on in Korea and vice versa. But clearly it could not have been coincidental. There were, of course, differences: the families that created the Japanese warrior-government that ruled into the nineteenth century came from provincial nobility, while the military rulers of Korea were more linked to the central aristocracy. Choe Chungheon came from a distinguished line that traced itself to famed Silla scholar and official Choe Chiwon. Still, the parallels are striking.

The two military clan governments resembled each other in another way: both patronized Zen Buddhism. Zen—or to call it by its Korean name, Seon, pronounced like the English word "sun"—was a form of meditative Buddhism that came to Korea from China. Its legendary founder, Bodhidharma, was a missionary from India who came to China and introduced a way of seeking enlightenment through quiet meditation. According to legend, Bodhidharma pulled off his eyelids so he wouldn't fall asleep, and they turned into tea plants. He meditated so long that his legs atrophied and fell off, which is why in Japan he is portrayed as legless.

Seon appealed to the military men for its discipline; it did not require ostentatious ceremonies or countless hours spent mastering sutras. Rather than having monks involving themselves in politics, the idea of having them engage in quiet meditation somewhere off in the mountains was attractive to the Choe military rulers, who were great patrons of Seon. An outstanding figure in Seon Buddhism was the monk Jinul, a contemporary of Choe U who founded the Seonggwangsa monastery on Mount Jogye in southern Korea, which is still a religious center. A unifier not a divider, his interpretation of Seon incorporated many of the practices of the rival Buddhist traditions. His sect, known as Jogye, after the mountain, is the largest denomination of Buddhism in Korea today.

The Mongols Arrive: Korea under Mongol Hegemony

We can only speculate how Korea might have evolved if the rule by the Choe shogunate had continued. Would it have developed a semi-feudal military system like Japan's? Would Korea have developed a samurai culture, too? There are reasons to think otherwise, since the

Chinese model of civil bureaucracy was very strong; even the Choe family respected the court and its traditions. In any case, it is impossible to know, since the Mongol invasions brought the period of military rule to an end.

Korea had seen many invaders from the great grasslands of Central Asia, but none as formidable as the Mongols. Numbering less than a million in all, the Mongols defeated almost every rival and created the greatest empire the world had seen. Goryeo had been threatened by the Khitans, then the Jurchens, but had been able to deal with these mounted warriors by resisting them, fortifying its borders, and, when necessary, paying them off with tribute. But none of these strategies worked when the Mongols came in the twelfth century.

The Koreans first encountered the Mongols in 1218. That year, the forces of Genghis Khan arrived at the border demanding that the Koreans pay tribute in the form of clothing, furs, and horses. The latter was particularly burdensome, since Korea's lack of grazing land made horses expensive. In 1225, the Mongol envoys were murdered by bandits and Choe U stopped paying. The Mongols, after a delay, sent an invading army in 1231. Faced with this mighty force, Goryeo agreed to start paying tribute, and the Mongols sent overseers to supervise the collection. The following year, Choe U murdered the Mongol overseers and stopped sending tribute, and the Mongols predictably returned with an even greater force under one of their great commanders, Sartaq. Choe, expecting a massive Mongol retaliation, had a plan.

As formidable as the Mongols were, they were not adept at moving across water. He therefore moved the entire government to the island of Ganghwa, a small ten-by-seventeen-mile island north of modern Incheon. An entirely new capital complete with palaces, offices, and temples was built on this tiny island just off the coast. From this bastion literally within shouting distance of the mainland—the Koreans would shout out insults to the frustrated landbound Mongols—the Koreans waged a war of resistance for the next twenty-six years. Sartaq's invasion ended when a monk killed him with an arrow and his forces left, but they soon returned. From 1233 to 1241 the Mongols launched continuous invasions, but failed to decisively defeat Goryeo. Finally, the Koreans agreed to pay tribute but would not leave the island.

Soon the Korean military leaders again refused to pay tribute, hoping the invaders would give up and leave them alone, but the Mongols resumed their invasions. This time they took up a new strategy of sending small forces to lay waste to the country. The results were devastating, with villagers massacred, homes destroyed, and fields burnt. A reported 200,000 people were captured and taken away as slaves. Korean histories record that the Mongols passing through a valley would kill every living thing, leaving not even a dog or a chicken alive. After four years of this, the last Choe ruler, Choe Ui, was killed in a coup—according to the chroniclers, he was too fat to climb over a wall and escape the conspirators. A new government agreed to truce terms, which this time included sending members of the royal family as hostages. Some military commanders still refused to accept Mongol suzerainty and continued to resist. The last Goryeo commander was defeated on what is now the modern resort island of Jeju in 1273.

The Korean resistance to the Mongols was certainly impressive. While it is true that the main attention of the steppe conquerors was on completing their conquest of China, no other state, other than the South Song in China, held off the Mongols for so long or endured so many repeated invasions.

From 1270 to 1356 Korea was a semi-autonomous client state of the Mongol rulers based in China. The Mongol leader Kublai Khan completed the conquest of China in 1279, which he and his successors ruled as the Yuan dynasty, making Beijing—or Khanbalig, as they called it—their capital. Goryeo, while a nominally independent state, was in reality an appendage of this empire. Members of the royal family spent time at the Yuan court in Beijing. After submitting to the Mongols and accepting them as overlords, the Korean king married his son to the daughter of Mongol ruler Kublai Khan. Goryeo kings also provided primary consorts to Mongol emperor king, linking the royal houses. Just to be sure of their continued loyalty, however, the Mongols also set up an Eastern Expedition Field Headquarters in Korea to keep an eye of the locals.

Lacking the expertise to build a navy, the Mongols ordered Koreans to build ships and supply sailors to transport a Mongol army to Japan in 1274. The invasion force sailed during the typhoon season; not surprisingly, after inconclusive fighting in western Japan, it had to return as a typhoon approached. For some reason the Mongols learned little from this experience. A second Korean-built armada landed in 1281—also in typhoon season—and was destroyed by a typhoon. The Japanese called these typhoons that saved them the kamikaze (divine winds) and later built a myth that their country was protected by the gods. But no gods protected the Koreans; these invasions and an aborted third one were costly burdens. Another burden, as well as humiliation, was having to provide women to the Mongol elite as tribute. For the women themselves this meant leaving their home country and family behind. But it sometimes worked out well, since many of them ended up married to wealthy and powerful Mongols. One, Lady Ki, the daughter of a low-level official, became the empress of the Mongol empire. The Ki family became one of the most powerful in Korea.

In some ways the Mongol-dominated period was not so bad for Korea. Korea maintained itself as a separate state with its traditional institutions and customs. There was only modest interference in internal affairs. The period of rule by the military lineages was over, and for the most part the pre-existing social structure and old ruling clans resumed their place in government. In fact, there was a significant positive benefit: Korea was now part of a great cosmopolitan empire. As never before or after, foreigners of all types entered the country. Koreans in Beijing and elsewhere mingled with Chinese, Mongols, Turks, Tibetans, Persians, Russians, and people from all over Eurasia. As a result, new ideas and technology were introduced to Korea, such as cotton and cotton weaving, and the use of gunpowder and the art of casting cannons. Another innovation that became important in Korean culture was distilled liquor; the colorless, potent, and popular Korean drink called *soju* dates from this time. New ideas about art and fashion were introduced; in fact, Korean traditional clothes still worn today on special occasions are partly derived from the fashions of the Yuan court. The most important influences came from China, especially Chinese literature and philosophy.

After the Mongols

By the mid-fourteenth century, the Yuan state had weakened. In 1356, Zhu Yuanzhang, a former monk, established the Ming dynasty in Nanjing and drove the Mongols out of southern China. In 1368, Ming forces captured Beijing and the Mongols were forced back to their homeland, where the remnant of their empire, now called the Northern Yuan, still controlled parts of Manchuria. Koreans became divided between those who remained loyal to the Mongols and those who sought alliance with China's new Ming dynasty. King Gongmin (r. 1351–74) saw an opportunity and turned against the pro-Mongol faction, abolishing the Eastern Expedition Field Headquarters. A few years later, Goryeo resumed its tributary relationship with China and adopted the Ming calendar.

Gongmin lost control of events when his Mongol wife died, however. Grief-stricken, he sat for hours each day staring at her portrait. Administration fell into the hands of his chief official, Shin Don, a monk from a slave background—two strikes against him in the eyes of the courtiers. Both the king and the monk were assassinated, and a couple of puppet monarchs sat on the throne while various strongmen and factions vied for power. An already volatile situation became more so when the Mongols tried a comeback, and Korea got caught up in the conflict between the Mongols and the Chinese Ming forces over control of Manchuria. Pro-Ming and pro-Mongol factions now contended for power in the capital of Kaesong. Meanwhile, a group of bandits known as the Red Turbans marauded the northern provinces, adding to the turmoil of the times. When the Ming began to build fortresses in the northern Hamgyeong province of Korea, the pro-Mongol faction in power at the time sent General Yi Songgye to attack the Chinese; he switched sides, however, and turned back and seized power in a coup. Proclaiming himself king in 1392, he ended the five centuries of Wang family rule and began the new Yi dynasty. The kingdom was renamed Joseon, and a new era in Korean history began.

The Mongols lost out in their attempted return to power and

ceased to be a factor in Korean affairs. Still, their invasions and domination of Korea had several consequences. They ended the period of rule by the military lineages, returning the rule of Korea to the civil aristocracy. The invasions themselves were terribly destructive and resulted in the loss of much of the country's architectural, artistic, and literary heritage. It is still painful to think of the cultural treasures that perished as the invaders pursued years of scorched-earth campaigns. The experience with the Mongols probably contributed to the fear of outsiders that characterized later Korean times. But being part of the Mongol empire also had the positive effect of exposing Koreans to foreign cultures and allowing for the flow of new innovations and ideas. Among the latter was the creed known today as Neo-Confucianism, which will be discussed in the next chapter. As this new ideology took hold, the Buddhist period effectively ended.

Legacy of Goryeo

Despite the ravages of the Mongols, Goryeo left behind a rich cultural legacy, including celadon ceramics, the *Tripitaka Koreana*, achievements in printing, and two great histories. Goryeo (Koryo) celadons were among the finest ceramics ever made; the beauty of the classic green-tinted vases and figurines with floral inlays has never been matched. They can be seen in a number of museums, and cheap reproductions are sold at virtually every souvenir shop in South Korea. Then there was the *Tripitaka Koreana*: 81,000 hand-carved wooden printing blocks containing the world's most complete Buddhist canon. On these blocks are carved fifty-two million Chinese characters—amazingly, without a single error! The blocks, which weigh 280 tons, would be as high as Paektu Mountain if they were stacked up. The *Tripitaka Koreana* that exists today is actually the second set, ordered by the king after the destruction of the original by the Mongols in 1232. The original set was made in the eleventh century over a period of eight decades, but the replacement set was completed just twelve years after they were started. Housed today in the beautiful Haeinsa Temple in southern Korea, the skill, effort, and care evident in the creation of this remarkable achievement are a testament to the strength of Buddhism in thirteenth-century Korea.

Printing was invented in China, but the Korean craftsmen, drawing on their highly skilled metal-casting techniques, developed the first moveable metal type, the basis of all modern printing. In 1234, two centuries before Gutenberg, the first known book was printed using this technology. The *Jikji*, an anthology of teachings by Seon monks printed in 1377, is the oldest such printed book in existence today. (To the annoyance of Koreans, it is kept at the National Library of France.) Of special importance to historians are the *Samguk Sagi* (History of the Three Kingdoms), mentioned earlier, and the *Samguk Yusa* (confusingly also translated as the "History of the Three Kingdoms"). Compiled by the monk Iryeon in 1279, the *Samguk Yusa* is as important for its fascinating collection of stories as for its account of historical events, although it does add to our overall knowledge of early history.

Perhaps the most important legacy of Goryeo was that it provided a long period during which Korea became a highly centralized state ruling over people with a common identity. The state was strong enough to survive the Khitans, the Jurchens, and the Mongols, and the identity proved durable enough to last to the present day. By the end of this period we can speak with confidence of a single Korean society and culture which is directly ancestral to the two Koreas of today.

CHAPTER 3

CONFUCIAN KOREA: THE JOSEON DYNASTY (1392–1910)

Frontier Warriors and Ideological Zealots: The Establishment of the Joseon Dynasty

Jeong Dojeon and his late-fourteenth-century colleagues had a vision of a virtuous society, one that would be in harmony with the Way of Heaven, where peace, prosperity, and human-heartedness prevailed. This vision, dubbed Neo-Confucianism by modern Western scholars, was based on a line of teachings derived from Song-dynasty Chinese interpretations of the ancient Confucian classics. The vehicle for fulfilling this vision was the newly established Joseon dynasty. To a remarkable degree, these scholarly zealots succeeded in their project of remolding Korean society in accordance with their understanding of the Way. Starting at the top with the king and his officials, they developed a set of institutions and values that penetrated deep into Korean society. It was a generations-long process, but by the eighteenth century Korea was the world's most thoroughly Confucian society.

When Yi Seonggye founded the new Joseon dynasty, he emphasized continuity over change. Even the name he chose harkened back to ancient times. He created no new institutions and conducted no massive purges. In fact, the new dynasty was for the most part dominated by the same families and officials that had served the old.

Rather than one dominant social group replacing another, a number of new people joined the ruling aristocracy of landed officials and scholars. Yi Seonggye was one of these: his father was an ethnic Korean who served as a minor Mongol official, and his mother was of Chinese origin. Yi came up through the ranks in the Goryeo army, where he distinguished himself in campaigns along the troublesome northern frontiers and against Japanese pirates. He was the last Korean leader with a military background until the twentieth century.

King Taejo, as Yi became known, had the support of some other military men and many officials who felt that the Wang family of Goryeo had lost the Mandate of Heaven, and of scholars who were eager for the opportunity to reform society. Taejo tried to gain acceptance, if not support, from the rest of the elite; many were won over to the new dynasty, but not all. The most prominent of those that resisted the order was the highly respected scholar Jeong Mongju (1337–92). Taejo tried to charm the learned man into accepting the new dynasty by exchanging poems with him, but Jeong was adamant in his loyalty to the Goryeo state. Taejo's fifth son, Yi Bangwon, less patient and more ruthless than his father, held a party in Jeong Mongju's honor and then had him murdered on his way home. It is said that bloodstains can still be seen on the bridge in Kaesong where this incident took place.

Even though the creation of Joseon in 1392 was not marked by a major upheaval, it was more than just a change of dynasty. Among Yi Seonggye's supporters were the Confucian scholars who had become enamored with a new form of Confucianism brought back from China. These scholars aimed at nothing less than to remake Korea according to their understanding of this ideology.

These Confucian zealots were all men of learning recognized by their peers, and were moral leaders in their communities. Though they have been termed "Neo-Confucianists" by modern historians, they would probably be puzzled by that designation, since they didn't believe they were creating anything new. Rather, their aim was to recapture the original line of teachings of the ancient sages that were refined by the old Chinese master, and to restore the moral standards that had been lost. It might be better to refer to them as they saw themselves: as Confucian revivalists. They often called themselves "followers of the Way," meaning the true way to virtue. To them, that meant living in harmony with the moral order of the universe, which, according to their beliefs, required placing the family and the state on a firm moral basis.

Many Confucian revivalists were teachers, but for most the highest calling was to serve in public office. In doing so, they could ensure that society was being governed according to correct moral principles. They were especially focused on the ruler, believing that he upheld the moral and social order of society through his personal example of virtuous conduct and by governing with concern for the welfare of his subjects. It therefore mattered greatly to them that the ruler maintained high ethical standards and a strong awareness of the moral dimension of his role in society. The leaders of this movement saw in Yi Seonggye and his family a new dynasty that could provide such rulers, and that could serve as a means of purifying Korean society.

Remaking Society in Accordance with the Way: The Neo-Confucian Revolution

The Confucian revivalist officials carried out their project with zeal, and succeeded in remolding Korean society to an extent that has no parallel elsewhere in East Asia. China never experienced such a sustained and systematic effort to remodel the institutions of its government and its society, nor did Japan or Vietnam, although both officially adopted Neo-Confucianism. Perhaps the best parallel to the efforts by the Neo-Confucian literati at creating a virtuous society can be found in the Islamic revivals prior to the mid-nineteenth century.

One way the Korean Neo-Confucian literati resembled the Muslim revivalists was their intolerance of any deviation from the orthodoxy. The Confucian revivalists were especially hostile to Buddhism. They chided monks for their moral laxity and their involvement in politics and criticized the expense of supporting temples and performing elaborate rituals. Monks produced nothing of value and relied on others to feed them, and Buddhism, in their opinion, did not respect the social relations that held society together. Its tradition of celibacy was a threat to family and lineage, and its concept of abstract universal love was inimical to the hierarchical love in Confucianism that gave primacy to family, then to friends, and then to neighbors. It encouraged withdrawal from society, not active participation in it. Buddhist monks devoting their lives to meditation and prayer were seen as self-indulgent, immoral people who neglected their duties to family and society.

However, this harsh antipathy toward Buddhism and other forms of worship such as shamanism was a minority view at the start of the dynasty. Members of the royal family continued to patronize Buddhism for the first century of the dynasty, and sometimes consulted with shamans. Indeed, the monarchs in general were less enthusiastic about radical change than the Neo-Confucianist reformers. Yet the reformers gradually got their way, and most of the temples in cities and towns closed. Buddhist places of worship were banished to the mountains and remote places where they continued to offer refuge and solace to those who needed it. Buddhism never disappeared, but it was marginalized, robbed of its political and economic influence as well as much of its intellectual and cultural vitality. Nor did shamanism and the worship of nature spirits disappear, but their role in society was weakened and shamans became socially stigmatized.

Confucian revivalists relied on several institutions to promote their reform agenda: the Censorate, the "Classics Mat" lecture program, and the civil examination system. The Censorate, which was originally borrowed from China and had existed in the Goryeo kingdom, became powerful during the Joseon period. It was, from a modern point of view, a peculiar and even sinister institution. It was a body consisting of mostly younger scholars—the idea being that people should be selected before they had a chance to be corrupted, while they still had energy and their idealism was undiminished. One branch of the Censorate focused on scrutinizing state officials, examining the backgrounds of both appointees and their families. Candidates for office not only had to have records of unblemished moral character, but had to come from families that were scandal-free; even a wayward grandparent could be grounds for disqualification. These members of the Censorate reviewed the conduct of officials in office to see that they were acting properly not only in public, but also in their private lives.

Another branch of the Censorate monitored the conduct of the king. Censors frequently admonished monarchs for unethical or otherwise improper behavior. In short, the Censorate were the moral guardians or moral police of the state. Since most censors were well schooled in the tenets of Neo-Confucianism and adhered to them faithfully, the Censorate functioned as one of the institutional bases for the great undertaking of making Korea a model Confucian society.

Another institution created by Confucian revivalists to reform government and society was the Classics Mat. Modeled on the Song China institution, the Classics Mat was a lecture program organized with a staff of twenty-one. It consisted of three sessions a day where the king would read and discuss the Confucian classics and commentaries on the classics by such luminaries as twelfth-century Chinese Confucian scholar Zhu Xi. The Classics Mat was designed to guide the monarch, and it served as an agency for promoting Neo-Confucian concepts at court. Kings were supposed to attend all three sessions; although they seldom adhered to this rather impractical arrangement, conscientious kings such as Sejong (r. 1418–50) did attend daily.

As if the lectures and scrutiny weren't enough for the king, he also had to deal with the historians. In most societies, historians might be read, but they are seldom taken seriously. Not so in Joseon Korea; the role historians played at court was nothing short of extraordinary. Two accompanied the king daily, one recording his words and the other his gestures and facial expressions. It was almost impossible for the king to have a private conversation with his officials without a pair of historians present; in fact, it was such a rare occurrence that when it did happen, it became a major scandal. At the end of each reign, the historians would compile a detailed record to be used as guidance for future monarchs. No king was allowed to see the historians' notes—any such requests were simply refused. Of course, it wasn't just the king, but all his officials who were observed in this way. Their every misdeed and failure to live up to the moral standards required of those in leadership would receive the final recorded judgments of the historians.

The Neo-Confucianists also used the curriculum of the civil service examinations to promote their ideals. Since passing the exam was the most important means of acquiring state office and validating one's status, basing the exams on the orthodox Neo-Confucian canon inculcated officials with its values and beliefs. State-sponsored schools trained young men of the *yangban* aristocratic class. Each county had an official school for local aristocratic boys to begin preparing them for the civil service exams. The brightest could go on to the prestigious Seonggyungwan Confucian academy in Seoul that was created early in the dynasty.

In these ways, then, the Joseon state became an ideologically oriented one.

Under a Virtuous King: Sejong, Hangul, and the Golden Age

Taejo had many sons—perhaps too many. His fifth son, Yi Bangwon, played a key role in his father's 1392 coup and expected to succeed him. The influential Jeong Dojeon, however, supported the eighth son, Yi Bangseok. Not to be deterred, Yi Bangwon, who had already killed the famed scholar Jeong Mongju, then had Jeong Dojeon and Yi Bangseok murdered. Depressed and weary, Taejo abdicated and placed his second son on the throne as King Jeongjong. But Jeongjong—fearing, with good reason, his ruthless younger brother—named Yi Bangwon crown prince and then abdicated after a brief reign.

Yi Bangwon, as King Taejong (r. 1400–18) kept intact the policies of Jeong Dojeon, whom he had murdered, and continued to promote the Neo-Confucian project. While in many ways an able leader, he was a ruthless tyrant, so suspicious of sharing his authority that he executed or exiled many of those who had helped him gain the throne, lest they try to cash in on their support or shift their support to another of Taejo's many offspring.

Taejong, in contrast to his father, had only four sons. His first was designated as heir, but was too fond of hunting and pleasure-seeking, and his second son became a monk, so in 1418, Taejong made his third son his heir and retired shortly afterward. This son, King Sejong, is considered by Koreans today as their greatest monarch, and there are compelling arguments to support this case. His greatness wasn't obvious at first: when he became king at age twenty-one, he was a semi-puppet, since his father continued to run the country from retirement. Only when his father died in 1422 was Sejong able to rule on his own. His talent for leadership soon became apparent. He led a series of successful campaigns against Japanese pirates in the south, bringing to an end their frightening attacks on coastal villages. In the north he personally led successful campaigns against the Jurchens, pushing the northern border to where it remains today, at the Yalu and Tumen rivers.

His string of military victories and skillful diplomacy would have been enough to insure his place in history; however, it was his sterling character and the cultural achievements of his reign that make him admired by Koreans. A sincere Confucian, he made an effort to act in accordance with the ideal of a virtuous prince who leads the people by moral example. He studied the Confucian classics and attended the Classic Mat lectures, which he took very seriously, and worked to promote and strengthen Confucianism. Sejong's earnest devotion to Neo-Confucian principles, and his energetic pursuit of both those principles and his own leadership abilities, contributed greatly to the progress of creating a morally sound society following the Way of Heaven.

Perhaps what Sejong is best known for is the creation of *Hangul* (also written *hangeul*), the Korean alphabet. Before his reign, Koreans mainly wrote in classical Chinese. Several systems had been developed since Silla times for writing Korean using Chinese characters, but none of them caught on. The problem was that two languages could hardly be more different than Chinese and Korean. Literacy in Chinese required mastery of thousands of characters, making writing in Korean extremely cumbersome. Sejong sought to solve the problem by creating a simple form of writing that was better suited for Korean; it would be easy to learn and phonetical, thus promoting literacy. He established a committee that studied the various writing systems they were familiar with and came up with a unique, ingenious system that works well for the complicated Korean language.

The *Hangul* alphabet not only accommodated the complex Korean sound system, but the letters themselves were based on stylized shapes of the tongue and mouth when making a sound. The result is the most scientific system of writing in the world. The work was finished in 1443 and was promoted in 1446 with a manual called the *Hunmin Jeongeum* (Correct sounds for instructing the people). For several centuries, Chinese was still widely used for government records and even for literature. Many *yangban* still looked down on the new writing system, denigrating it as "vulgar script" or "women's script"—the latter implying it was only good for untutored females. But in the twentieth century it became the main form of writing in Korean, as well as a symbol of Korean identity and cultural achievement.

The good king's reign was also a time of technical innovation. Many inventions were aimed at insuring good harvests and promoting knowledge of agricultural techniques. To keep track of rainfall, the state set up a system of rain gauges, called *chugigi*, throughout the kingdom, establishing what remains the world's longest record of measured rainfall. There were attempts to improve on the calendar and the measurement of time. Jang Yeong-sil, a particularly talented tinkerer, developed a highly accurate self-striking water clock and a sundial. Security being another major concern, experiments were made in weaponry, including a multi-barreled cannon and the world's first ironclad ships.

In his last years, Sejong had to deal with diabetes, the loss of his eyesight, and worries about leaving an heir who was very sickly and unlikely to be able to provide the strong leadership he hoped would continue to fortify the kingdom. Yet he could look back with pride. He had secured the borders, brought the country to an economic and cultural height, promoted Confucianism in society, and left behind the *Hangul* writing system, which was both a symbol of Korean identity and a vehicle for it.

Not all Joseon kings were models of Confucian behavior. Yeonsan'gun (r. 1492–1592) was the anti-Sejong, a cruel and vindictive tyrant. In his first few years the young monarch governed reasonably enough, but then went bad. He attempted to abolish the Censorate when it issued criticism of his conduct, and banished or killed many officials who challenged his authority. He even had the body of an official dug up and the remains mutilated. He shut down the main Confucian academy, the Seonggyungwan, and turned a major Buddhist temple into a pleasure palace in which he gathered women and horses from around the country. Upon his orders, 20,000 Seoul residents were evicted so he could turn their neighborhood into a royal hunting ground. Commoners were forced to labor on these projects. When they began to put up posters in *Hangul* mocking him, he had the new script banned. All this was too much, and his own officials deposed him. He was posthumously downgraded from a king to a prince, since no king could have acted in such a manner. Like all Joseon kings, Yeonsan'gun discovered that there were limits to royal power.

The Not-Always-Virtuous Politics of Joseon

Joseon politics hardly resembled the picture of staid aristocrats peacefully seeking office by mastering Confucian texts and triumphing on the civil exams. Rather, the five centuries of the dynasty can be read as a fierce and unending story of intrigue and struggle among aristocratic factions as they competed for power. Vying for public position among the *yangban* was a high-stakes game: to an even greater extent than in earlier times, holding prominent office was the main way for individuals and families to maintain high status, gain access to power, and secure their family's wealth.

Factional politics, focused on jockeying for key positions at court, was couched in the language of Confucian principles. The very attempt to create a virtuous society added to the viciousness of politics, since in this Confucian society, proper personal behavior by officials and the correct performance of rituals at court were necessary to maintain the harmony and prosperity of the state. Misbehavior and incorrect performance of duties could jeopardize the whole project and bring the wrath of Heaven down upon society. As a result, even seemingly trivial matters became the cause of serious disputes. For example, when King Hyojong died in 1659, it was unclear whether his mother the queen dowager should mourn for one year since he was her son, or for three years since he was a king. The canonical texts being unclear on this, one faction argued for one year and another for three. There were many other equally arcane disagreements, and their consequences were not trivial. Being on the losing side of one of these disputes could mean not only the loss of one's position in government, but could result in banishment or execution. Losers were banished to remote locations such as small islands off the south coast, where a *yangban* would be far from the court and cut off from his family, with only illiterate fisherfolk as his companions. There was nothing to do but study, read, and hope that the fortunes of his faction would take a more positive turn.

Life as a Ritual: Marriage, Family, and Death in Joseon Korea

Amidst factional strife, the project of shaping society according to the Neo-Confucian literati vision continued. During the Joseon era, the country became a Confucian society to a greater extent than it had ever been a Buddhist one. Confucianism emphasized the importance of family relations, the hierarchical nature of society, the necessity for order and harmony, respect for elders and for authority, and the importance of a clear distinction between men and women. Most of these were held as important in all premodern societies, but Confucianism made them its central principles, reinforced by rituals and ceremonies and by the study of the classic texts. Confucianism begins with the family as the basic unit of society; all other institutions are patterned on it. The state, for example, is sort of a big family with the king as the father. Families were bound together by a web of obligations reinforced by rituals and ceremonies, with each member performing his or her role. The most important principle that held the family together was *hyo*, or filial piety.

One's duties and obligations extended not only to the living but also to past and future generations. That is, one always had to be aware of one's conduct in light of what the ancestors would say about it and how it would affect one's descendants. Each family kept a careful record of their lineage and maintained ancestral gravesites. The graves of the ancestors were visited on special days. Family members prostrated themselves three times before the ancestor's grave and presented them with food and wine. Rituals to the family ancestors were performed regularly at home as well: memorial tablets with the names of family ancestors were taken out and the head of the household performed prostrations before them. These ceremonies for the family ancestors, known as *jesa*, became central to Korean ritual life.

Children were taught to show respect, obedience, and unquestioning love to parents, who reciprocated with their devotion to their children. This was symbolized on New Year's Day, when children in their best clothes bowed before their parents, and the parents in turn gave the children red envelopes containing money. Three years of mourning were carried out when a parent died, and the date of their death was commemorated annually thereafter by a special ritual ceremony. Everyone had a duty to marry to continue the family lineage. This was so important that a man or woman would be addressed as a child until they married. If a young person died before they wedded, they were often wedded posthumously to a boy or girl who had also died prematurely, ensuring that no family members went unmarried.

Virtuous Women: Being Female in Joseon Korea

No other feature of Korean life was more strikingly transformed under the influence of Joseon Neo-Confucianism than the relations between men and women. A society where men and women mixed so freely, and where women had so much independence that it seemed scandalous to the Goryeo-era Chinese visitor Xu Jing, became one of the most gender-segregated and male-dominated lands outside the Arabian Peninsula. Women had to be chaste and loyal to their husbands. Widows were no longer allowed to remarry, since they had to be loyal to their husbands for eternity. Girls were often married in childhood, and even if their husbands died before they were fully grown—which was not uncommon in premodern times with high death rates—they still had to remain widows. Women were held to a high standard of chastity. Any questioning of women's virtue could bring dishonor to her entire family. Young girls were given a *paedo*—a small knife with which they would take their own life—if that should happen. A woman who was seduced, raped, or even rumored to have had an affair or been violated was expected to use her *paedo* to protect her family's reputation. Women did not socialize with men who were not relatives. They were to be silent in men's presence; in fact, talkativeness was grounds for divorce.

Since "distinction" between men and women was a cardinal virtue in Confucianism, women were never to assume a man's role. Joseon-era laws prohibited women from riding horses or playing sports. In fact, the spheres of the two genders were kept so separate that houses had different entrances—one for men and one for women. Inside the home, the men's and women's quarters were separated by the kitchen. Late in the Joseon era, concern for keeping men and women apart went even further. To make sure that they did not mix in public, there were certain hours of the day, marked by ringing a bell, when only women could be on the street. At all other times, only men could move about. Many upper-class women lived their entire lives secluded behind high walls, with little exposure to men other than relatives. There were tales of girls on swings—swinging was a popular pastime—going high enough to get a glimpse at the world beyond the walls. If they got sick, they were treated by specially trained women or were separated from a male doctor by a curtain. In the latter case, the doctor could only feel his female patient's pulse with a string that ran under it. Of course, such restrictions were impossible to impose on lower-class women, who had to work in the fields alongside men at busy times. But the idea of the strict separation of the sexes and male control penetrated to all levels of society.

Two exceptions to the restricted life of women were *kisaeng* and *mudang*. *Mudang* were shamans, a role that during the Joseon period became principally occupied by women. While officially frowned upon as ignorant superstition, shamanism always remained a significant part of Korean life. How else to deal with the ghosts of the dead and other malevolent spirits that troubled people? Even kings and members of the royal family consulted them. The *mudang's* social status was low, but this was not reflected in the respect her powers were given. Women also served as *kisaeng*, the Korean equivalent to the Japanese geisha. These were selected as young girls, usually from poor commoner or even low-born families, and were trained to entertain and serve men. Literate and often artistically accomplished, they offered aristocratic men the kind of intellectual and playful companionship that was absent in their ritually circumscribed marriages.

A few *kisaeng* such as Hwang Jini (1506–60) became famous poets. Hwang is worth noting. Famed in her day for her beauty, wit, and independent spirit, she won recognition as a writer. She was a master of the *shijo*, the short, suggestive poem similar to the Japanese *haiku*. Only a few of her poems survive today, but they are enough to maintain her reputation as an important poet. Hwang Jini is a popular subject of film and literature today, admired in both North and South Korea. Yet even this talented woman could not escape the limitations of her status as a woman and a non-aristocrat. All *kisaeng* had constricted lives; at best they could become a concubine or secondary wife of a wealthy *yangban*.

Men in White: Being a Privileged Male in Joseon Korea

Creating a virtuous society meant establishing a stable social order where everybody had their place. Theoretically, this meant a meritocracy where all rose or fell according to their virtues and talents. Yet, theory aside, Korea remained a highly rank-conscious society divided into social classes determined by bloodline. Only *yangban* were allowed to take the civil-service exams—not in theory but in practice. The lower orders of commoners and "mean people" were excluded. Neo-Confucian literati were concerned that everyone should know their rank so that order could be maintained. To this end, they developed the *hopae* system, in which people wore identity tags indicating their status. *Yangban* wore yellow poplar tags; commoners small wooden ones, and there were big wooden ones for slaves. *Yangban* serving as high-ranking officials wore ivory identity tags, while lower-ranked officials wore ones of deer horn. Each contained the name, date, and place of birth of the wearer. The *hopae* system also served to aid in tax collection and in catching runaway slaves. Such an elaborate effort to control society was unusual in premodern times, and while only intermittently enforced, it was a sign of how far Joseon officials were willing to go to make sure everyone was in their place.

Yangban had to be model Confucians, and were held to a high standard of moral behavior; they had to make a show of carrying out elaborate rites to their ancestors and conspicuous displays of filial piety. For example, so assiduously did *yangban* men observe the mourning rites for parents and grandparents that they began wearing white—the color of mourning—all the time. As a result, the white clothes of *yangban* men, along with their black horsehair hats, easily distinguished them. So did their pipes: when tobacco became popular in Korea in the seventeenth century, aristocratic men smoked it in pipes with stems so enormously long that they required a servant to light and stoke them. *Yangban* were different from aristocrats in Europe in that ostentatious shows of wealth were avoided, and there were no palatial mansions; most lived in modest homes with simple furnishings. Despite their modesty, however, their homes had heated floors and sliding doors to let in air and light, making them more comfortable than the castles and estates of their Western counterparts.

Yangban derived their wealth from land usually worked by tenant farmers or slaves. Many were large landowners, but some had only modest holdings and lived just a bit above the poverty level. Even poorer *yangban*, however, could be proud of their social status; most importantly, they had the opportunity to sit for civil service exams and gain public office. The greatest goal of the *yangban* was to serve in government. Most began tutoring their sons to pass the civil-service exams from an early age, as this was the main way to achieve that aim. Young men then attended a local state-sponsored school or one of the several hundred *seowon*, private academies that prepared them for the exams and served as centers of Confucian scholarship. Whether or not they became officials, *yangban* prided themselves as scholars and moral leaders of society. In a society without a clergy, it was the local *yangban* who provided ethical guidance, often giving public lectures to the commoners. They acted as informal adjudicators of disputes, since most commoners tended to avoid the royal courts, where plaintiffs and witnesses were routinely tortured to determine the truthfulness of their testimony.

In spite of their moral pretensions, there was a hedonistic side to *yangban* life. Aristocratic men often spent time at the *kisaeng* house, and frequently became patrons of a particular lady. Pornographic literature and art were discreetly circulated, and *yangban* men could be heavy drinkers. No doubt many *yangban* wasted their rather leisurely lives lounging around the *kisaeng* houses, gambling, or dissipating their energies in petty factional politics. Some, however, were men of accomplishment. A few distinguished themselves as poets and amateur artists; others compiled histories. Some *yangban* came to close to being the men of virtue that Confucian revivalists had worked to create. Yi Hwang (1501–70) and Yi I (1536–84), better known by their respective pen names Toegye and Yulgok, were the most revered of the Confucian philosophers. Both appear on today's South Korean currency. Other *yangban* devoted their time to practical matters, writing treatises on medicine, economics, and social reform.

The Weight of Poverty: Being Poor in Joseon Korea

The Neo-Confucian project of transforming the country to a truly virtuous one was aimed at the elite, but gradually trickled down to commoners. Most ordinary folks adopted the ritual practices of their betters and internalized many Confucian values. A few older traditions survived—for example, mixed drinking and dancing between men and women remained common. Yet even commoners faithfully carried out the rites to the ancestors and accepted the Confucian concepts of virtue.

Virtuous or not, life for commoners remained rough and hard. Most peasants did not have enough land to support their families, and had to work part of the time on *yangban* estates. When bad weather damaged the harvest, hunger was widespread. Grain was stored for these occasions in government granaries, but it was lent, not given, and thus could put a poor commoner family deep into debt. Rice farming, with its transplanting and weeding, was labor-intensive work, but there were times for recreation, such as attending markets held once or twice a week—that is, every five or ten days (a Korean week had ten days). There were weddings and festivals; card games were popular, as were wrestling matches and, always, drinking. But these were brief respites in a hard life.

Commoners could not rise in status; there was little social mobility in Korea's rigid society. Still, the poorest commoner could console himself that he was not a slave or an outcast. Slavery was quite common in the early Joseon period, with as much as a third of the population being enslaved. In no way did this resemble slavery in the Americas, however; there were no big plantations, nor ethnic or racial distinctions, and freed slaves easily blended into society. In fact, Korean slavery was complicated. There were four legal classifications. Some were chattel slaves with virtually no rights or property; others were landowners, differing from ordinary peasants in status but not much else. A few landowning slaves who became wealthy were—as strange as this may seem—slave owners themselves. Slave families usually lived in their own section of a village and did not, as a rule, intermarry with commoners.

One group of commoners who tended to prosper more than most were the merchants. Korean commerce, however, was not as sophisticated as China's or Japan's. Cities were smaller, the merchant class more modest and less wealthy, and the volume of trade smaller than in neighboring countries. Geography explains much of this: China, like Europe, had great rivers that provided easy highways facilitating transport; also like Europe, Japan had protected seas linking population centers—most significantly the Inland Sea. Korea had neither of these; the mountains and hills made overland travel difficult, the rivers did not connect regions of the country; furthermore, the high tides and sandbars made coastal navigation challenging. As a result, trade often consisted of peddlers burdened with A-frame backpacks making their way over narrow mountain footpaths. But geography can be overcome, and Koreans were able to construct a fairly centralized and uniform government in spite of living in a country of valleys and small plains separated by mountains.

Geography was not the only explanation for such a modest level of commercial development; cultural norms hindered commerce as well. Confucianists looked down on trade. Merchants and bankers were viewed as villains who got their wealth from others but produced nothing themselves. Even the innkeepers who housed them were lumped in with butchers and gravediggers as outcasts. The officialdom who governed the country, for the most part—and there were exceptions—failed to appreciate the role or importance of commerce in strengthening the kingdom and promoting the welfare of its people. Businesses were restricted to licensed shops and hobbled by government price controls. Government decrees prohibited the mining of the silver and gold that the country possessed, lest it attract China's attention and cause it to demand tribute payments of precious metals. This did not help commerce, either. In the absence of precious metals, money was restricted to clunky copper coins that had to be strung together in heavy ropes of cash. Bolts of cotton were often used as another even more cumbersome medium of exchange.

One aspect of society that did not change, despite the efforts of the Neo-Confucianists, was the importance of the spirit world among commoners. While Confucianism acknowledges no gods, afterlife, or eternal soul, most Koreans lived a world of inhabited by *gwisin* (spirits). There were spirits of the dead that could haunt them or bring disease and misfortune; these required a shaman to placate. The natural world of mountains, trees and rock outcroppings were the abode of spirits. The most important, the mountain spirit Sanshin, had a shrine in almost every Buddhist temple. The women of the house made offerings to household gods, like those of the kitchen and the gate, and those dwelling in the storage jars; there was even a god that protected the outhouse. In every village there was a shrine for the local guardian god. And *pungsu*—or geomancy, as it is called in the West—was practiced by everyone; even the state employed geomancers. Buildings and gravesites, even the capital Seoul, were situated according to geomantic principles, often with the aid of professional geomancers.

Fending Off the Invaders: Foreign Policy

In the early fifteenth century, the Jurchens outside the northern borders were subdued; those inside the border were brought under control and eventually assimilated into Korean society, and the Japanese pirates that plagued the south were defeated. Relations with the Ming, though a bit shaky at first, improved. Korean rulers, seeking the legitimacy that recognition from the Chinese emperor conferred, sent tribute missions to Beijing. At first these were sent every three years, then annually, and then three times a year, starting with the New Year's mission. These missions provided opportunities for trade and cultural exchange: the Koreans exported cloth and ginseng and brought silk, medicines, books, and Chinese porcelains into the country. Tribute missions could number in the hundreds, and were a great opportunity for Koreans to travel and keep up with the intellectual, cultural, and fashion trends in China.

The long period of peace carefully established in the early Joseon came to a sudden end with the Japanese invasion of Korea in 1592. While they covered a shorter period and were less destructive than those of the Mongols, the Japanese invasions remain more strongly seared into the memory of the Korean people—reinforced, perhaps, by Tokyo's colonization and rule in the first half of the twentieth century. The Japanese military hegemon and megalomaniac Toyotomi Hideyoshi (1536–98), emerging as the effective ruler of Japan after a long series of bloody conflicts, launched his plan to take Korea by force and use it as a base to conquer China. He assembled a force of a quarter-million fighters in what was probably the greatest overseas invasion in history prior to the twentieth century. The Korean court discounted warnings of a possible attack, including alerts from Yi Sunshin, a military official who was out of royal favor at the time, and was thus caught unprepared when the initial force of 53,000 men landed in Pusan. The well-trained Japanese forces, equipped with muskets as well as swords, pikes, and arrows, marched through the country slaughtering the ill-equipped, hastily assembled Korean forces. In only three weeks they captured Seoul, and crowds of Koreans jeered and threw rocks at their king and his courtiers as they fled northward.

The Chinese quickly responded to Joseon's request for help and were able to stop the Japanese advance at Pyongyang. The war became a stalemate for a while, paralleling the later Korean War where one side held the southern part of the country and another the north. In 1597, Hideyoshi sent a second wave of invaders. This time the better-prepared Koreans with their Chinese allies were able to contain the Japanese advance to the south. Stalemated on land and harassed on sea, the Japanese withdrew shortly after Hideyoshi's death in 1598.

The East Asian War of 1592–98, as it is called by some modern historians, was one of the major international conflicts of the premodern era, with hundreds of thousands of combatants and vast casualties. A reminder of its brutality and scale can be seen today in the Mimizuka (Mound of Ears) in Kyoto, where the pickled ears of 38,000 Koreans and Chinese—trophies of war—are buried. The hero of the war was the aforementioned Admiral Yi Sunshin (1545–98). Although Yi came from a family of civil officials, he chose to take the military test rather than the more prestigious civil exam. A victim of factional politics, he was out of power and his entreaties for military preparedness were ignored at the time of the Japanese invasion. Called back to office by the chastened court, Yi supervised the construction of a fleet of ships that carried on a successful naval campaign, sinking hundreds of Japanese ships and making it difficult for Hideyoshi to continue sending forces to the peninsula. One of Admiral Yi's innovations was the *geobukseon* "turtle ships," which were the world's first ironclad vessels, predating the Monitor and the Merrimack in the US Civil War by more than two and a half centuries. These ships resisted Japanese naval gunfire and were well designed to ram and sink enemy ships.

Admiral Yi Sunshin died in combat toward the end of the conflict. Today he is a national hero whose statue stands prominently in downtown Seoul. No doubt a military strategist of the first order, he certainly earned his fame. However, he and his men were not the only Koreans who gave a good account of themselves. Thousands of peasants fiercely resisted the Japanese even after they were abandoned by the hapless government. And then there were monks who had lost their status in society, but not their martial traditions. Among these was Seosan (1520–1604), who remains famous in Korea today for organizing monks to resist the invaders. Also on the list of heroes was the famous *kisaeng* Non'gae, who killed a Japanese commander by holding him in her arms and throwing herself off a cliff, taking him along. It may be just a myth but one that has entered the mainstream of Korean narrative histories.

Hardly had Korea recovered from the Japanese invasions when

it was invaded again, this time from the north. In the early seventeenth century, Nurhaci, the leader of a Jurchen group known as the Manchus, united the peoples of Manchuria. In 1616 Nurhaci founded the state of Jin and began to carry out his ambition to conquer China. The Ming, having rescued the Koreans from the Japanese, now called on them to assist in fighting the Manchus. The Korean ruler Gwanghaegun (r. 1608–23) sent troops to help, but being conscious of how vulnerable his state was to attack from this new barbarian threat, he instructed his military commanders to see which way the battle was turning. When the Manchus began emerging victorious, the Korean forces surrendered without a fight and adopted a policy of neutrality. This might have made practical sense, but it outraged many officials and other members of the elite who felt obligated to help their nominal suzerain in its struggle. What an un-Confucian breach of loyalty this was! Gwanghaegun was removed by a coup, and like Yeonsangun was posthumously downgraded to the status of royal prince, having acted in a manner unworthy of a king.

In 1627, the Manchus reacted to the pro-Ming coup by invading Korea, forcing the court to flee to its traditional place of safety on the island of Ganghwa. Out of harm's way, the king negotiated a treaty establishing a tributary relationship with the Manchus. However, as they had done with the Mongols before, once the immediate threat passed, they reneged on the agreement and resumed a pro-Ming policy. Nurhaci's successor Abahai—now calling himself the emperor of the Qing dynasty—invaded Korea again in 1636. The court once again retreated to Ganghwa, but this time Abahai's forces managed to capture the island. The king, who had retreated to a fortress south of Seoul with his army, surrendered. The Manchu invasions were less destructive than those by the Japanese, and the interruption of relations with China proved only temporary. In 1644, the Manchus seized Beijing and began ruling China as the Qing dynasty, and Korea's tributary relations with China resumed.

The "Hermit Kingdom": Korea in the Aftermath of Invasions

Koreans never really accepted the idea that the Qing were the legitimate rulers of China, or even that they were fully civilized. To them, China was under "barbarian rule." This was unfair to the Qing rulers, who had assimilated much of Chinese culture and acted as good Confucianists. Koreans also looked down on the Chinese elite who had compromised their Neo-Confucian principles and their dignity by submitting to the alien Manchus. Not all Koreans held the Qing state in disdain; in the eighteenth century some Joseon writers praised the commercial development in China. In general, however, Koreans after the mid-seventeenth century saw China as a society that had compromised civilized values by submitting to barbarian rule. Nonetheless, they maintained correct tributary relations with them.

Korea also reestablished proper relations with Japan under the Tokugawa shogunate, sending periodic diplomatic and cultural exchange missions to Edo (Tokyo). There was just one problem: the missions could not present their credentials to the emperor of Japan, because, as all good Koreans knew, there was only one emperor—the celestial ruler in Beijing. To smooth this over, the Japanese created a special title, *Taikun* ("great prince"), for the Koreans to use when addressing their ruler. (This title was picked up by Westerners and is the origin of the word "tycoon.") Korean visitors came back impressed by the prosperity of Japan but disgusted at the freedom with which men and women socialized and the incomplete adherence to Confucian norms that they observed. They also found some Japanese customs disgusting, such as the women painting their teeth black. In general, Japan, like Qing China, was found wanting.

With China compromised by the rule of a barbarian dynasty and the Japanese tainted by outré customs, Koreans often saw themselves as the truest adherents of the Way and their society as the most civilized. Their kingdom might be small and militarily weak, but they were morally pure and superior to their neighbors. To maintain that purity, and most of all to avoid harm from foreigners, from the seventeenth century Joseon attempted to limit contact with the outside world. The nickname "Hermit Kingdom," which nineteenth-century Westerners applied to the country, comes from this deliberate seclusion. The lengths that were taken to impose isolation on the nation were extraordinary. Koreans were not allowed to travel abroad except on authorized missions. The size of boats was restricted to prevent fishermen or merchants from sailing to another country. Foreigners were not permitted to enter the country. When several Dutch sailors washed ashore in 1627, they were put to work building guns for the military, but were not allowed to leave. In 1653, thirty-six Dutch seamen were stranded on the island of Jeju when their ship wrecked there; they, too, were prohibited from leaving. Eight managed to escape, and one, Hendrick Hamel, wrote the first account of Korea in a Western language.

There were two exceptions to the prohibitions against outsiders entering the country. Japanese merchants were allowed to trade at Busan, but were confined to a walled compound called the Waegwan ("Japan House"), where they had virtually no contact with Koreans except authorized merchants. The other was the embassies that were sent from China. These traveled overland across Korea to Seoul along a prescribed route, and Koreans were forbidden to have contact with them. They entered Seoul through a special gate and stayed within a walled compound; only authorized Koreans were allowed to interact with them. As a result, the only foreigners in the country saw as little of it as possible and met few local people—not unlike the restrictions that are imposed on visitors to North Korea today. By the nineteenth century, Korea was perhaps the most isolated major state in the world.

The Calm before the Storm: Late Joseon

If the reign of Sejong marked a high point in the history of premodern Korea, the reigns of King Yeongjo (1724–76) and his grandson Jeongjo (1776–1800) constituted another final golden age before the turbulent nineteenth century changed Korean society forever. Yeongjo promoted political stability by appointing officials from all the major factions and managed to take some of the heat out of the political intrigues. Perhaps the most skilled leader since Sejong, he also led by moral example, trying hard to fit the Confucian model of kingship. He dutifully performed rituals and held himself to a personal standard of moral rectitude while paying close attention to the governing of the state. After half a century of rule, he was succeeded by his able grandson Jeongjo. Both were skilled at maintaining the loyalty of the powerful aristocratic families while keeping them from openly attacking each other.

Yeongjo and Jeongjo reigned during good times. The country was at peace with its neighbors and prospered at home. Lighter plows and hoes, greater use of fertilizer, more effective intercropping, and some good forest management had improved farm output just enough to support a growing population and keep it well fed—most of the time. Commerce, while still modest in scale, flourished, with the country adopting a more monetized economy. In literature, it was the great age of the novel—popular novels from this period are still read today. The best known of these is *The Story of Chunghyang*, a tale of a young lady who falls into the clutches of an evil local official but is rescued by her lover. Some of Korea's greatest painters were active at this time as well, including Kim Hongdo, whose depiction of everyday life—farmers in the field, weavers, people attending village markets—are a delightful record of the times. Other painters devoted themselves to capturing the scenic spots of the country, while still others recorded its beautiful women. The prevailing interest in the past is reflected in the number of histories written at this time, works showing impressively high standards of scholarship. One, composed by Yu Teukkong in 1784, began the controversy over whether Korea was really unified by Silla or there were two Koreas—the other being Balhae—a controversy that continues today. Other scholars compiled maps and geographies of the country.

The tranquility was not complete: factional rivalries were still present, and threats to the Confucian order popped up from time to time. One such incident involved Yeongjo's son, the crown prince Sado. His behavior became increasingly bizarre, showing signs of serious mental illness, which represented a true crisis for the monarchy. The king ruled by the Mandate of Heaven; he had to maintain harmony among the people and demonstrate that he and his lineage were worthy of Heaven's trust. Failure to maintain harmony and lewd or unseemly behavior could result in the loss of that mandate. And a mentally ill heir to throne? What could be a clearer sign that the Yi family was losing the pleasure of Heaven? Sado's illness had to be kept a secret. On his father's orders, he was suffocated in a rice chest that muffled his cries while his wife, Lady Hyegyeong, was ordered to lie beside him as if nothing was wrong. Her extraordinarily insightful account of it all makes for compelling reading. The scheme worked: his death was ruled as natural, and the crown passed to Sado's son, who became King Jeongjo.

On the Edge of a Storm

The eminent civil servant Kim Jeonghui died in 1856 at the age of seventy. From a family of *yangban* in Chungcheong province in central Korea, he had passed the civil service exam at age twenty-four. Trained for a life of public service, he distinguished himself as a calligrapher. He was interested in old things, the treasures of his country's long traditions. He made a study of old Buddhist texts and had a great passion for collecting inscriptions found throughout the kingdom. Kim also wrote about geology, history, and Confucian doctrine. He witnessed political crises, and was once exiled to the island of Jeju himself. Yet his life was overall a good one filled with pride in his nation's past, its institutions and culture, all of which were still flourishing when he passed away.

It is doubtful that Kim Jeonghui could have possibly imagined just how radically Korea's history was about to change. A well-informed Korean in 1856 might have been aware that there was a new threat abroad, that Western "barbarians" had launched a major attack on China and forced that country to open its ports to trade. But he would not know that this was only the beginning of a great storm soon to sweep across the land, altering the course of Korean history.

HEAVEN LAKE Heaven Lake, located at the top of Baekdu Mountain on the North Korean/Manchurian border, is Korea's tallest and most sacred mountain. The mountain was supposedly the base of operations for Kim Il Sung's anti-Japanese guerrilla campaign. *Photo: Megapixl © Cczbb.*

GANGHWA DOLMEN An ancient dolmen (megalith) on Ganghwa Island near Incheon, this stone is one of more than ten thousand dolmens found throughout Korea. Most were built between 1500 and 300 BCE. Amazingly, Korea accounts for 40 percent of all the world's dolmens. *Photo: Megapixl © Artaporn.*

GOGURYEO TOMB MURAL This tomb mural from Goguryeo illustrates the mix of Chinese and native influences found in the art and culture of this warrior-dominated state. Originally based in southern Manchuria, Goguryeo moved its capital to what is now Pyongyang in the fifth century. *Photo: Wikimedia Commons © ddol-mang.*

JEULMUN POTTERY Also called combed pottery because of its distinct design. The origins of Jeulmun pottery date to at least 8000 BCE, making it among the world's oldest pottery. The more mature form depicted here appeared around 4000 BCE, and is associated with the beginnings of agriculture in Korea. Jeulmun pottery was replaced with undecorated Mumun pottery around 1500 BCE, when rice cultivation became common. *Photo: Wikimedia Commons © Ismoon.*

RICE PADDY For the past three thousand years, the Korean countryside has been dotted with rice paddies like this one near Gyeongju. *Photo: Wikimedia Commons.*

EMILE BELL The Silla era produced many huge bronze bells, some of the largest ever made. This massive example is the Emile Bell commissioned by King Seongdeok in the eighth century. It is the biggest bronze bell in Korea and probably the most well known. *Photo: Wikimedia Commons.*

BULGUKSA TEMPLE The eighth-century Buddhist Bulguksa temple in Gyeongju is the finest example of Silla architecture that survives today. *Photo: Wikimedia Commons © Eimoberg.*

CHEOMSEONGDAE OBSERVATORY Cheomseongdae is an ancient astronomical observatory located in the Silla capital of Gyeongju. The oldest such observatory in Asia, it is still standing today. *Photo: Megapixl © Sangapark118.*

GOLDEN SEATED BUDDHA FIGURINE This golden seated Buddha figurine from Gyeongju is designated a national treasure of South Korea. It exemplifies the highly refined Buddhist art of the Three Kingdoms and the Silla period. *Photo: National Museum of Korea.*

TOMB OF KING GONGMIN The Goryeo-period ruler Gongmin freed Korea from domination by the declining Mongol Empire in the fourteenth century. During the last years of his reign, after the death of his beloved Mongol wife, he lost interest in his royal duties, turning much of his authority over to a Buddhist monk. *Photo: Megapixl © Zlotysu.*

TRIPITAKA KOREANA The *Tripitaka Koreana* contains some 81,000 woodblocks used to print the Buddhist canon. Carved in the thirteenth century during the Mongol invasions, the blocks are housed in the Haeinsa temple in southeastern Korea. It is the most complete set of Buddhist scriptures in the world today. When printed, the text numbers more than 6,000 volumes, and if lined up they would stretch sixty kilometers. *Photo: Wikimedia Commons © Ken Eckert.*

JOSEON LANDSCAPE (Left) This fifteenth-century painting by artist Seo Munbo typifies Korean landscape painting and its avoidance of bright colors. *Photo: Museum of Japanese Art Yamato Bunkakan.*

KING SEJONG This modern statue of King Sejong in Seoul is based on his surviving portraits. It honors the fifteenth-century ruler, who is today considered to be Korea's greatest monarch. Admired as a model of Confucian virtue, he directed the creation of the Korean Hangul alphabet. It was also under Sejong's reign that the northern borders of Korea were fixed to where they are today. *Photo: Megapixl © Siraphol.*

TAEDONG GATE Built in the seventeenth century, the Taedong (Eastern) Gate in Pyongyang is all that is left of the wall that once surrounded the city. It is one of the few surviving structures from the city's ancient past in the North Korean capital. *Photo: Wikimedia Commons © David Stanley.*

TURTLE SHIP (Above) This is a modern replica of one of Admiral Yi Sunshin's "turtle ships," the world's first iron-clad vessels. Turtle ships were employed to great effect against the Japanese during Hideyoshi's invasions of Korea. *Photo: Megapixl © Jackbluee.*

PORTRAIT OF KING TAEJO (YI SEONGGYE) (Left) General Yi Seonggye led a coup in 1388, and in 1392 made himself the first monarch of the new Joseon dynasty. Although Yi reigned for only six years, his family ruled for more than five centuries until the Japanese annexation of Korea in 1910. Here he is portrayed in a typical royal pose. *Photo: Wikimedia Commons © Sithijainduwaraparanagama.*

THRONE OF JOSEON KINGS This throne is in Geyeongbok Palace in Seoul. Korean kings wielded considerable power, but not as much as the Chinese emperors whom they often modeled themselves after. For all the ceremony and ritual associated with their position, their actions were constrained by the scrutiny and moral authority of Confucian scholars and by the influence of the major aristocratic families. *Photo: Megapixl © Vansinsy.*

WATER CLOCK The Burugak Jagyeongnu (water clock of Boru-gak Pavilion) dates to the time of King Sejong of the Joseon dynasty. Many water clocks were built in Korea; Silla even had a special department of water clocks. *Wikimedia Commons © InSapphoWeTrust.*

PRAISEWORTHY LOTUS (Left) Sin Yun-bok's "Praiseworthy Lotus" is a Joseon-era painting from the *Hyewon pungsokdo* album that depicts *yangban* aristocrats amusing themselves with *kisaeng* courtesans.. Sin (1758–1813) was known for his realistic depictions of everyday life. He was also known for his paintings of beautiful women, especially *kisaeng*, the professional courtesans of premodern Korea. *Photo: Gansong Art Museum, Seoul.*

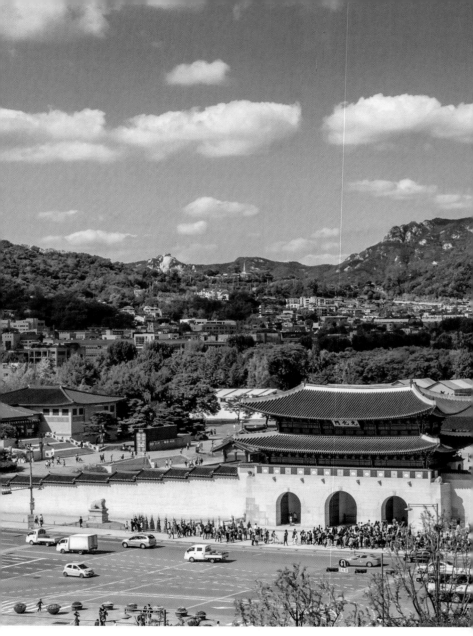

GYEONGBOKGUNG PALACE Built in 1395, the Gyeongbokgung Palace, located in Seoul, was the main royal palace of the Joseon dynasty. At one time the palace grounds covered 40 acres and contained 500 buildings, being a

royal city within the center of the capital. Most of the buildings were
destroyed during the Japanese colonial occupation, but some are still standing
in downtown Seoul. *Photo: Megapixl © Vincentstthomas.*

TRADITIONAL KOREAN HOME A traditional Korean home in Bukchon Hanok Village in Seoul, one of the few such neighborhoods to survive the country's rapid modernization. Traditional homes were surrounded by walls; the entrance was a gate, often brightly colored, that opened to a small courtyard. This was intended to ensure privacy, especially for the women of the household. *Photo: Megapixl © Nattanai.*

HYANGGYO Gate to a *hyanggyo*, a state-sponsored county school where young men were trained for civil-service exams by the Joseon government. Each of the more than 200 counties had a *hyanggyo* that was generally open only to men of the *yangban* aristocratic class. Few of these structures survive today. *Photo: Megapixl © Sungboklee73.*

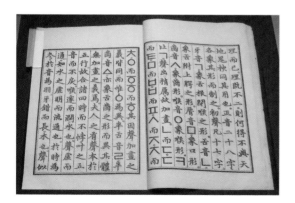

HUNMINJEONGEUM This document, issued in 1446, explains the creation of a new Korean alphabet, which is known today as Hangul. This writing system, devised by a committee of scholars at the behest of King Sejong, did not fully replace the use of Chinese characters until the twentieth century. *Wikimedia Commons © Kbarends.*

JAPANESE OFFICERS ON HORSEBACK Japanese officers are seen here riding through a Korean street during the early period of colonial rule. The Japanese colonial administration resembled a military occupation. The governor-general, always a military man, presided over a large network of troops and a national constabulary that was a visible presence in almost every community. *Photo: Cornell University Library.*

EAST GATE OF SEOUL This photo, taken around 1900, is of the East Gate in Seoul, a major entrance to the city and the site of one of the main city markets. Note the *yangban* in their customary white clothes and black horsehair hats. The only hint of the early modernization of the city are the telephone lines. *Photo: Cornell University Library.*

CHAPTER 4

FROM KINGDOM TO COLONY: KOREA UNDER IMPERIAL DOMINATION AND COLONIAL RULE (1876–1945)

Hermit Kingdom No More

In the seventeenth and eighteenth centuries, some Korean visitors to Beijing encountered European Jesuits who had a mission there. They brought back telescopes, clocks, maps, and a few Chinese translations of Western books on math and science, which were read with interest. Some were impressed by the Europeans' skill in drawing up calendars and making astronomical calculations. Others became fascinated with the new religion espoused by the Jesuits; in the late eighteenth century, a small number of Koreans converted to Catholicism, although their grasp of Christianity was a bit shaky.

So Koreans in the early nineteenth century were not oblivious to the West, but few fully appreciated the threat posed by Western imperialism or the momentous changes occurring in the world powered by the Industrial Revolution, global capitalism, modern science, and new ideas about political and social organization. Several events did make them notice. From 1839 to 1842, the Chinese suffered a humiliating setback at the hands of the British in the Opium Wars. And in 1858–60, China suffered a second setback culminating in a brief Anglo-French occupation of Beijing, while the Russians annexed some Chinese territory on the Korean border. Then there was the forced opening of Japan in 1854 by Commodore Perry and the upheavals of the 1860s that followed. A new government replaced the old Japanese shogunate, led by men who—and this was truly shocking—dressed like the Western barbarians.

The Korean response was to stand firm. They rebuffed several attempts by British, French, and Russian ships to open trade, reasserting that the country was not interested in commerce or relations with distant lands. A particularly hard line took place under Daewongun, who came to power in 1864 as the father and regent of young King Gojong. The strongest, most energetic leader Korea had seen in generations, Daewongun was determined to strengthen the monarchy and protect the nation. In 1866, he cracked down on Christianity, executing several thousand Korean Catholics and a few French priests who had smuggled their way into the country. The French responded to the killing of their citizens by sending an expedition in October of that year consisting of seven ships and six hundred men. They landed on Ganghwa Island, the former refuge of the Korean court. The French forces, hindered by the lack of good maps and encountering stiff resistance from Korean soldiers, left without accomplishing much.

In the same year, the *General Sherman* incident took place, an event known to every schoolchild today in North Korea, but one few Americans have ever heard of. A heavily armed American merchant ship, the *General Sherman*, with a crew of Americans, British, Malays, and Chinese, sailed up the Daedong River to Pyongyang, hoping to trade. They were politely told by the local official, Pak Gyusu, that foreigners were not permitted and they had to leave. The ship got stuck on a sandbar; there was an exchange of fire; and at some point the locals set fire to the ship, killing the crew as they jumped off. There were no survivors. For a while, the disappearance of the ship was a mystery, but the Koreans told the Chinese what had transpired.

When in turn the Chinese informed the US mission in Beijing, the American response was typical of the times—when the "natives" cause trouble, send in the gunboats. And this they did. In 1871, a punitive expedition consisting of five ships and 1,200 men led by

Admiral John Rodgers and Frederick Low, the US minister to China, sailed for Korea with a letter demanding an account of the missing ship. Landing on Ganghwa Island, they captured and destroyed the fortifications and killed hundreds of Korean defenders, but were unable to find their way to Seoul, and in the face of continued fierce resistance they left. Although the American press labeled it "a splendid little war against the heathens," it was a failure; the only thing it accomplished was to convince Daewongun that his policy of uncompromising opposition to the opening of the country was vindicated. Proud of fending off the French and Americans, he had stone signs erected, proclaiming, "Western barbarians invade our land. If we do not fight, we must appease them. To urge appeasement is to betray the country." This was a lesson later taught to North Koreans: stand up to foreign aggressors.

Daewongun's policies, however, only postponed the inevitable. The country was soon "opened" not by Western gunboats, but by Japanese ones. Some Japanese were itching for an intervention. When the new reform-minded Meiji government attempted to establish relations with Seoul, the Koreans, disgusted by their barbarically dressed neighbors, rudely rebuffed them. Japan, imitating the Americans under Commodore Perry, decided to open Korea to their merchants and establish a presence within their strategically located neighbor. An excuse to do so occurred in 1875, when Koreans fired upon a ship Tokyo sent to survey the Korean coast. In retaliation, Japan landed forces on Ganghwa Island in February of the following year. Meanwhile, Daewongun had lost out in a domestic power struggle. His son, Gojong, declared his independence from his father and was persuaded by Pak Gyusu—the same gentlemen who had ordered the *General Sherman* to leave—and others to negotiate. A sophisticated and intellectually curious official, Pak had become convinced that it was time for his country to engage with the world. In the Treaty of Ganghwa, Korea agreed to open selected ports to Japanese trade and enter into formal diplomatic relations with Tokyo.

Suddenly Exposed to the World

Realizing that the world around them had now changed and they had to change, too, the Korean government dispatched missions to Japan and China to learn about reforms. In 1882, they opened relations with the US and sent a mission to Washington. They arrived at the White House and prostrated themselves before a startled President Arthur. It was, however, the Koreans who were startled most often by the contrast between their society and the rest of the world. The wealth and power of Europe and America was a revelation of just how weak and vulnerable their society was.

As a result, it was immediately clear to many Koreans that their country needed to find ways to adopt to this new reality. They sought advice and a model to follow—but advice from whom, and which model to follow? Koreans traditionally viewed China as a center for culture and learning, so that was one place to look. The Chinese were carrying out what they called their "Self-Strengthening" program of cautiously borrowing Western technology (especially military technology) and engaging in Western-style diplomacy while maintaining their basic political institutions and values. Japan offered a more radical response to imperialism: a thorough adaptation of Western legal, political, and educational institutions while maintaining their imperial house as a symbol of their own traditions. Another possible path was to learn directly from the West, primarily by going to the United States or learning from the American missionaries that were arriving in the country in the 1880s.

Koreans were not only suddenly flooded with new ideas about government, society, science and technology, and international affairs all at once; they had to find ways of applying them to their society. As if this were not enough of a challenge, they found themselves in the middle of three empires: the declining Chinese, the expanding Russian, and the rising Japanese. All three were seeking to gain some measure of control over Korea and were actively intervening in its affairs.

Each power had its own motives for being interested in Korea. Tokyo saw Korea as "a dagger pointing at the heart of Japan." The new government of Meiji Japan was primarily seeking survival by being strong enough to maintain its sovereignty, already compromised by unequal treaties it had been forced to sign with Commodore Perry and the other Western powers that had followed the Americans. But it hoped for more: to be an internationally respected, strong, prosperous state. This involved gaining control over its periphery. The Japanese annexed Okinawa to the south in 1874, began a systematic settlement of the wild frontier area of Hokkaido to the north, and turned their attention to Korea to the west. To prevent Korea from being a springboard for a foreign invasion of the Japanese archipelago, Tokyo needed it to be a friendly pro-Japanese state strong enough to defend itself, or a weak Japanese-controlled puppet-state. If neither of those options worked, it could annex Korea directly. Meiji leaders pursued all possibilities, eventually deciding to annex their neighbor.

China's main concern was keeping their empire intact. To this end, Beijing encouraged settlement in Manchuria to further integrate that territory into their empire, put down Muslim rebellions at their western frontiers, and sought to exercise control over Korea. Beijing's aim was not to annex Korea, but to make it subordinate to Beijing and keep it out of the hands of other powers, as a Korea under foreign control would represent a direct threat to them. Russia, too, was interested in Korea. An expanding empire in the Pacific region, it had annexed a part of China to Siberia in 1860, thereby becoming Korea's neighbor. It now looked at the peninsula to the south, eyeing its warm-water ports and its resources. Thus the Koreans were seeking advice from their neighbors while trying to avoid being swallowed up by them.

Grappling with a Changing World
Considering the length and depth of Korea's isolation, it is surprising how quickly so many of the Confucian literati and educated commoners came to grasp the need for major change. They just couldn't agree on how. Those who went to China advocated for Chinese-style reforms; those who went to Japan advocated for following that nation's path. Meanwhile, the government proceeded cautiously, creating some new institutions, including a new body for conducting foreign relations and some soldiers trained in modern methods by Japanese officers. These modest beginnings were

too slow for a group of young educated men who had visited Japan and who saw the need for more radical change. Known as the Enlightenment Party, these scholar-official reformers now sought to remake Korea. Inspired by a new vision of society based on what they had observed taking place in Japan, they exhibited the same zeal that their Neo-Confucian ancestors had in adopting new ideas learned abroad and using them to remake society.

As impatient as they were zealous—and one can understand their sense of urgency—they carried out a coup attempt in late 1884. The leader of the group was Kim Okkyun. At thirty-three, he was the oldest of this small band of radicals; most were in their twenties, and all were young, idealistic, and determined. On December 4, during a banquet commemorating the opening of the new postal service in Seoul, the plotters started a fire in a nearby building and set off some explosions. In the confusion that followed, they murdered several conservative ministers and the heads of the military units in the capital and took the king into protective custody. They then proclaimed a new government with a sweeping set of reforms—abolishing *yangban* status, tax reform, creating a modern army and police force, and cancelling all debts held by the poor. Their coup was short-lived, however; the Chinese, who had some troops stationed at their legation, intervened and the coup plotters were killed or fled. Kim went to Japan; another plotter, Seo Jaepil, who had briefly served as defense minister, fled to the US, where he became an American citizen under the name Philip Jaissohn.

The Gapsin Coup, as the events of December 1884 are called, was in retrospect a tragedy for Korea. It removed a group of talented potential modernizers from the political stage, strengthened the hand of conservatives, and led to a decade of Chinese-dominated government. From 1884 to 1894, the Chinese exercised a great measure of control over Korea through their representative Yuan Shikai, a young general who would later become the ruler of China. It was a lost decade for Korea, which didn't have much time lose if it was to modernize fast enough to survive. For ten years, the Chinese hindered Korean efforts to carry out any reforms that might lessen China's grip on the country. They made it difficult for Koreans to travel abroad, pressured the Joseon government to order students abroad to return home, and blocked efforts by Seoul to open embassies in Western countries. But the Chinese could not keep out the foreign missionaries who opened schools and hospitals and exposed young Koreans to new ideas. Nor could they keep out the Japanese and Russians who opened businesses and engaged in political intrigue.

China's period of dominance came to an end in 1894, when the Donghaks revolted. The Donghak ("Eastern Learning") movement was founded in 1864 by Choe Jeu, who mixed Korean religious practices and Confucian ethics and cosmology with ideas derived from Christianity: belief in a single divinity and the concepts of universal brotherhood and equality. A panicked government in Seoul called for Chinese assistance, but before troops could arrive, Korean officials were able to negotiate with the Donghaks, promising to look into their grievances, and things quieted down. Though they were no longer needed, the Chinese forces arrived anyway, as did—uninvited—troops from Japan: Tokyo was not going to allow China to consolidate its hold on the peninsula. Instead of fighting the Donghaks, the Japanese and Chinese forces fought each other, and Japan's modernized forces carried out a crushing defeat of the Chinese forces. With the Chinese driven out and the Japanese in effective control of Seoul, Tokyo sponsored a new reform government, which included Gapsin veterans returned from exile in Japan.

Carried out under the tutelage of Japan, the Gabo Reforms, as the measures of 1894 are called, brought about sweeping changes. *Yangban* status was abolished, as was slavery; equality before the law was established. Child marriage was prohibited, widows were allowed to remarry, and the civil service exams were ended. A new Western calendar was adopted and the tributary status with China officially came to an end. Topknots were prohibited, since they symbolized the old ways, and the state ordered men to adopt Western-style haircuts. The last order met with considerable resistance. The Gabo Reforms, enthusiastically enacted by Korean reformers who had been out of power for the past decade, marked the beginning of the end of the old order and the beginning of modern Korea. But the reformers never freed themselves from the taint of having acted under the influence of Japanese bayonets. It didn't help that the Japanese minister in Korea undid whatever goodwill his country might have earned by having Gojong's wife Queen Min, who was staunchly anti-Japanese, murdered by Japanese thugs. In a horrific act of violence, after killing her they covered her body in kerosene and burned it. Events at this time were an unfortunate preview of the period of Japanese rule that began in 1910, a period marked by a mixture of good-willed reform efforts and competent, sophisticated administration combined with arrogance and brutality.

Japan's elimination of China from the Korean scene served to draw Russia in. In early 1896, a pro-Russian faction at court spirited King Gojong out of the palace and past the watchful eyes of the Japanese over to the Russian legation, positioning the king to rule from a location protected by Cossacks. At this point, a group of Korean progressives formed the Independence Club led by Yun Chiho, who was American-educated, later joined by Gapsin Coup veteran Seo Jaepil, who returned from the US with an American education, an American wife, and his American name—Philip Jaisohn. The club called for a modern representative government and an independent foreign policy. In a break with tradition aimed at emphasizing Korea's cultural independence from its neighbors, their newspaper was printed in *Hangul* rather than Chinese characters.

In 1897, they renamed their nation the Great Korean Empire; Gojong was proclaimed emperor. This put Korea on an equal footing with its imperial neighbors and was a reassertion of Korean pride and autonomy. But the king and his conservative officials saw the Independence Club as a threat and shut it down in 1898. Its leaders once again fled into exile, joined by Yi Seungman, a graduate of an American missionary school. Yi barely escaped arrest by fleeing to the US embassy and spent the next half century in America, where he took the name Syngman Rhee.

From the Korean Empire to the Japanese Empire

Tokyo had invested too much in Korea to let it slip under control of Russia or an unfriendly government. In 1904, it attacked the Russians, launching the Russo-Japanese War. To the amazement of the

West, Japan emerged victorious from this conflict in 1905. Russia conceded Korea and much of Manchuria as a Japanese sphere of influence. President Theodore Roosevelt, who brokered the peace settlement, tacitly gave Tokyo a free hand in Korea in return for its recognition of the American presence in the Philippines. Britain, too, as part of an alliance with Japan, recognized Japanese primacy over the peninsula. In 1905, with the blessing of the great powers, Japan declared Korea as a protectorate. Western states closed their embassies, and Korea became a Japanese possession in all but name. Korea sent representatives to a peace conference in The Hague in 1907 to protest Japan's violation of its sovereignty, but the outside world showed little interest in its plight.

Japan's takeover of Korea from 1905 to 1910 was a step-by-step process initially supervised by Ito Hirobumi. Ito, Japan's most respected elder statesman, the author of its constitution, and the single most important architect of its modernization process, carried out the task with skill. Japanese advisors were attached to ministries, effectively taking charge of them. In 1907 the army was disbanded, and when Gojong began to act too independently he was forced to abdicate in favor of his mentally incompetent, easily controlled son Sunjong. In 1909, Ito was assassinated by Korean nationalist An Junggeun in Harbin, China. However, the policy of absorbing Korea into the empire continued, and in 1910 Korea was formally annexed. Although its legal status was couched in ambiguous language—the term "merger" was used—Korea was in effect a Japanese colony, and would remain so for thirty-five years.

Koreans responded to their loss of sovereignty in many ways. A few were enthusiastic about joining the Japanese empire, a fact that causes discomfort among modern Koreans but made sense in the context of the time. To their eyes, Japan was an agent of progress and prosperity, an Asian entity with a culture similar to theirs, which was able to stand up to the West. Their own dynasty seemed weak and inept in comparison. Some high-ranking officials were bought off by the Japanese, who awarded them pensions; many others among the elite simply accepted the inevitable.

Reactions of those opposed to annexation varied. Some officials resigned rather than serve the Japanese, and withdrew into private life. Some felt despair. Prominent diplomat and official Min Yeong-hwan, overwhelmed by the tragedy of what was happening to his country and his sense of helplessness to do anything about it, committed suicide. Peasants in the countryside often resented the presence of the foreigners and remained loyal to the royal family, but most just went on with their lives.

Some Koreans fiercely resisted the Japanese takeover. When the army was disbanded in 1907, many ex-soldiers joined with scholar-officials such as Yi Donghwi, forming "righteous armies." Between 1907 and 1910, about ten thousand Koreans died fighting the Japanese, many in small guerrilla bands, before they were suppressed by the superior weapons and organization of their colonizers.

It is easy to look back on those last years of Korean sovereignty and view the nation as an ineffective, pathetic, and even hopelessly backward state. Yet the short-lived Great Korean Empire was not all that incompetent—the king was, certainly, but not the entire state. It carried out legal reforms, established the basis for a modern education system, carried out a systematic land survey, and signed contracts with foreign investors to construct modern infrastructure. In 1899, for instance, the first railroad opened, linking Seoul to the port of Incheon, and the first electric streetcar began operating in the capital. Many individual Koreans began embracing change: starting newspapers, establishing modern schools, opening businesses. A small number of intellectuals absorbed Western ideas, reading Western political, economic, and scientific works, usually in Japanese translations. Shin Chaeho, for example, wrote a work on Korean history in 1905 that was the first to present Korea as a nation in the modern sense.

In fact, one wonders what might have happened had Japan not taken over the country, had China, Russia, and Japan not interfered in Korean affairs. Would it have been another Japan? Would the modern, prosperous Korea of today (South Korea, that is) have come about even earlier? We will never know the answer to these questions. The modernization that took place after 1910 was under the direct supervision of the Japanese, and was intended, first and foremost, to serve the needs of their homeland, not of Korea.

Colonial Korea

Korea's colonial experience was an unhappy one. In many European colonies, the colonizers ruled indirectly through local chiefs, rajas, or emirs, but Japan ruled directly and thoroughly. By the 1930s, when the colonial government was at the peak of its intensity, about a quarter of a million Japanese civilian, military, and police personnel were employed in Korea. This was roughly equivalent to the British presence in India, which had more than fifteen times the population, and ten times greater than the number of French in Vietnam, a colony with a population similar to Korea's. While an Indian or African peasant might encounter a British or French colonial official only rarely, ordinary Koreans encountered them every day—the Japanese schoolteacher, the village policeman, the postal clerk. The police were particularly intrusive, with the power to judge and sentence minor offenses, collect taxes, oversee local irrigation works, even to inspect businesses and homes to see that health and other government regulations were being enforced. It was a top-down administration with all officials, police, and military directly answerable to the governor-general. Koreans served mainly in the lower ranks of the bureaucracy and were excluded from any meaningful participation in decision-making.

Furthermore, Japan's colonial rule had the feel of an occupation, with a highly centralized national gendarmerie and strategically located officials. Military garrisons were positioned throughout the country. The governor-generals were all military men who wore military uniforms. Japanese officials—even schoolteachers in the early years—carried swords. The governor-general himself had far more power than any Korean king ever had; he answered only to the prime minister of Japan, and was accountable to no one in the peninsula.

The harsh military character of the colonial administration was partly a response to the hostility with which many Koreans greeted the Japanese; the colonial administration had not begun well. Terauchi Masatake, a hardened army general who came to Korea as the first governor-general, was met upon his arrival with an assassination plot. He launched a sweeping crackdown on the opposition, arresting seven hundred Koreans. One hundred five were convicted of being involved after being tortured and confessing. Their forced and often far-fetched confessions, a forerunner of those elicited in North Korean show trials, were often so outlandish they drew the attention of the Western press. This, along with the fact that most of those targeted were Christian, attracted too much bad publicity; an embarrassed Japanese government released many of them. But the colonial authorities took no further chances, and the early years of their rule were a continual reign of terror, with tens of thousands of Koreans arrested, beaten, and tortured. Korean-language publications were subject to strict censorship when they were approved of at all, which was seldom. Especially humiliating for a people proud of learning, education for Koreans was restricted to just a few years of basic schooling.

Daehan Manse!: The Birth of Modern Nationalism

Resentment against Japanese rule burst into the open in a most dramatic way in 1919—on March 1, 1919, to be precise—a date that is still celebrated today as the inception of modern Korean nationalism. At the end of World War I, US president Woodrow Wilson declared the principle of national self-determination. This was meant to apply only to Europeans, but it galvanized many victims of imperialism across the world, and Koreans were among the first to be animated by this promising turn of international events. In late February, representatives of various Protestant, Cheondogyo, and Buddhist groups decided to issue a declaration of independence as a kind of peaceful protest statement in a park in Seoul. They planned to sign it and send a petition to the peacemakers who were meeting in Paris, requesting that Korea be given its back its freedom. It was a modest and symbolic gesture, yet it proved—probably to the surprise of the organizers themselves—to be the spark of a conflagration that swept across the peninsula and would be a turning point in modern Korean history.

The timing was potentially explosive, because not only were many intellectuals discussing what the principle of self-determination meant for Koreans, but thousands of their countrymen were gathering in the capital to attend the funeral of the former King Gojong, whose death reminded Koreans of what they had lost. Added to this combustible mixture were rumors circulating that the Japanese had poisoned him. Worried by the tight security imposed in the capital, the religious representatives decided to meet in a restaurant instead of the park on February 28, intending to issue their declaration and sign the petition there. When their declaration was read to a crowd by a person who happened to have a copy, the reaction was electric. Demonstrations broke out in the city and soon swept the country, taking place in every province and city. An estimated half million to one million men and women of all backgrounds participated. The March First Movement, as it came to be called, was the first great outburst of modern national sentiment. The concept of Korea as a sovereign nation-state, of the Korean people as a nation, leapt from the teahouse conversations of a few intellectuals to the shouts and dreams of hundreds of thousands, if not millions, of ordinary people. Today Korean historians often justifiably see this as a turning point in the growth of modern Korean nationalism.

Although almost all the demonstrations were peaceful, the Japanese reaction was not. Several thousand were killed and many thousands arrested in a wave of repression. In one incident, a group of protesting Christians was forced into a church, perishing when it was torched by colonial police. One tragic case was that of Yu Gwansun, a bright young girl born in central Korea who received a scholarship to study at the American missionary-run Ewha Women's high school; her teachers recounted her impressive ability to memorize texts. Only sixteen when the March First Movement began, she became an activist and helped organize a demonstration in her region. When a thousand demonstrators assembled, the Japanese opened fire, killing many, including both her parents. Yu was arrested and offered release if she would give the Japanese the names of her fellow organizers. She refused and died in prison a few months later from injuries caused by torture. Yu became a symbol of the movement and the resistance to Japanese rule.

Under the Admirals: The Liberal Decade

Koreans didn't get their independence, but the March First Movement did bring about a brief decade of greater freedom. In 1919, a
shocked and embarrassed government in Tokyo decided to shift the
administration of the colony from the hardline Prussian-style army
over to the more liberal Anglophile navy. Two admirals served as
governor-generals during the next twelve years. Inaugurating what
they called their "culture policy," the Japanese authorities permitted
Koreans to open newspapers in their own language again. This was
followed by a number of Korean-language magazines and other publications. The colonial administration promised to expand public
education and extend the length of schooling for Koreans so that it
would be equal to what Japanese received. Instruction would be
given in both Korean and Japanese, and schools could teach Korean
language and history alongside mandatory courses on Japan. Koreans were allowed to assemble and form organizations, including
those that discussed political ideas, but could not advocate for independence or challenge the authority of the colonial regime.

Koreans responded quickly to this chance to express themselves
more openly, and the 1920s saw a short-lived cultural renaissance.
Educated Koreans explored new ideas, reexamined their cultural
heritage, and charted new courses for the future of their society.
They did so in newspapers and glossy magazines and in societies
that advocated cultural, educational, and social reforms. Yet even
with the reforms, Korea was still far from a bastion of free expression. The 1925 Peace Preservation Law gave police broad authority
to crack down on political activity, and the notorious Thought Police
kept an eye on all Koreans. Almost every Korean organization had
police spies. Koreans who crossed the ambiguous boundaries of
what was permitted were arrested and routinely tortured. Most were
forced to publicly recant any anti-Japanese statements or sentiments
and were then released. All Koreans were completely shut out of
higher government posts. In short, the "liberal" 1920s seem liberal
mainly in comparison to the harsh 1910s and the years after 1931.

"New Women" and "Old Ways": A Society Undergoing Change

Leading the cultural renaissance of colonial Korea was the emerging middle class. This was a new social group of teachers, doctors, accountants, businessmen, bankers, and civil servants in the colonial bureaucracy who were plugged into the modern world. They represented a huge break from the past, wearing Western-style clothes, living in houses with electricity and—if they were well off—maybe a radio. These modern men and women read newspapers and magazines, and modern literature by foreign writers in translation, or by Korean authors who were writing Western-style novels and short stories. They sent their children to modern schools, where the curriculum included science and math as well as civics, history, and literature. This new middle class included a group of modern entrepreneurs. The old stigma against commerce was diminishing, and many educated Koreans entered into businesses of all kinds. Some operated rice mills, textile plants, trucking companies, banks. Members of this small Korean business class worked closely with their Japanese counterparts, but had their own separate chamber of commerce in Seoul. Among the most prominent were Kim Seongsu and his brother Kim Yeonsu; they owned the Gyeongbang Textile Company, one of the largest and most successful businesses in Korea. The Kim brothers were of *yangban* background, and their ancestors would have rolled over in their graves to see them and their colleagues running businesses like rice mills and textile companies. Some of the new entrepreneurs, such as Pak Heungshik, came from a more humble background. Pak owned a chain of retail stores, including the Hwashin department store in Seoul, and by the 1940s had become the richest man in Korea. Although modern industry and banking in colonial Korea were dominated by the Japanese, the presence of a small class of Korean factory owners, bankers, and modern retailers like Pak and the Kims, who often worked closely with and learned from their Japanese counterparts, was a valuable asset for South Korea after its liberation in 1945.

While men of the new middle class wore clothes that would not have looked out of place in New York or London, Korean women were more likely to wear the traditional *hanbok* dress. Attitudes toward women changed slowly, and few women appeared in public life, yet things were changing for them, too. Many left home to take jobs in factories, where they made up a substantial portion of the workforce. And women were getting educated, although the purpose of educating women was not to prepare them for professional life, but for their roles as "wise mothers, good wives." The thinking was that a woman could better supervise the schooling of her children and be a more useful companion for her husband if she was educated.

A few women, however, broke from even this changed role, becoming writers, educators, artists, and political activists. Feminist Kim Wonju was one of these "new women," as they were sometimes called. In the 1920s, Kim published *Shin Yeosoeng* (New Woman), a magazine aimed at the modern woman. Some of these women wore Western-style clothes, listened to jazz, smoked and drank in public, and freely socialized with men. No women broke with tradition more than Pak Gyeongwon, a wealthy farmer's daughter who left home and studied industrial arts in Japan. After returning to Korea and working in a textile mill, she went back to Japan and became a driver—a very unusual job for a woman—and then a pilot. She won a number of flying contests before being killed in a plane crash. The crash could be viewed as symbolic, showing that she flew too high for her times—but the fact that she flew at all was evidence of a major change in this conservative Confucian society.

During this period of change, the old *yangban* lost their monopoly on public office and suffered the humiliation of all colonial subjects—being lorded over by foreigners. But otherwise, they didn't make out too badly. Many took advantage of their knowledge of the colonial system to acquire lands from peasants who were unable to establish legal ownership. The *yangban* were no longer a distinct social class, but they still represented much of the wealthier, more dominant sector of Korean society.

Factory Workers and Foragers: Ordinary Koreans under Colonial Rule

Below the landowning elite and the new middle class were the vast majority of Koreans, who saw little or no improvement in their lives.

A small industrial working class emerged in the early years of colonial rule, and grew by five- or six-fold between 1931 and 1945. Industrial workers were also assigned to the more menial tasks; Japanese brought over from the home country filled the managerial and skilled jobs. Wages were low as well, with Korean workers paid only a third of what their Japanese counterparts earned. Resentment among Korean workers was high, and strikes and protests were common. Despite their modest numbers, the strikers were concentrated in cities and exposed to new ideas, and they were often militant. Many formed "red labor unions"—so called because they were sometimes organized by communists. But by the mid-1930s the colonial authorities had cracked down on them so hard that labor unions ceased to function, or did so only underground.

About three-quarters of the people were farmers, and for most of them, life under colonial rule became harder. Land ownership declined and the great majority of peasants became tenant farmers. A small percentage of farm families owned most of the land, while the others owned either no land or not enough to support a family. To survive, they had to rent land from a landowner or work in his fields. Typical rents amounted to half of a farmer's crops, leaving barely enough to feed a family in a good harvest. The Japanese carried out systematic land surveys that caused many peasants to lose their land because they could not prove ownership, which was often based on custom. Even those small farmers who had legal title to land where they grew some crops for market found that the increasing commercialization of agriculture subjected them to sharp market fluctuations, forcing them to borrow. They frequently accumulated high levels of debt as a result. Nothing better illustrates the hardships and exploitation of Korean farmers under colonial rule than the scarcity of rice. Rice production increased but it was for export to Japan. Instead of rice, poor Koreans—and most Koreans were poor—ate millet imported from Manchuria. Millet, while nutritious, was traditionally dismissed as a "coarse grain" eaten only as an emergency substitute when rice was not available.

Population growth also put pressure on the land, since the number of mouths to feed increased faster than new land opened to cultivation. Among the farmers who had it worst were those who moved into the mountain forests and squatted on public land. They would burn trees and bushes, sow a crop, then move on to another field, barely eking out a precarious existence. This contributed to the deforestation of the country, as the traditional customs that had protected the woodlands broke down. Photos from the period depict treeless mountainsides, as if colonial rule had stripped the country bare.

The More Militaristic 1930s

In 1931, as the Great Depression engulfed much of the world, Japanese army units carried out a takeover of Manchuria. The Japanese government in Tokyo now moved into an increasingly militaristic, ultra-nationalist direction. Instead of international cooperation with the Western powers, the Japanese bragged about their uniqueness while creating an empire in eastern Asia that would give them the resources, markets, and manpower to be free of reliance on the Euro-American–dominated global economy. For Korea, this meant that the "liberal period" was at an end. As it expanded into China, imperial Japan saw Korea as a base for further expansion. Tokyo began industrial development in the north and returned the administration of the colony to the army, which re-imposed some of the more repressive policies of the past. This accelerated after 1937, when Japan invaded China.

Both the Japanese homeland and Korea were then mobilized for what had become a major war effort. As part of this general marshaling of the population, the governor-general began shutting down Korean organizations and replacing them with large-scale state-sponsored ones. Writers belonged to the writers' association designed to direct their efforts toward wartime propaganda. Young people were channeled into the Korean Federation of Youth Organizations. The Korean Association for Imperial Rule Assistance, the Korean League for the General Mobilization of the National Spirit, and the Korean Anticommunist Association all had branches throughout the country. In 1940, the entire country was organized into 350,000 Neighborhood Patriotic Organizations, each consisting of ten households.

These new organizations functioned as vehicles for the collection of contributions, carrying out rationing, and assigning people tasks for volunteer labor. The first day of each month was Rising Asia Service Day, on which everyone was required to perform voluntary tasks. By 1940, the colony was taking on the character of a totalitarian society in which all activity was directed toward the goals of the state. As the war continued, it was increasingly difficult for any prominent Korean to avoid being a cheerleader for the regime.

When the war expanded in late 1941 from a conflict with China to one with the United States and the British Empire, hundreds of thousands of Koreans were conscripted to work in Japan. School terms were shortened so that students could carry out voluntary labor, and many young people were among those sent to Japan as laborers. In fact, by 1945 a sizeable portion of the total labor force in Japan was Korean. A most tragic development that remains a sore point in Korean–Japanese relations today was the use of up to 200,000 young Korean women as "comfort women." Recruited under false pretenses, they were forced to serve as prostitutes for Japanese troops. Returning home in disgrace, many had to carry the shame of this experience their entire lives. One recalled how, as an eighteen-year-old, she was offered a good job at a restaurant, then found herself shipped off to Burma with seventeen other young women and forced to service thirty men a day. Living under virtual imprisonment, five in her group committed suicide. Yet the comfort women were not the only tragic figures among the many Koreans caught up in the war started by their colonial occupiers.

Koreans Become Japanese: Japan's Bizarre Attempt at Forced Assimilation

Imperialism is never pleasant for its victims. Even if the rulers' motives are benign, having so much power over others often tends to bring out the worst in people. But few colonial rulers during the great heyday of imperialism before World War II left a legacy as bitter as the Japanese in Korea. There are many reasons to explain the hatred the Koreans had toward the Japanese. For one, Korea's colonizers were a familiar neighboring people that shared many East

Asian traditions and who had invaded Korea in the past. The Japanese colonial rule, as we have seen, was more intrusive and intensive, taking on many features of a military occupation. And unlike other colonized nations—India, say, or Indonesia or those in Africa—Korea was an ethnically unified society with more than a millennium of political unity and self-rule.

Korean resentment over Japanese rule was only compounded by the way the colonial authorities pursued changeable and contradictory policies. Tokyo could never quite decide what Korea was. Was it simply a frontier region of Japan, like Okinawa, that was to be absorbed into the homeland? Was it a foreign colony inhabited by an alien people who were to be treated as colonial subjects? Or was it—as some policymakers considered it, especially after 1931—a kind of junior partner in the Empire, inhabited by somewhat inferior cousins? Thus, colonial policies were inconsistent and confused. One idea was for a substantial colonization of the peninsula by ethnic Japanese, which would be part of a process of gradually absorbing Korea into the home country. But few Japanese farmers were interested in relocating to Korea. Many Japanese worked for the state and state corporations; some worked at private Japanese businesses, but Japanese only made up 3 to 4 percent of the total population in Korea.

Another policy was to make Koreans Japanese. As part of the process of making "Korea and Japan One Body," as it was sometimes termed, limitations were placed on the use of the Korean language. The big push for forced assimilation began after the war with China started. From the late 1930s the use of Korean in the schools was restricted further and further until students could be punished for speaking it. Korean-language newspapers were shut down, and virtually all publications in Korean ceased. All Koreans were required to register at Shinto shrines, which now appeared everywhere. In Japan, Shinto had been used as a state cult to bind the Japanese together, but it was an alien religion to Koreans. For many, especially Christians, being forced to observe Shinto ceremonies was offensive. Then came the Name Order: in 1940, Koreans were required to change their names to Japanese ones. Most did this by selecting Chinese characters that were the same as or similar to their own and pronouncing them in the Japanese way. This "loss of names" was especially traumatic in Korean society, where the veneration of ancestors and preservation of family lines was so important. It was more than a loss of identity; it was a betrayal of one's forebears.

A few Koreans accepted the reality of being part of the Japanese Empire and sought to adopt Japanese culture. Yet no matter how hard they tried, Koreans were not really accepted by Japanese as equals; nor did they mix socially. An insular, racially exclusive people, the Japanese kept apart from Koreans, and intermarriage was rare. Rather than creating harmony and unity between the two peoples, colonial policies did quite the opposite, fostering a strong sense of Korean nationalism.

Inventing Korea: The Painful Birth of Modern Korean National Identity

Colonial Korea was therefore the great incubator of modern nationalism. From the March First Movement on, Korean nationalism was a powerful force. It was not a movement—that would imply a unity that Korean nationalists never possessed. Korean nationalists all shared the same goal: to regain their nation's independence. And they didn't just want to be independent again; they wanted to be part of a prosperous, strong nation that was in the forefront of a progressive, civilized humanity. What they didn't agree on was how to get there. Gradualists like the influential writer Yi Gwangsu felt that Korea had to first improve itself, educate the people, and learn to become modern; then, when the Korean people had achieved a sufficient level of maturity and "modernity," Korea could become independent. Many educated Koreans ascribed to this view. They looked at their own history with a certain amount of shame and blamed Confucianism, the lazy and self-serving *yangban* class, and the country's subservience to China for its pathetic weakness and loss of independence. A free and independent Korea was their aim. However, it would be a long-term project, led by people like themselves who would be simultaneously cooperating with the Japanese while establishing schools, newspapers, and self-improvement societies that would lead the ignorant masses into the modern world. Only then would Korea be ready to join the world of sovereign states. Thus they were able to persuade themselves that they were supporting the independence movement by collaborating with the colonial occupiers. It is easy to ridicule the obvious self-serving nature of these moderate, gradualist nationalists; still, most were sincere.

Moderate nationalists promoted education and efforts to establish a Korean university. Some, like the northern landowner Cho Manshik, were influenced by Gandhi's nonviolent, noncooperating nationalist movement in India. Cho established an organization to encourage Koreans to buy locally made products and boycott Japanese imported goods. These more moderate forms of protest and national consciousness-raising could not survive the more repressive administration of the 1930s. During the war, the Japanese insisted that all prominent Koreans actively support the war effort, which meant that most of the moderates were pressured into giving speeches or other public displays of support. This weakened their nationalist credentials and would haunt them after liberation.

For many Koreans, the gradualist approach toward reform and liberation was completely unsatisfying. They turned to radical explanations and radical solutions for the country's plight. A few of them were attracted to anarchism; many were attracted to communism after the Bolshevik Revolution of 1917. Lenin's denunciation of imperialism and his offer to help victims of colonial oppression excited young Koreans. When Lenin called an international conference of the Toilers of the East in Moscow in 1922, Koreans were the largest group to attend. In fact, considering the poverty and geographical and political obstacles to reaching Moscow, it is surprising how many participated. They returned with a new vision for society.

Marxism was especially attractive since it offered an explanation for the country's weakness, its poverty, and its victimization at the hands of the Japanese. It was an all-embracing philosophy, which like Neo-Confucianism offered a blueprint for a virtuous, harmonious, prosperous society. In fact, Korean Marxists were very much like their Neo-Confucian ancestors, coming back from abroad with a prescription to cure society's ills and lead it to a bright future. They were not gradualists, but believed in violent revolution, opposed cooperation with the colonial authorities, and held the moderate nationalists in contempt. They saw the latter as not only collaborators, but as elitists in the tradition of the *yangban*. And they wanted more than independence; they wanted a social revolution that would be led by the masses, the common peasants and workers.

In the early 1920s, young Koreans, many of them students returning from Japan, formed several Marxist "study clubs." In 1925, members of the clubs established a Korean Communist Party. They were quickly rounded up and arrested by the ever-vigilant Japanese police. Three more communist parties were organized over the next three years; each attempt was short-lived, since the police quickly found out and arrested the members. Japanese police efficiency made any type of organized activity aimed at independence extremely difficult. Nonetheless, they could not eliminate the domestic communist movement. The Korean Communist Party reappeared as a secret underground organization led by Pak Heonyeong. Pak spent time in and out of jail for leftist activities. He was arrested for the last time in 1933, but was released in 1939 after faking mental illness. Traveling around the country as an itinerant bricklayer, he kept the domestic communist movement barely alive. A number of writers and intellectuals, avoiding activism, quietly maintained their communist beliefs.

Resistance from Abroad: The Exile Movements

Colonial rule created a diaspora of exiled Koreans who became active in the nationalist independence cause. However, rather than being part of a unified movement, they were divided by ideology, disagreements on tactics, and geography. Most independence movements among Asians and Africans during the heyday of colonialism had a principal overseas base of operations—London, Paris, Switzerland, New York, and so on—but Korean nationalists were scattered all over the globe. Some worked in Tokyo until the repression of the 1930s made that no longer viable. Others were in Shanghai, Manchuria, western China, Siberia, Hawaii, and the US mainland. The efforts of these globally dispersed groups were largely uncoordinated. In 1919, a number of groups tried to combine their efforts, forming the Korean Provisional Government in Shanghai. This organization proved too ideologically diverse to be effective.

The first president of the Korean Provisional Government was Syngman Rhee, who actually lived in the US. Rhee was an interesting character. As noted above, he was an American missionary-educated youth of modest background who fled the country when the Japanese cracked down on the Independence Club. After earning a Ph.D. in political science from Princeton University, he became active in the small Korean community in the United States. His reputation as an outspoken opponent of Japanese rule, and his prestigious degree—Koreans always admire academic distinction—made him a prominent and respected leader. But he had no real organizational base other than being the nominal head of the Korean Provisional Government.

In contrast to Rhee, another prominent independence leader, Kim Gu, had little formal education but earned a reputation as a man of action. A member of the Donghak, he murdered a Japanese trader whom he mistook for a policeman in a fit of outrage over the death of Queen Min in 1896. Escaping from jail, he became a monk and then joined the resistance movement in China. He and his followers carried out assassination plots, including a close but failed attempt on Emperor Hirohito. His most famous terrorist attack took place in Shanghai in 1932, while the Japanese were celebrating the emperor's birthday. Two top military commanders died and another official, Shigemitsu Mamoru, lost a leg. Later, as foreign minister, Shigemitsu would limp across the deck of the USS *Missouri* to sign the terms of Japanese surrender in front of a seated General MacArthur. The famous scene captured the sense of a defeated Japan crippled by war—but in fact, Shigemitsu had been crippled by the Korean resistance. During World War II, Kim Gu headed the small Korean Restoration Army that fought the Japanese as allies of Chiang Kai-shek's Kuomintang. Like most other exiled nationalist groups, it remained small and isolated.

Thousands of Koreans joined forces with the Chinese Communist Party, some making the Long March to Yenan with Mao Zedong. During the war, a unit of Korean communists—the Korean Voluntary

Army under the leadership of Korean communist Mu Jeong—fought with the Chinese communists. In a completely different area of operation, a few thousand Koreans fought in the mountains of Manchuria along the northern border of Korea. During colonial times, hundreds of thousands of Koreans crossed into this region. There many young people joined the guerrilla bands that were coordinated by and under the command of the Chinese Communist Party.

The most famous of the Manchurian guerrillas was Kim Seongju, whose father had emigrated to Manchuria from the Pyongyang area when he was nine years old. Kim joined the Chinese communist resistance to the Japanese sometime around the age of twenty, changing his name to Kim Il Sung (Kim Ilseong). At the young age of twenty-five he led a small guerrilla raid on the border city of Bocheonbo, briefly capturing it from the Japanese. This raid in June 1937 made Kim Il Sung modestly famous, since it was widely reported in the Korean-language press. The Japanese formed a special unit to track him down, but failed. Although little more than pinpricks to the mighty Japanese military establishment, these guerrilla attacks were troublesome enough to spur them into action. Tokyo carried out a military campaign in 1939 that largely wiped out the Chinese and Korean guerrillas, forcing the survivors, including Kim Il Sung, to flee across the border into the Soviet Union.

The Colonial Legacy

By most standards, Korea's colonial experience was fairly short in duration—thirty-five years—yet it was a very traumatic one. The country experienced direct foreign rule for the first time in its history. It underwent radical economic and social changes. The colonial occupation was intense and intrusive; no one was left alone. Especially during the last years, a near-totalitarian system was created, accompanied by mystical nationalism—the cult of the emperor—and characterized by the mass mobilization of society. For Koreans it was a new type of government and a new type of state with highly concentrated power, where all activity was directed toward state-sponsored goals. In many ways, both North and South Korea were heirs to this regimented, goal-oriented type of government. North

Korea in particular can be seen, at least in part, as a reincarnation of the late-colonial totalitarian society characterized by militarism and ultra-nationalism and centered on the all-embracing cult of the semidivine family line.

The Japanese bequeathed Korea some major industrial development and an impressive rail system with almost as many miles of track as there were in China. But the industries, mainly concentrated in the north, were operated by and for the Japanese, and the rail system was designed to serve Japan's needs, not Korea's, bringing products to ports to be exported to Japan and transporting troops across the peninsula to Manchuria and later to the Chinese heartland. The deliberately slow development of the education system never met public demand for schooling, resulting in unlicensed informal schools and a surprising number of young Koreans being sent to Japan by families that somehow scraped together enough money to pay for it. And while Korean businessmen and some skilled professionals prospered under colonial rule, there is little evidence that most ordinary people benefitted at all. In fact, for the majority who were peasants, life became worse than ever. Furthermore, the absurd attempts to erase Korean identity at a time when Korean national consciousness was rising contributed to the bitterness toward the Japanese.

When Japanese rule ended in 1945, it left a legacy of people frustrated that their opportunities for education and advancement had been blocked by Japanese discrimination, of farmers unhappy about the loss of their land, of repressed artists and intellectuals, of angry nationalists, and of millions disoriented by the upheavals of wartime mobilization that had uprooted them from their homes. It was a restless population ripe for radical change.

CHAPTER 5

KOREA BECOMES TWO STATES: DIVISION AND WAR (1945–1953)

The Arbitrary Division of Korea

On the night of August 10, 1945, the State-War-Navy Coordinating Committee instructed Colonel Dean Rusk and Colonel Charles Bonesteel to draw up a proposal to divide Korea into separate Soviet and US occupation zones. Looking at a modest scale map, the colonels noticed that the thirty-eighth parallel divided the country into roughly two equal halves, and that Seoul was just below it in the southern half. They proposed that this be the line separating the two occupation zones.

The hastily called meeting carried a sense of urgency. On August 6, the US had dropped the atomic bomb on Hiroshima; two days later, the Soviet Union had declared war on Japan. Having agreed to do so within three months after the German surrender, Stalin waited right until the deadline. Almost immediately, Soviet forces advanced on the Japanese in Sakhalin, Manchuria, on their short border with Korea. The Japanese forces, depleted of men and material, quickly gave way. Washington, hoping to keep the entire peninsula from falling to the Soviets, offered to create separate occupation zones, as had been done in Germany and Austria. But since US forces were nowhere near Korea, there was no reason to expect Moscow to agree to halt its advance at the thirty-eighth parallel. To the surprise of many, however, Stalin instantly agreed. These odd circumstances were behind Korea's division in two: a temporary act of expediency became a permanent and tragic reality for the Korean people, one that would haunt them for the next three generations.

It is unlikely that anyone involved appreciated what they had wrought. One of the world's most ethnically and culturally homogeneous nations, with a history of political unity unbroken for a millennium, was now severed in two. The arbitrary line not only divided a country, but separated provinces, valleys, and families. It was not based on any historical, cultural, or geographical distinctions; it was just a straight line across a map. Modern history offers (pardon the pun) no parallel case of this happening. Germany was divided, of course, but that country was a collection of little states and one bigger one, Prussia, which had only been cobbled together by Bismarck in 1871. Korea, by contrast, was an ancient state that had been established back when Germany's forebears were still tribal peoples gathering acorns in the forest. Of course, it did encompass regional differences, but there were fewer of these than in Germany or most other states of its size, and in any case they had no relation to the boundary between the two Koreas. The demarcation was set by people who knew little about Korea; no Koreans were aware of the decision, and it is unlikely that any would have approved it.

The division of Korea was one of the great tragedies that the twentieth century brought to the country, comparable to its annexation by Japan in 1910. In some ways it was worse, as it lasted longer and left deeper scars. Done out of expediency, it was not intended to be permanent, but it became so. Almost all Koreans regarded the division of their country as unacceptable, and almost all, in both North and South, wanted reunification.

A Brief Moment of Joy: The End of Japanese Rule

On Sunday, August 15, 1945, Koreans were told to gather around the nearest radio to hear an announcement from the emperor. This was most extraordinary, since the remote, godlike Japanese emperor never addressed his subjects; the general public had not even heard his voice. As they listened, few could make out his words, since most Koreans could not understand Japanese well, and those who could had trouble comprehending the archaic form of the language the imperial family used. But the message got through: Japan was surrendering. To people isolated by strict censorship and accustomed to hearing only reports of victories, the news came as a shock. They may have known the war was not going well, but they had not expected this. Almost immediately, Koreans broke out in spontaneous celebrations—singing, weeping, and dancing in the streets. Symbols of Japanese authority were destroyed and the families brought out hidden *taegukki*, the Korean national flag, or improvised them, and proudly displayed them. At night the landscape was lit by Shinto shrines that Koreans had set on fire.

Koreans expected the Japanese surrender to result in independence, but the Allies had different ideas. At the Cairo Conference in December 1943, Roosevelt, Churchill, and Chinese leader Chiang Kai-shek agreed that Korea would gain its independence "in due course" upon the defeat of Japan. When the news of this spread, mainly to the Korean exile community, it was assumed that "in due course" meant immediately. However, Franklin Delano Roosevelt, who like most Americans knew little about Korea, had proposed that the country be placed under some sort of allied trusteeship after the fall of the Japanese Empire. Later he proposed that it be placed under a UN trusteeship for forty years, until Koreans were ready for independence, not appreciating the fact that Koreans had many centuries of experience in being an independent state. Stalin agreed, but suggested shortening the period to between twenty and thirty years.

Koreans, being unaware of this in 1945, began to prepare for independence within days of the announcement of Japan's surrender, forming People's Committees in Seoul and elsewhere. These were ad hoc groups of prominent local citizens of all political views who met to prepare for the restoration of independence and to handle practical matters such as ensuring adequate food supplies and avoiding clashes between Koreans and Japanese. Within two weeks, People's Committees had been formed in all provinces and major cities and towns. In early September, representatives of the various committees declared a Korean People's Republic.

Made in Moscow? The New North Korean State

To say that neither the Soviets nor the Americans were prepared for the occupation of Korea would be an understatement; they were totally unprepared. Moscow and Washington simply had not given Korea much thought, and Japan's capitulation came sooner than expected. Neither side even brought Korean-speaking interpreters with them, nor did the military commanders of either occupation zone have clear orders on what they were supposed to do when they arrived. Both occupations were improvised, but the Soviets had a clearer sense of the kind of society they intended to create than the Americans, who seemed to have had no idea of what they expected to accomplish.

Because of their proximity, the Soviet forces occupied their zone first. On August 11, the 25th Red Army crossed the border into northeast Korea. Over the next two weeks they took control of the industrial northeast region, carting off equipment and engaging in unofficial looting. On August 26 they entered Pyongyang. The Soviets found that the People's Committees were already carrying out many of the functions of local government, so they worked with them. The head of the Pyongyang People's Committee was Cho Man-shik, a Christian nationalist and an advocate of nonviolence who served as the nominal leader in the region. But the Soviets were looking for more reliable partners—communists they could work with. The local communists who emerged from hiding or jail had few contacts with Moscow; they took orders from the Korean Communist Party, whose leadership was, rather awkwardly, in the American zone. The Soviets didn't want to work with Christian nationalists and regarded the local communists as unreliable. Furthermore, they desperately needed Russian-speaking Koreans just to communicate with.

Into this situation came Kim Il Sung and his partisan comrades. After fleeing to Siberia in 1940, they had become part of the 25th Red Army's 88th Special Reconnaissance Brigade. When the war ended, Kim and his fellow partisans tried without much success to return to Korea. Finally, Kim and sixty of his comrades managed to get a ride aboard a ship sailing to the port of Wonsan on the East Sea. On September 19, they arrived in northern Korea. It was the first time Kim had been in Korea since he was twelve; for some of his fellow Manchurian guerrillas, it was the first time ever. Wearing Soviet military uniforms, familiar with the Soviet army, speaking some Russian, and with unimpeachable nationalist credentials, this small group of former Manchurian guerrillas was just what the Soviets were looking for. Although not the most senior member, Kim Il Sung was the best known and also managed to impress the Russian officers who interviewed him. Having found the leader they needed, they almost immediately began promoting him. The Soviets introduced him to the public by having him deliver the keynote speech at the massive welcoming ceremony for the Red Army they organized on October 14. From then on it was clear that the Soviets were preparing Kim for a leadership role.

However, Kim Il Sung and his guerrilla companions were not the only Korean communists who were playing important roles. The occupation authorities managed to find hundreds of bilingual Soviet-Koreans from all over the USSR who provided technical expertise. Particularly valuable was their familiarity with Soviet government and Communist Party organization. At the same time, thousands of Korean communists returned from China. These so-called Yenan Communists included the prominent leader Kim Dubong, who formed the rival New People's Party. At the insistence of the Soviets, this party merged with the North Korean Branch Bureau (as the Korean Communist Party in the North was called). Furthermore, as the Americans and their allies in the South began to crack down on communism, most of the communist leaders there fled north, forming a "domestic Communist" faction under the leadership of Pak Heon-yeong. Thus, Kim Il Sung had to share power with many others, but he was still the one the Soviets were promoting. His portrait was hung in public places alongside Stalin's, and composers were instructed to write songs about his heroic deeds as a partisan fighter. The Soviets however, could not have known what they were creating: a dictatorship with a cult of personality that would outdo that of Stalin, and a dynasty that would long outlast the USSR.

At first, Moscow entertained the idea of establishing a unified Korea from the two occupation zones that would be friendly or at least neutral, rather than establishing a separate government in their sector. But in early 1946, they took steps to create a new Soviet-style state. Carefully managed elections produced a national People's Committee that carried out sweeping reforms. Industries were nationalized—a rather easy step since most were owned by Japanese who had fled or been repatriated. They instituted an eight-hour workday and a minimum wage. Other laws established equality between men and women and made divorce easy. Mass adult-education campaigns reduced illiteracy, and compulsory universal education was enacted.

The most significant measure was land reform. In a country where most people were tenant farmers or agricultural laborers, nothing could have done more to win support for the new political and social system the Soviets and their communist allies were establishing. All the property of the big landowners was confiscated—most landowners fled south of the parallel—and more or less equally distributed to all farmers. Heavy land taxes and the small size of the farms meant that their material existence improved only marginally, but the peasants were now working their own land.

With these measures, a radically new society was emerging in the North: one based on equality, in which everyone was to address each other as "Comrade," in which formerly humble peasants and workers were told they were the new elite of society, and in which the old *yangban* class that had dominated society for many centuries was gone. But it was also a regimented society that brooked no dissent. Protest demonstrations—mostly by Christian groups—were brutally repressed. Writers and artists were enlisted as propaganda agents of the state, and much as had been done in wartime under the Japanese, everyone was mobilized for various campaigns directed toward state goals. An elaborate security apparatus was developed under the direction of former Soviet police officer Bang Hakse. North Korea soon had all the makings of a Soviet-style totalitarian government except a prison system—political prisoners were simply carted off to the Soviet Union's gulags—and an army. The latter was created in early

1948, when some of the security forces were converted into the Korean People's Army.

Americans Create Their Own Korea

The Americans, like the Soviets, arrived in Korea ill-prepared, lacking interpreters and a coherent plan; like the Soviets, they had few contacts in the country and were not sure who to work with. And like the Soviets, they lacked clear instructions from their government. But in most other ways the US occupation was different. Unlike the Soviets, the Americans refused to work with or even acknowledge the People's Committees. They were slower to delegate authority to locals, and had real difficulty in finding local leaders they felt comfortable with. Within months the Soviet administration undertook a clear, orderly, systematic transformation of the country, while the US occupation had a chaotic, confused quality during all of its three years. When they arrived in Seoul, the Koreans cheered the American liberators wildly, but their goodwill dissipated immediately when the US military commander, General Hodge, a good soldier but ill-suited for the task of nation-building, ordered that the Koreans continue to obey the Japanese colonial authorities. This was meant only as a temporary measure of expediency to ensure order until the Americans could put their own administration in place. However, Koreans were stunned at being told to obey the oppressors that they had just been liberated from. The Americans quickly realized their mistake and sent the Japanese home, but they never fully regained the trust of the people they had been sent to govern.

A major problem for the Americans, much as for the Soviets, was finding people they could work with, and it was one the US never solved satisfactorily. South Korea became a confusing mix of groups competing for power: the communists under Pak Heonyeong, who hoped to work with others to bring about a socialist revolution; various radical and left-leaning groups not affiliated with or willing to work with the communists; the conservative landlords and businessmen; right-wing independence fighter Kim Ku, who returned from China; and some moderates such as Kim Gyushik and Yeo Unhyong. The split between moderate and radical nationalists that had emerged in the 1920s came out in the open with liberation. The US occupation authorities outlawed the Korean Communist Party, and most of its members fled to the North. However, both communist-leaning and non-communist radicals continued to stir things up. A wave of labor strikes, student demonstrations, and pent-up griev-ances of all sorts emerged. Occupational authorities saw the hand of communists everywhere, and the right-wing conservatives who operated the police force arrested tens of thousands, until there were more Koreans in jail for political offenses than there had ever been under the Japanese.

The Americans gravitated to the wealthy landlord elite. Some could speak English, and most had enough understanding of West-erners to know how to please their foreign occupiers; they were, of course, also fervently anti-communist. Some of them, such as the industrialist Kim Seongsu, were decent enough people, but they had two strikes against them as plausible leaders of a new Korea. Firstly, most had not only prospered under the Japanese, but had willingly or under pressure actively supported the regime, especially during the war, thus undermining any nationalist credentials they might have had. Besides being tainted as collaborators, they owned the land that the country's millions of poor farmers wished to have, and thwarted attempts at land reform. Not only did the Americans align themselves with this elite class, but they appointed Koreans who had served in the Japanese police and military to run the South Ko-rean police and national constabulary (the forerunner of the later South Korean army). This, of course, did little to endear the occu-pation government to most Koreans.

One early candidate for a leader in the South was Syngman Rhee. Well known in Korea, the independence leader from the US had un-tarnished credentials as an uncompromising opponent of the Japa-nese and as an articulate spokesman for the independence cause. After Pearl Harbor, Rhee had left Hawaii for Washington to lobby for support for Korean independence. At the end of the war he some-how finagled a ride on General McArthur's private plane to Seoul, arriving on October 16. At first, the Americans thought they had found their leader. This was suggested by his formal public introduction by General Hodge. But they soon found Rhee to be a stubborn, independently minded old man who was difficult to work with. He was nobody's man but his own. Rhee led a campaign opposing the trusteeship and calling for immediate independence. This caused trouble for the US and only contributed to the atmosphere of disorder. But it served Rhee: he could gain popularity, since everyone hated the idea of a trusteeship, while also demonstrating he was no one's puppet. Conservatives found in Rhee a person they could support and who in turn could protect them from charges of collaboration. So an alliance of Rhee and the conservatives gained the upper hand in the South.

With politics polarized between left and right in the South, more moderate leaders—the left-leaning Yeo Unhyeong and right-leaning Kim Gyushik—formed the Coalition Committee to create a centrist government. For a moment the Americans saw hope, especially in the dashing, handsome, well-spoken Yeo. But in July 1947 Yeo was assassinated by an unknown assailant. Out of desperation, the Americans brought back Seo Jaepil, the aging former Gapsin coup leader, as a figure moderates might rally around. Seo's return was an extraordinary event, made even more so by the fact that someone who had briefly served as defense minister in 1884 and had led the Independence Club in the 1890s could still be around. Seo was not only very, very old, but dying of cancer. He came home, had a look around in the country he had not seen in half a century, and returned to the US to die. Thus, with the leftists mostly suppressed, the communist leadership having fled north, and the moderates rendered ineffective, the leadership in 1948 passed to Rhee and his conservative backers.

Untrustworthy Trusteeship: The Creation of Two Koreas

The original plan was to create a UN trusteeship, but there was no trust on any side. The Americans didn't trust the Soviets, the Soviets didn't trust the Americans, and the Koreans—at least in the South—didn't trust either of them. In December 1945, the US, the Soviet Union, China, and Britain met in Moscow to discuss setting up the trusteeship. It was to last four to five years, realistically reduced from the previous plan of twenty years. An American-Soviet Joint Commission was created to work out the details. Up to that point, Koreans had known nothing of the secret wartime plan for a UN trusteeship, and they reacted to the news with spontaneous outrage. On both sides of the parallel, massive demonstrations took place. At first these included the members of the Korean Communist Party, but when Moscow told them to support the plan, they fell in line. The Soviets then used opposition to the trusteeship as an excuse to clamp down on non-communist political groups in their sector. In the South, demonstrations continued, adding to the sense of disorder there and making it hard for the Americans to govern.

Meanwhile, nothing was accomplished by the Joint Commission when it met in 1946. A stumbling block was Moscow's stipulation that any political groups that opposed the trusteeship be barred from participating in the self-governing process. Since all political groups except for the Soviets' communist allies were adamantly against the idea of trusteeship, this was an obvious non-starter. In reality, by the spring of 1946 it was probably already too late to create a unified governing entity. The border between the two zones was being treated as a permanent one and the outlines of a separate state in the North were already being established when the Joint Commission met. The body's second meeting the following year also got nowhere, after which the US, seeing no progress and wishing to extricate itself from the peninsula, turned the question of independence over to the United Nations. The UN formed a Temporary Committee on Korea, which decided elections would be held in the spring of 1948.

When it was clear the Soviets would not cooperate, the UN held elections anyway, in the areas that were accessible to them; that is, in the South. This meant there was to be a separate election in the South, which would in all likelihood mean a separate government. Some South Koreans were appalled by the possibility that the division could become permanent. Kim Gyushik and others made a desperate last-minute attempt to work out some agreement with the North, but this got nowhere. In May the elections took place, and a National Assembly was elected in the South. Three hundred political parties participated, but of course, the Communists were absent.

In July, the Assembly elected Rhee as president, and with the UN's blessings the Republic of Korea (ROK) was declared in Seoul on August 15.

Separate preparations for independence took place north of the parallel. A constitution was drawn up for the new state, modeled on the 1936 Soviet Union constitution. In fact, it was drawn up in Moscow by Soviet officials who had it translated from Russian into Korean and then presented to their Korean clients. The North then carried out its own elections, which they claimed were secretly conducted in the South as well. An assembly met—two-thirds of the delegates were supposedly southerners—and approved of the new government. They then proclaimed the Democratic People's Republic of Korea (DPRK) on September 9. What is important to bear in mind is that both of these Koreas claimed to be the only legitimate one. In fact, the constitution of the DPRK specified Seoul as the capital (Seoul actually means "capital" in Korean). Pyongyang was only supposed to be the temporary government headquarters.

The new Republic of Korea in the south got off to a bad start. First, Seoul was plunged into darkness when the North cut off its electricity; almost all of the peninsula's power was generated in the far north. Then the government stumbled into semi-chaos as the executive and legislative branches quarreled. Rhee's government was at odds with the National Assembly; it may have elected him, but its largely independent members soon challenged the actions and appointments of their president. A major issue was Rhee's use of men who had served as officers in the hated Japanese police force to staff and command his security forces. The commanders of his newly created ROK army also had been officers in the Japanese army. One of the top generals was Kim Seokwon, who had headed a special unit to track down Kim Il Sung in the late 1930s. Unable to work with the Assembly, Rhee often ignored it and ruled in a semi-dictatorial style, using his Japanese-trained police to lock up opponents, who soon filled the jails. He also made use of an army of thugs known as the National Youth Corps, led by Yi Beomseok. Yi, who had been educated in Nazi Germany and later in China, was an admirer of Chiang Kai-Shek's Blueshirts, which in turn were patterned after Mussolini's Blackshirts. Under the slogan, "Nation first, state first," they paraded around and beat up and intimidated anyone who they regarded as a threat to the newly established political order. Rhee, meanwhile, saw communist infiltrators everywhere. Schools were purged of teachers; government offices fired civil servants; and institutions of all types dismissed employees suspected of being sympathizers. Protesting students were beaten and jailed.

Unrest was greatest in the countryside, which was filled with peasants excited by talk of land reform but frustrated by the government's failure to move on it. Some rose up in revolt. The worst violence was on Jeju, a beautiful island province that is now a popular vacation spot known as "Korea's Hawaii." Local citizens in this rural place staged an armed rebellion, taking advantage of the miles of tunnels and the caches of weapons the Japanese had left behind as a measure for a last-ditch defense of Korea against an Allied invasion that never came. In the appallingly violent struggle that followed, some 10 percent of the island's 300,000 inhabitants perished before the rebellion was put down. Rhee sent in his new army to bring Jeju back under control. In October 1948, just weeks after command of this force was transferred from the Americans to ROK officers, the army was assembled at the port of Yeosu to land on the island. Instead of putting down the revolt, however, the soldiers themselves rebelled. Some waved banners calling for the overthrow of the government. Loyal troops were found who could put down the mutiny, but only after heavy fighting. Some of the rebel soldiers that managed to evade capture became part of the anti-government guerrilla bands that were popping up in the mountains.

The Rhee administration's anti-communism was reinforced by the thousands of former landlords and businessmen, Christians, and other conservatives who had fled from the North and wielded strong political influence. And of course, there was real fear of the North. For one, its allies Russia and China were neighbors, whereas the Americans were far away and their support was uncertain. Thus insecurity fed into the anti-communist hysteria. In 1949 the government forced 300,000 former communists, suspected communists, and anyone thought to have loyalties to North to join the National

Guidance Alliance in order to keep them under the watchful eye of the state. Even members of the armed forces were not above suspicion. A young Japanese-trained military officer, Park Chung Hee (Pak Jeonghui), for example, was nearly executed on the grounds of being sympathetic to the communists, but was exonerated. He would serve loyally in the ROK army, lead a military coup in 1961, and head a staunchly anti-communist government.

North Korea took advantage of the turbulence in the South to foment more of it. Pak Heonyeong and his fellow southerners trained hundreds of agents to sneak into the ROK and lead or organize revolts. Within a year of its independence, guerrillas were active in several mountainous areas. They also had agents stirring up trouble elsewhere, so Rhee's paranoia had a real basis. However, most of the unrest in the South was locally generated.

While the South was floundering, the North was consolidating. Kim Il Sung—not yet an absolute ruler—and his partisan comrades shared power with the Yenan and Soviet Korean leaders, and especially with Pak Heonyeong and his fellow domestic communists. They all followed the Soviet blueprint on how to create a modern industrial state backed by military strength. In 1949 they implemented a two-year economic plan to increase electric generation and industrial production and to construct infrastructure. Propaganda teams traveled to villages and neighborhoods, bringing the goals of the socialist revolution to the people through films and songs. Everyone was organized into state-sponsored women's, youth, farming, and labor organizations, which functioned as means to recruit voluntary labor for public projects while instilling loyalty to the regime. And real progress was achieved. There was little disorder, since all opposition had been eliminated prior to independence and the peasants had gotten the land they wanted. Many citizens were genuinely excited about the new progressive state, even if they disliked the mass campaigns and were saddened by the division of the country, which often meant loss of contact with relatives below the parallel.

Meanwhile, North Korea was quickly building a powerful Korean People's Army. With the proclamation of the People's Republic of China in 1949, tens of thousands of Koreans who had fought under the Chinese People's Liberation Army began returning to Korea, providing a large corps of experienced fighters. Moscow was generous, equipping it with artillery, tanks, and other weapons. It is not surprising, then, that Kim was confident that reunification under the DRPK was inevitable.

Reunification by Force: North Korea's Invasion of the South

On June 23, 1950, a UN team of observers completed an inspection tour of the 38th parallel. There had been frequent clashes along the border, some instigated by ROK forces, and there was always the fear that war would break out. The UN team reported finding nothing unusual, having apparently totally missed the quiet military buildup of the DPRK forces. Two days later, on June 25, North Korea began an artillery barrage followed by infantry advances. And thus on that day began what became known to the South Koreans as the "June 25th Incident"; to the North Koreans as the "Great Motherland Liberation War"; and to the Americans as the "Korean War."

Kim Il Sung's plan was to head directly to Seoul. He believed that if that city was captured, the ROK army would begin to collapse, South Koreans would rise up, and in a matter of days the war would be over. Initially, the invasion went as planned; after two days, the Korean People's Army (KPA) was in Seoul. South Korea was caught completely by surprise. There was panic in the capital; soldiers retreated and thousands of civilians fled in nightmarish scenes of utter chaos. Symbolizing the horror of these hours was the Han Bridge Incident. There was only one bridge across the mighty Han River that formed the southern border of the city. ROK forces, in an attempt to slow the advancing forces, blew it up prematurely while it was packed with escaping civilians, killing hundreds of them. Roads became rivers of families heading south ahead of the advancing KPA—men, women, and children moving mostly on foot and carrying whatever they could on their backs.

The South Koreans were not the only ones caught completely by surprise; the Americans were, as well. At first they were confused about the reports, but when they realized that a full-scale invasion was underway, they reacted quickly. On June 27, President Truman ordered General MacArthur, who was busy with the occupation of Japan, to come to the aid of the ROK army. The Americans went to the UN to ask for a resolution giving them the authority to intervene, and received it almost immediately. The Soviet Union, which could have vetoed the resolution, was boycotting the UN in protest of the international body's refusal to allow the representatives of the People's Republic of China to replace Taiwan's Nationalist government seat at the UN. This proved fortunate for the Americans, since there was no obstacle to getting United Nations approval. In fact, the US entered the war under the banner of the UN. Eventually a number of countries joined the UN effort, including 12,000 British, 8,500 Canadian, 5,000 Turkish and 5,000 Filipino troops and a few more from other countries. These allied forces served to support the pretense that this was an international effort; it was in reality an American operation.

Truman's decision to enter the war had a profound impact on Korean history. Just as the hastily called meeting in August 1945 led to the division of Korea, the president's hasty decision to intervene made that division permanent. Why did he choose this course of action? North Korea didn't expect an American intervention, and Moscow probably didn't either. Even Rhee could not have counted on it. While the Americans couldn't wait to extricate themselves from Korea, and many were willing to write off the regime, Truman felt he and his Democrats could not politically afford to "lose Korea." Just the year before, the Chinese Nationalist government of Chiang Kai-shek, despite billions in foreign military aid, had fled with the remnants of his army and government to the island of Taiwan. As many Americans saw it, Moscow had just consolidated control over most of Eastern Europe; now the world's most populous nation could be added to the column of communist advances. The policy of "containment" appeared to have been undermined from its very inception. So Truman, not wanting to "lose" yet another country to the Reds, decided to make a stand in Korea.

But saving South Korea was not easy. Most US troops were in Europe. The nearest ones at the government's disposal were the occupation forces in Japan, numbering about 100,000, but they were not very combat ready and it took a while to mobilize them. When

American forces did arrive, on July 5, they were defeated by the KPA and forced to retreat south. The KPA, meanwhile, was advancing steadily southward. Its main target was Busan, in the extreme southeast corner of the country, where Rhee's government had fled and was now based. As its fall would mark the effective end of the regime, North Korea's forces were racing there to capture it before American forces could arrive in large numbers. But Kim Il Sung and Pak Heonyeon's plans did not go as expected. Instead of capitulating after the fall of Seoul, ROK forces put up more resistance than expected, making the conquest of the South slower and more difficult than anticipated.

Another problem was the reaction of the people to being liberated by the KPA As the North Korean forces captured cities and towns, they set up People's Committees to govern them. They rounded up suspected ROK officials and class enemies, executing many, and promised to redistribute the land to the farmers. But the liberated southerners did not react as the North Korean leadership expected. A few students and intellectuals came forward to serve the new political order, but most South Koreans were less than enthusiastic about being liberated. Many were angry that their own people—fellow Koreans from the northern part of the country—were invading them. Others feared what the communists would do. When young men declined to volunteer to serve in the North Korean armed forces, they were drafted against their will. Tens of thousands of these impressed soldiers were forced to retreat with the KPA when it was driven back into North Korea, and most were never heard from by their families again. In short, the brief North Korean occupation mainly generated hatred for the communists rather than support. There were some guerrillas who fought for the North, but they were mostly the remnants of those that had fought in the mountains before June 1950, not new recruits.

All this meant that the KPA was unable to advance fast enough to complete its conquest before the arrival of substantial UN forces. Still, by early August most of South Korea was under KPA occupation; the South Korean government controlled only a little corner in the southeast within a mere forty-mile radius of Busan. But it was enough to provide a foothold for the massive numbers of US troops when they arrived. By this time, the Chinese were already becoming alarmed. Mao decided to send troops if the war went really badly and Pyongyang itself was in danger of falling, and sent out messages to the US to this effect. If the Americans decided to liberate the North, he would bring in "volunteers" to defend it. Unfortunately, the US had no diplomatic relations with the communist regime in Beijing, so the message was delivered through Indian diplomatic channels, which the Americans did not take seriously.

Trapped in the southeast corner of the country, the American military commander, General MacArthur, decided to execute a bold move. Against the advice of many in Washington who thought it too risky, he moved 80,000 Marines and 260 ships and landed them at Incheon—not an easy feat, since he had to navigate the notoriously tricky seas off the west coast. His forces landed in early September, almost five years to the day from the first arrival of American forces in Korea. As planned, the North Koreans were taken by surprise. Within days, the UN forces had fought their way back to Seoul, and by the end of September, the KPA was in disarray. Kim Il Sung, panicking, pleaded to Stalin and Mao to send forces to save his faltering army in the South. His attempt at reunification had clearly failed.

Had the Americans and South Koreans stopped at this point, the war would have soon come to an end, and South Korea would have been secure. The war had already been a bloody one, with more than 100,000 military and civilian casualties, but this figure was only a tiny fraction of the eventual loss of life in the Korean War. Unfortunately, both MacArthur and Rhee were determined to press onward. For Rhee and his government, it was nearly impossible to stop at this point when the reunification they so passionately desired seemed possible. They had the support of MacArthur, who sought the same total victory and unconditional surrender of the enemy that he had achieved five years earlier against Japan. For Truman, while he was less enthusiastic about pressing on with an invasion of the North, a rollback of communism would be a political victory. Therefore, on October 7, at the request of the US, the UN passed a vaguely worded resolution that approved the use of UN forces to cross the thirty-eighth parallel and destroy the KPA forces. Two days later MacArthur moved his troops into the DPRK.

ROK forces didn't wait; they began crossing over even before they had approval to do so. On October 10, the first major city in the North, Wonsan—the port where Kim Il Sung had first arrived—fell to South Korean forces. In a radio broadcast, Kim ordered his people to "fight to the last drop of blood" and then fled to safety near the Chinese border. Within a few days, the swiftly moving UN and ROK forces captured Pyongyang. On October 20, President Rhee made a triumphal entry into the former North Korean capital. By late November, almost all of the North was under was under ROK and UN control; reunification was nearly complete.

South Korea's occupation of the North was remarkably similar to the North's brief occupation of the South, and the response from locals was similar as well. ROK forces told the people they were being liberated, but North Koreans showed little enthusiasm for their liberators. Some fled; most were largely passive. While few resisted, not many embraced the new regime. Rhee, furthermore, did little to ingratiate his government with the local population: thousands were arrested, and the ROK authorities threatened to punish those who had collaborated with the communists—but that, of course, included almost everyone. Worst of all, they announced that illegally appropriated land would have to be given back to the rightful landlords. One could hardly imagine an announcement less likely to win hearts and minds. Meanwhile, Kim Il Sung and his government were still hanging on in Kanggye, a small city in the remote rugged mountain area near the Chinese border. He was advised by Moscow to leave for China, a signal that his Soviet allies were about to abandon him. But he was saved by the Chinese.

In late November, MacArthur, promising his men that the war would be over before Christmas, launched the last mopping-up effort to secure the area along the Chinese border. He ignored intelligence reports indicating that Chinese forces under the guise of Chinese People's Volunteers—that is, they were not official Chinese forces, but supposedly just volunteers—had begun quietly crossing over into North Korea several weeks earlier. On November 27, the

Chinese counterattacked the UN and ROK forces. The Americans were caught as unprepared as the North Koreans had been at Incheon a couple of months earlier. Led by veteran military commander Peng Duhuai, the Chinese advance was rapid and relentless. Once confident of total victory, the UN forces now retreated on all fronts—so rapidly that at times it became a rout. On December 6, the Chinese and North Koreans retook Pyongyang, and on January 4 they were in Seoul. They continued marching until they reached the thirty-seventh parallel, well inside South Korea. Eventually, the Chinese advanced beyond their supply lines, and the UN forces were able to regroup and begin pushing them back. On March 15, UN forces retook Seoul, which had changed hands four times in nine months. By the summer of 1951, the war stalemated at roughly where it started—along the 38th parallel, with the Chinese and North Koreans holding some territory south of it at the western end toward Seoul, and the UN and South Koreans holding some territory north of it near the east coast.

Truman fired MacArthur when he chafed at being denied another try at moving into the North; the Americans had no desire to expand the war. Neither did Mao; he saved his ally, fought the Americans to a draw, and was willing to accept a divided Korea and call it a victory. In July 1951, the two sides began negotiations for a peace settlement. For Kim Il Sung and Syngman Rhee, returning to the status quo was not acceptable, but they had little choice in the matter. Once again, Koreans saw their fate decided by the great powers. Kim, sidelined by the Chinese, was no longer effectively in command of the military situation. Instead he focused on consolidating his power at home and casting blame for the failure to reunify the country on others. He carried out a number of purges and began rebuilding the Korean Workers' Party by recruiting new members from the rank and file.

Rhee was also busy consolidating his power and fending off threats to it. His administration was riddled with corruption. For example, he created National Defense Corps to mobilize all available men for the war effort, but the organization proved a vehicle for its officers to line their pockets with the military aid funds that were flowing in. Unable to find enough allies in the National Assembly to re-elect him, he declared martial law, had many of the legislators arrested, and intimidated others in sufficient numbers to have them pass a constitutional amendment that allowed for direct election of the president—which, of course, he won. He also created his own party, the Liberal Party, that soon gained a well-deserved reputation for corruption. Throughout the war, the government in Busan had carried out extrajudicial killings of those suspected of disloyalty, beginning with the initial North Korean invasion. At that time, 30,000 suspected Pyongyang sympathizers were rounded up and nearly 3,000 of them executed as a preventive measure.

While Kim and Rhee were eliminating enemies at home, the UN and the Chinese carried out talks. Yet, despite negotiations that started in July 1951, the war dragged on, largely confined to a narrow strip of land along the border. Frustrated, the US stepped up its bombing of the North. This was accelerated with "Operation Pressure Pump" in July 1952. Thousands of bombing raids destroyed every possible military and industrial target, including the dams and dikes that irrigated the rice fields. Pyongyang and other northern cities began to look like Hiroshima and Nagasaki after the A-bomb, with only a few buildings standing. More bombs were dropped by the Americans on this little country of hardly more than eight million than the allies had dropped on either Germany or the Japanese Empire in World War II. As a result, the North Koreans were forced to move underground. The entire country became a bunker state, with industries, offices, and even living quarters moved to hundreds of miles of tunnels. Nonetheless, civilian casualties in these bombing raids were appallingly high.

By 1953, all parties were ready to end the conflict. Newly elected President Eisenhower had promised to end the war, and since the Chinese had achieved what they needed, Mao was ready to end it, too. For the Soviets, the war was not so bad; it tied down American forces and lifted some of the pressure on Europe at a relatively low cost to them. The Soviets supplied weaponry, and some of their pilots pretended to be North Koreans and flew DPRK planes, but it was the Chinese, not the Soviets, who supplied the troops. Yet even the Soviets were getting tired of the conflict, and after Stalin's death in March 1953 they were ready to end it. Kim Il Sung, realizing that his hope for reunification had been thwarted—at least for the time being—and needing a respite from American bombing, was ready for fighting to cease. Only South Korean president Syngman Rhee was opposed to peace. There was less domestic pressure on him to capitulate, since the war was now confined to the border, away from the civilian population, so the South was not experiencing the level of death and destruction that the North was. Above all, Rhee refused to give up the hope of reunification.

In fact, Rhee became a real problem for the US. He organized mass rallies in his country calling for a more aggressive stance, and lobbied conservative Americans to pursue victory. A stumbling block in the peace negotiations was the exchange of prisoners. Some North Korean and Chinese prisoners did not want to go home, but the Chinese and the DPRK insisted that they all be returned. Rhee attempted to sabotage the peace negotiations by releasing Chinese and North Korean prisoners. The Americans became so frustrated with Rhee that they drew up a secret plan to remove him from office and replace him with someone easier to work with, but it was never carried out. On July 27, 1953, the UN, China, and North Korea signed an armistice that was enacted without Rhee's signature.

Division Made Permanent: The Impact of the War on Koreans
The Korean War could be characterized as a war in which almost everyone lost. Pyongyang and Seoul both failed in their efforts to reunify the country. The Americans stopped South Korea from falling to the communists at a cost of 40,000 lives, but they ended up where they did not want to be—stuck in the peninsula, with the threat of the resumption of war always present. The war didn't cost the Soviets much, but they didn't gain anything, either; it did not divert US attention from Europe. China could claim some success—defending an ally and fighting the Americans to a draw may have enhanced the prestige of the new regime—but it came at a cost of perhaps 300,000 Chinese lives. The war also preserved an ally that would later prove troublesome to the Chinese. It strengthened the US military presence near their border, and it cost them Taiwan:

when the war broke out, the US sent its navy to defend the last province held by Chiang Kai-shek's Nationalists just as the PRC was about to take it. Most of all, the Korean people lost: perhaps more than a million and a half men, women, and children died in the war. The death and destruction were truly horrific, and yet the one thing almost all Koreans wanted—reunification—was now farther away than ever.

For the DPRK in particular, the war was a disaster. The country was in ruins. Just how many lives were lost is uncertain—it is estimated that up to 8 or even 10 percent of the population perished, a casualty toll matched by few countries in modern history. The war was certainly a failure for the regime, since rather than reunifying the country on its own terms, it ended up strengthening both the South Korean regime and the US commitment to defend it. The failure of the South Korean people to rise up and support the KPA must have been a demoralizing blow to Kim and his comrades. Even more troubling was the passive response of the people in the North to the occupying ROK forces.

The extent of death and destruction was not as great in the South, but it was still horrible. Seoul was a jumble of half-standing buildings and rubble. More than 200,000 South Korean soldiers were killed, along with at least an equal number of civilians. Tens of thousands of South Koreans—mostly young men but also intellectuals and others of various ages—were taken to the North and never seen or heard from again. Millions of South Koreans were forced to flee, forming one of the world's largest refugee populations. Perhaps most tragic were the millions of South Koreans who were now totally cut off from family members. In most cases they would never learn what had become of their siblings, parents, children, or spouses.

Not only was the Korean War a bad war for almost all—it didn't end. The agreement in July 1953 was only a cease-fire. It certainly didn't end for Kim Il Sung, who never gave up his plans for reunification. Over the next several decades he sought to learn from his mistakes and prepare for final victory. And what were the lessons? —To make sure his country was militarily and industrially strong enough to carry out a war without the support of allies. To make sure the citizens of the Democratic People's Republic were well indoctrinated so they would give all their efforts and would not cooperate with the enemy. To foster the revolutionary forces in the South until the people were ready to turn against their regime and support the North, and to gain international support for his efforts at reunification and prevent the US from interfering. These goals were exactly what his regime worked to achieve.

The war didn't end for the South, either. It left the Republic of Korea with one of the world's largest armed forces—600,000 citizens under arms—and with a large US military presence in their country. It hardened the attitudes of many in South Korea who were outraged by the North Korean invasion and appalled at the way its occupation had conducted itself. An entire generation of South Koreans was now ardently anti-communist and pro-US, and even if they were often critical of the government in power, they accepted the legitimacy of the Republic of Korea as the real successor to the historical Korean state. Unlike the leadership of the North, South Korean leaders knew that they could not reunify the country by force, but like their northern counterparts, they believed that they had to create an industrially and militarily strong society that would eventually be able to achieve victory in a renewed conflict. Both Koreas would now engage in an economic development race to better prepare themselves for the next outbreak of fighting, while at the same time demonstrating the superiority of their system to their own people and to their neighbors across the demilitarized zone.

CHAPTER 6

THE RISE OF NORTH KOREA: THE YEARS OF RAPID DEVELOPMENT

Total Victory of the Partisans: Kim Il Sung's Consolidation of Power

Kim Il Sung's attempt to liberate the South had been a disaster. When the fighting stopped in July 1953, his country was in ruins. He had brought death and destruction upon his people on a vast scale and had nothing to show for it. Rather than reuniting the country, he had hardened the division within it and now faced a heavily armed Republic of Korea with a substantial US military presence. Many leaders would not have survived such a setback, but Kim not only survived, he consolidated his power, eliminating all his rivals, and forged ahead with his plans to create a modern industrial socialist state.

This might seem surprising, but Kim Il Sung proved to be a nimble survivor. First, he shifted blame for the failure to liberate the South on the domestic communists. Only one week after the signing of the armistice, he began to purge them. Pak Heonyeong and his mostly southern comrades were held responsible for the failure to reunite the country, since they had promised uprisings in the South that did not materialize. Kim conducted a Stalinist show trial of the twelve most prominent domestic communists, all originally from the South. It turned out that they all were secretly in league with enemy and had deliberately sabotaged the liberation. Each confessed to being a South Korean or American agent. All were then executed. Only Pak Heonyeong was spared, but not for long; he was arrested and executed two years later, when it turned out that he, too, had been secretly plotting with the Americans. In fact, he had been covertly working for the Americans since the late 1930s. So it was not Kim's blunders, but a massive conspiracy by his rivals that had brought about defeat.

Kim Il Sung didn't stop there. In 1955, he purged Pak Ilu, a prominent Yenan faction member, whose personal connections with Mao failed to save him. Then, in 1956, he faced a challenge from the Soviet and Yenan factions. While away on a visit to the Soviet Union and Eastern Europe, drumming up aid for his development plans, some of his comrades began intriguing against him. Weeks earlier, in February, Khrushchev had denounced Stalin's cult of personality, and Moscow was beginning to nudge the "little Stalins" from power. These were the leaders that they had promoted in their Eastern European satellites, each with a personality cult patterned on Stalin's. This emboldened Choe Changik of the Yenan group and Pak Chang-ok of the Soviet group to challenge their own "little Stalin." But Kim, upon returning, had them removed from office. Only intervention by Beijing and Moscow saved them and their associates from arrest or worse.

The reprieve was temporary, however. In 1957, Kim began a massive purge that lasted three years. About 100,000 people were arrested, amounting to almost 2 percent of the adult population, and about 2,500 were executed. A few Soviet and Yenan group members managed to flee to the safety of the USSR and the PRC, but most were not so lucky. By the end of the purge, almost all of the key positions and most of the mid-level positions in the Party, the state bureaucracy, and the military were held by Kim's former guerrilla comrades or their clients. One Yenan group member, Kim Changman, still held a high post. He had become one of Kim Il Sung's most ardent supporters early on, denouncing his fellow Yenan group members and anyone else whose absolute loyalty to the Great Leader was questioned. In the end, however, being more Catholic than the pope didn't save him, either, and he disappeared a few years later.

By the 1960s, only Kim Il Sung's comrades from the Manchurian mountains, his relatives, and some of his comrades' relatives held positions of authority. And what a group this was to lead the modernization of the country! Few had completed middle school, and some had no formal schooling at all. Few had any foreign experience; some had never even been to a large city until they arrived in Pyongyang. Isolated, provincial, and not even having grown up in the country they were now governing, they may have been among the least educated ruling elite of any modern country. When Kim Il Sung died in 1994, the leadership roster was largely the same lineup as it had been in the late 1960s, minus those who had died of natural causes over the years. Thus this small band of a several hundred guerrilla veterans and their families retained their grip on power for half the century. As they died off, they were replaced by their sons, in-laws, and close protégés. It was a small, tight-knit, increasingly intermarried elite that held most of the key positions in the Party, military, and bureaucracy under three generations of the Kim family.

North Korea's Great Leap Forward: Recovery and Rapid Industrialization

While Kim and his partisans were eliminating all possible challengers, they were also busy rebuilding and remolding their society. North Korea literally rose from the ashes to become an industrial nation. By almost any measure, its economic development from 1953 to the 1970s was an impressive achievement. In a little more than two decades it went from a mostly rural agricultural society to a mostly urban industrial one. It emerged as a modern society with levels of education and healthcare that were among the highest in Asia.

North Korea recovered from the wartime destruction with remarkable speed. Within three years, factories were rebuilt and industrial production had recovered to about where it had been at the start of the war. It had more than a little help from its friends. The Soviet Union and its Eastern European allies such as East Germany provided generous support, and China put the large number of its troops still stationed in the country to work on construction projects, making for what may have been the largest international socialist aid effort in the history of communism. Still, all this assistance was smaller than the amount of aid the US was pouring into South Korea with much less impressive results. While the aid the DPRK received was crucial, much of the country's successful recovery can be attributed to the government's ability to organize and direct its population and limited resources toward the recovery effort. Mass-mobilization campaigns put almost every available person to work, toiling long hours at clearing rubble and building new houses and other structures.

The reconstruction effort demonstrated just what could be done by concentrating all available manpower to work at centrally directed projects. Unfortunately for North Koreans, no one was more impressed by this achievement than Kim Il Sung and his comrades. For the next six decades, they would follow this same pattern of marshaling the masses in an effort to achieve economic feats. In the early days this produced sometimes spectacular results, but after the 1960s the campaigns became less and less effective.

The showcase reconstruction project was the city of Pyongyang. Since American bombing raids had reduced it to rubble, Kim Il Sung had to construct a virtually new city. This he did with enthusiasm, personally supervising the project. It was a display city, designed to demonstrate the power of the state and the effectiveness of the revolution to everyone who lived or visited there. It had broad streets and wide plazas that were perfect for mass rallies and military parades, along with grandiose public buildings and ubiquitous monuments to the revolution and its leadership. Nothing remained of the old Pyongyang and its 2,000-year history; it was an entirely new, Stalinesque modern urban space. Later Kim added more and more monuments to himself and a subway system that functioned as a giant fallout shelter, buried so deep underground that it could withstand almost any air attack. Few cities in modern history were built to reflect the vision of a single person so comprehensively. Unfortunately, it was the vision of an aesthetically challenged, egocentric tyrant with a middle-school education.

Meanwhile, the economy was completely socialized. Elsewhere in the world there were communist states that opted to allow some private businesses and private farming, but North Korea went for complete socialization, making only the most minimal of concessions to private ownership; only Maoist China could match the degree to which free enterprise was eliminated. By the end of 1957, all farms had been merged into state-owned "cooperatives." Peasants who had achieved their dream of owning their land a few years earlier now lost it; everyone became a salaried laborer working for the state.

Kim Il Sung then force-marched his country into the industrial age, beginning with his first Five-Year Plan in 1957. This started off as a Soviet-inspired effort at developing a modern industrial state. Then in 1958 Mao began his Great Leap Forward, an attempt to overcome a shortage of skilled technicians and capital and achieve amazing leaps of development by mobilizing the entire population, instilling in them a revolutionary fervor and then instructing them to build a great industrial, socialist state. It is not clear how successful Mao was in inspiring his masses to heroic feats of reconstruction, but he did inspire Kim, who quickly altered his Five-Year Plan in imitation and radically revised his economic targets upward. When Mao announced that China would surpass Britain in steel production, Kim announced that he would surpass Japan in per-capita industrial output in ten years. When Mao consolidated the state farms into giant communes, Kim merged the 13,000 village-based cooperatives into 3,800 large-scale ones. Like Mao, he shifted much of the industrial production to local authorities.

Kim never used the phrase "great leap forward" but instead came up with the term *cheollima*, a reference to a flying horse in Korean mythology that could leap 1,000 *ri* (1 *ri* being approximately 400 meters [1,312 feet]) in a single bound. It symbolized what could be accomplished under the right direction. The inspiration for the *cheollima* movement—or so the story goes—came from an incident in which Kim visited a steel mill that was falling far short of its targets, and stepped in to personally direct the work. When the management began listening to the needs and advice of the workers themselves and solving practical problems on the spot, the factory met its goals, then exceeded them, and then far exceeded them, finally becoming a virtual cornucopia of steel.

Kim Il Sung became known for such miracles. In 1960, he spent a number of days on a cooperative farm listening to and instructing the farmers, and the output shot up. The following year he worked his magic at a factory near Pyongyang. These became models of how officials could accelerate production by working directly with the farmers and factory hands—providing inspiration and guidance and listening to their suggestions. Kim himself would make endless on-the-spot guidance trips—thousands of them over the years—personally overseeing and inspiring the workers. His son and grandson would continue the tradition. Later economic plans were accompanied by "speed battles" to step up the pace of production. There were 70-day, 100-day, 200-day speed battles in which work was intensified, and people were expected to "volunteer" to labor well beyond the 40-hour legal workweek. Workers were told to drink less soup so that they could take fewer restroom breaks. Campaigns called for workers to "see the morning stars"; that is, to arrive at work early to put in extra labor. College students were often sent to farms and work sites to set up red flags and shout slogans to spur the workers on. Office workers were not spared, but also were asked to work on farms during planting or harvest times or even on construction projects.

The impressive results that Kim's use of mass-mobilization campaigns for unrealistic targets—constantly subjecting the people to extra "volunteer hours" of labor and motivating them by exhortations rather than material rewards—achieved in the early years only encouraged him to keep using the same tactic. And as mentioned, he continued with ever-diminishing returns. A Seven-Year Plan for 1961–67 made impressive progress, but fell short of its unrealistic targets and was extended by three years. Then a Six-Year Plan for 1971–76 came up still shorter. And so it went, with each new development plan missing its goals by a greater and greater margin, until by the 1980s the economy was hardly growing at all. Nonetheless, Kim stuck to the same old strategy of relying on mass labor and revolutionary zeal rather than searching for better methods and new approaches.

Achieving Political Autonomy

No goal was more important to the North Korean leadership than achieving political autonomy. Kim Il Sung and his partisan comrades viewed their history as a story of how foreigners and their collaborators had subjugated the people and held the country back. It was their task to prevent this from happening again by making the country as strong and free from outside control as possible. Because of this fierce desire for independence, Kim Il Sung was wary of both Moscow and Beijing—yet he needed aid and military support from the Soviets as well as the Chinese. The problem for him was how to get the support of the communist giants without being drawn into their orbit.

A big opportunity came with the Sino-Soviet rift that came out in the open in 1961. Kim was able to triangulate, learning to establish good relations with both without being a satellite of either. It was a skill he learned the hard way by making costly miscalculations. First, he cleverly signed treaties of friendship with both communist neighbors, promising military support in the case of conflict—in fact, the treaties were signed in July 1961, just one day apart. But then he began to tilt toward China in the early 1960s and became openly critical of Moscow's bullying of other communist countries. The Soviets responded by reducing aid sharply, which was a blow to the North Korean economy. A chastened Kim Il Sung used the fall of Khrushchev in late 1964 as an excuse to improve relations, and the flow of aid resumed. Then relations with Beijing deteriorated during Mao's Cultural Revolution in the late 1960s. But the two sides made up in 1970, and for the next two decades Kim was able to skillfully maintain positive relationships with both communist giants, distancing himself from their rivalry.

While continuing good relations with Moscow and Beijing was essential for maintaining his autonomy and fueling his economy, Kim Il Sung's main focus was on reunification. For a while he put the issue on the back burner, concentrating on economic development, but not for long. In 1964, he spelled out his threefold plan for reunification. The first step was to build North Korea into an impregnable fortress. This meant creating a powerful military and literally fortifying the country so it could withstand an invasion or another bout of massive air attacks. It also meant indoctrinating the entire population so they would fiercely resist an invasion and unquestioningly obey orders from their leader. In the first decade after the Korean War, the regime's energies had been focused on economic development. Military buildup was important, but less of a priority. Now, needing to beef up his armed forces, Kim adopted his "equal emphasis policy," which would direct most of the country's scarce resources into creating a powerful military. In practice, this meant the nation could never sustain the same level of growth or fulfill the promises to materially improve the lives of its people.

The second part of the plan was to foster the revolutionary forces in the South. Kim believed sending his army to liberate his countrymen below the parallel before they were ready for revolution had been the great mistake of 1950. Sooner or later the South Korean people would rise up against the corrupt, incompetent South Korean regime, which was composed of Japanese collaborators and American stooges. Pyongyang's policy was to be a shining example of independence and progress, continuing to aid and abet progressive elements in the South who were living under the thumb of the US imperialists until they were ready to rise up.

The third part of the strategy for reunification was aimed at isolating the South Korean government and getting the Americans to withdraw from the peninsula by promoting and uniting revolutionary forces throughout the world. Put another way, Kim's strategy for reunification was to strengthen the North, weaken the South, and get the Americans out. Over the next thirty years of his extraordinarily long rule, Kim Il Sung and his comrades never deviated from this threefold strategy for reunification. It was the guiding principle behind North Korea's foreign policy.

In the late 1960s, Pyongyang became a little impatient with the speed of the revolutionary forces in the South and decided to step up pressure on the regime. It may have hoped the American involvement in Vietnam would keep Washington preoccupied, or that the anti-government demonstrations in South Korea following the peace treaty with the Japanese might be indications of a latent revolutionary surge. In 1967 the North instigated numerous incidents along the DMZ, including exchanges of gunfire. In January 1968, it landed commandos along the eastern coast and attacked the Blue House, the ROK president's residence, in a failed attempt to kill Park Chung Hee, who had assumed the presidency of the ROK in 1963. Later that year they landed eight infiltration teams along coastal areas where they attempted to incite villagers to rebel, telling them they were being liberated and lecturing them on their need to rejoice and support the revolution. Instead of embracing their liberators, however, the locals quickly turned them in to the police.

On the same day that the Northern commandos attacked the presidential mansion, DPRK forces seized the US naval intelligence ship *Pueblo* and held its eighty-two crew members captive for eleven months. The crew members wrote a hilariously absurd confession filled with puns and insults that the North Koreans apparently didn't understand. As funny as this was, it was the DPRK that had the last word—they kept the ship, which is still anchored near the spot where the *General Sherman* was burned, and preserved it as a museum of US imperialism.

The provocations didn't end. The North Koreans shot down a US spy plane the following year. However useful these actions might have been in testing the responses of the US and the ROK to military provocations, Kim must have been disappointed with their failure to ignite the revolutionary forces in the South. He had the generals in charge of the attacks removed, and then switched tactics. In 1972, the DPRK imitated Beijing's rapprochement with Washington by proposing peace talks with Seoul. Kim sent his brother to the South for negotiations. A few exchanges back and forth between Pyongyang and Seoul by representatives of both sides led to nothing, and the talks petered out the next year. Kim's demand that the US withdraw before things could go further was a non-starter, rendering the talks useless. He then tried direct negotiations with Washington. Since the US was disengaging from Vietnam, maybe it could be induced to sign a peace treaty with Pyongyang and leave the Korean peninsula, too. But the Americans simply ignored this transparent attempt to get them to abandon their South Korean allies.

With a peace offensive getting him nowhere, Kim returned to provocations. In 1974, for example, a Japanese-Korean acting on DPRK orders attempted to assassinate Park Chung Hee while he was giving a televised speech. The shooter missed his target, but hit Park's wife. The iron-willed Park, after a pause, continued with his speech. In addition, several tunnels big enough to drive armed vehicles through were discovered under the DMZ. Furthermore, in 1976, North Koreans killed two Americans who were trimming a tree along the DMZ, causing a major incident and provoking a US show of strength. In 1981 and 1983, Pyongyang made attempts to assassinate Chun Doo Hwan, Park Chung Hee's successor as ROK president. These continual provocations gave the Americans and other outsiders the impression of a dangerous, irrational regime—a perception that was only half right. The DPRK might have been dangerous, but it wasn't irrational: the acts of terrorism and military clashes served the regime's purposes. Kim and his successors used them to probe the South for its revolutionary potential and to test the Americans' resolve to defend Seoul, as well as to keep their forces and their people prepared for the day of liberation.

Meanwhile, North Korea joined the Non-Aligned Movement in 1975 in an effort to both create international pressure on the US to withdraw and to diplomatically isolate the regime in Seoul. At first, the North Koreans were successful at getting UN resolutions passed calling for the withdrawal of all foreign forces from the Korean peninsula, and Pyongyang's cause gained support from many third-world countries. A stream of heads of state—especially from countries in Africa and other developing nations—paid visits to Pyongyang; no matter how small their country was, they would receive a massive, enthusiastic welcome from city residents who were dutifully obeying orders. But the clumsy manners of North Korea's inexperienced diplomats were counterproductive, and after a few years the Non-Aligned Movement lost interest in supporting Pyongyang's cause.

Up until 1980 reunification was still far off, but Kim Il Sung had not given up hope—well, perhaps "hope" is not the correct word. He was fairly confident that eventually the tide of events would turn his way and he would be the leader of a united Korean nation.

Creating a Dynastic State: The Kim Dynasty and the Rise of Kim Jong Il

No feature of North Korean society struck outsiders as being more bizarre than the cult of Kim Il Sung and his family. The cult originally began under the direction of the Soviets, and was closely patterned after that of Stalin. In the 1960s it was influenced by Mao Zedong's cult, which went beyond Stalin's. During the Cultural Revolution, millions of Chinese waved their Little Red Books containing quotes by Mao; praise for his leadership blared from public loudspeakers; and mass rallies took place, with multitudes waving the "mighty red banner of Mao Zedong Thought." Yet, Kim outdid Mao with a cult so extreme as to make even Mao blush; it was so central to all aspects of life that North Korea became a cult-state.

Kim Il Sung called the Cultural Revolution "idiocy," but he was influenced by it, and in 1967 he began his own more modest version. There were no Red Guards smashing things up and harassing officials, but he did emulate Mao by intensifying his personal cult and creating his own "thought." He began to be addressed as *suryeong* ("leader"), a term that had previously been reserved for Lenin and Stalin, and it became customary to preface it with *widaehan* ("great"), so that he was now almost always referred to as the Great Leader. He also became a great thinker. His thought was called *juche*. His various proclamations and speeches were gradually edited into an encyclopedia-length compendium of "*juche* thought," also referred to at times as "Kim Il Sungism." Their content, which stressed self-reliance and a number of mind-numbingly repetitive statements on achieving revolutionary objectives, promoted what was perhaps the world's most tediously boring ideology. But it elevated Kim Il Sung from being not only a peerless patriot to a peerless thinker. In the 1970s and '80s, the state spent scarce foreign exchange funds and distributed free translated copies of *juche* thought abroad; many can still be found, dusty and unread, in libraries across the world. And it set up *juche* study societies in a number of countries. In the new 1972 constitution—this time written by Koreans in Korean—*juche* was enshrined as the ideological foundation of the state.

A few years after the Cultural Revolution was launched in 1966, the adulation of Mao Zedong's subjects toward their leader began cool down a bit. This was not the case in North Korea, where the cult of Kim Il Sung continued to intensify into the 1970s and never diminished. Glorification of the Great Leader was raised to a new level on his sixtieth birthday on April 15, 1972, which was celebrated with extravagant fanfare; thereafter, his birthday became the most important holiday on the Korean calendar. Then there were those badges with his picture on them. In the late 1960s, only officials had worn them, but after 1972 everyone was expected to do so. The Great Leader's picture hung in virtually every room in every building; his statue appeared in almost every public square. There was no escaping his words and visage. Even the mountains in the remote wilderness were adorned with massive inscriptions quoting or praising him. His heroic leadership in the anti-Japanese struggle—or that of his comrades operating under his inspiration—became the main subject of plays, operas, songs, paintings, and movies.

Kim's cult differed from those of Stalin, Mao, and other modern authoritarian rulers in that it extended to his family as well. In this way, it was very Confucian—very Korean. From the late 1940s, mention was made of the family line of patriot-heroes that Kim was descended from. Over the years North Koreans learned of his father, Kim Hyeongjik, who was credited with leading an anti-Japanese movement; and of his mother, Kim Bangseok, another great patriot (although her Christian background was omitted). Then there was his great-grandfather Kim Eungu, who, in a fabricated account, led the attack on the *General Sherman*, now a key event in modern Korean history. By the late 1960s the history of modern Korea was intertwined with the story of the Kim family, who were placed at the center of the struggle to create a modern, strong, independent nation. While the immense importance Koreans attached to family lineage explains some of this, there was another motive: Kim Il Sung was worried about his succession.

Although he was still a very healthy, vigorous man in his fifties, Kim Il Sung began to prepare for his succession in the 1960s. At first he groomed his younger brother Kim Yeongju, but there were some problems with this choice. Kim Yeongju had never fought or played any role in the resistance or the Party in its early years, and was also said to have health issues, although he ended up living well into his 90s. In any case, at some point Kim Il Sung turned to his eldest son, Kim Jong Il, and made him his anointed successor.

According to official biographers, Kim Jong Il was born on the sacred Paektu Mountain on February 16, 1942, in the secret forest headquarters of the national anti-Japanese resistance headed by his father. Amazingly, a rainbow appeared and flowers bloomed on the mountain even though it was the depth of the bitterly cold northern winter. In actual fact, he was born in 1941—in Siberia, where his father was working for the Soviets. (Why even the year of his birth was changed is uncertain, but it follows a pattern of official histories changing details of the past for reasons that are often obscure). He attended a special school for the children of high-ranking officials, then enrolled in Kim Il Sung University, where the elite studied. While still in his twenties he was appointed to some important Party posts as a junior member. Being artistically inclined, he moved to the wonderfully named Propaganda and Agitation Department of the Korean Workers' Party, where he directed his attention to producing plays, operas, and movies glorifying his father. He even wrote a treatise on film, which became mandatory reading for anyone in the cinematic world of the DPRK.

His emergence as successor was carried out in a rather careful way. Sometime around 1974, he was designated as the successor by his father, but this was only known to Party insiders. Not until the Sixth Party Congress in 1980 did Kim Jong Il appear in public under that designation for the first time. Even afterward, he never spoke publicly, but pictures of him standing alongside his father became ubiquitous and his pronouncements on various topics were given the same weight. His name, when it appeared in print, was set in the same special large type previously reserved for his father. His birthday, February 16, became a holiday, and the period between that date and April 15, his father's birthday, became the "loyalty season." Kim Jong Il became the "Dear Leader"; he was also referred to as "great leader," but with the word *jidoja* used to mean "leader," which sounded a bit less exalted than *suryeong*, the term used for his father.

With Kim Jong Il as the heir apparent, North Korea became a dynastic state. Kim Il Sung's cult expanded to include almost all members of his family, including his first wife, as well as his second, Kim Jong Il's mother Kim Jung Suk, who was called the "mother of Korea." In reality, the DPRK had become a monarchy and the Great Leader's lineage the royal family.

Everybody Has a *Seongbun*: The New Hierarchy

North Korea's leadership, being good communists, called for the end of economic and social inequality. Yet what they created was a rigidly hierarchical society. In fact, in many ways it was a mirror image of the old Korea, with social ranks simply reversed—workers and peasants on the top and *yangban* at the bottom. As in the old Korea, in this new socialist one, status was based on bloodlines. In early times there were the bone-ranks, and later the sharp differences between *yangban*, commoners, and low or "mean" people; these were replaced by new hierarchies in the DPRK. In the 1950s the regime undertook a careful background check of the entire population, placing each person into one of three categories (*gyecheung*). At the top there was the "core class" consisting of those with politically reliable and socially desirable backgrounds—landless peasants, industrial workers, and those who had fought in the anti-Japanese resistance. Next came the "wavering class," a somewhat less reliable group. At the bottom was the "hostile class" who had undesirable backgrounds: landowners, businessmen, those who had served in the colonial government, Christians, those who had been Buddhist priests or shamans. It also included those with relatives in the South and Southerners who had been captured or kidnapped and brought north during the Korean War.

The three groupings were based on the degree to which their loyalty to the communist regime could be counted on. The core class were called "tomatoes" (red all the way through); the wavering class were "apples" (red only on the outside); and the hostile class were "grapes" (not red at all). Each class was hereditary, based on one's parents or grandparents, and was in turn passed along to one's children. About 30 percent of the population were in the core class; 50

percent comprised the wavering class, and 20 percent were in the hostile class. In the late 1950s, many members of the hostile class were relocated to more remote areas, such as the northeast. They were generally forbidden to reside in the capital, Pyongyang—the most desirable place to live—or near the border with South Korea.

This class system—though it might better be described as a caste system—was further refined in the 1960s. The three classes were subdivided into fifty-one subgroups called *seongbun*, graded by reliability. Twelve *seongbun* made up the core class: those with worker backgrounds, former farmhands and landless peasants, KWP members, etc. Near the top were relatives of deceased revolutionaries, national liberation fighters, or war heroes. Nine *seongbun* made up the wavering class, and thirty made up the hostile class. The latter included all manner of bad backgrounds—those who had engaged in pro-Japanese or pro-American activities, or who had family members who were charged with political crimes, or who were originally from the South, and so forth. A few more categories were added later. *Seongbun* were never publicly mentioned; they were listed in secret government files, but everyone pretty much knew where they belonged. One's *seongbun* determined one's life chances—it would designate things like eligibility for desirable jobs and entry into good schools. Children from bad *seongbun* became aware of the fact at around the age of twelve, when they were barred from donning the red scarf of the Kim Il Sung Youth with the other kids. They were unlikely to be admitted to a university or ever live in Pyongyang. It was possible, but difficult, to rise in status, and easier to fall to a lower rung if one got into political trouble of some sort.

Life was certainly hard for those in a bad *seongbun*, but it was hard for most people. The real gap was between the upper levels of the core class, who formed the true elite of high-ranking Party members and their families, and everyone else. The elite lived in special neighborhoods, went to special schools, and enjoyed a life of privilege and relative comfort. Making up about 1 percent of the population, they had access to imported luxury goods and could automatically expect their children to go to top schools—Kim Il Sung University being at the apex of the system. They had their own special hospitals with up-to-date medical care; a few had foreign luxury cars and drank imported cognac. This small elite of Party officials, high-ranking military officers, and the upper echelon of the bureaucracy was still subordinate to the innermost elite: those related to, or with some close personal connection to, Kim Il Sung and his family.

North Korea also retained its traditional pattern of male dominance, even though the regime claimed to practice gender equality. Women did have access to equal education, could share inheritances, and could divorce; theoretically, all occupations were open to them. Indeed, this was a major change in Korean society. Part of this push for gender equality was to deal with the labor shortage, since economic development was dependent on mobilizing manpower and so many young men were in the military. Women made up the majority of the labor force in light industries. Free day-care centers were available, and working women were given additional rations. However, they did not have to work, and some stayed home to take care of children and do the housework.

All this rhetoric and legal framework for gender equality was a façade disguising the reality that it was a man's world. Women seldom held high-status jobs. Many were schoolteachers, but few were professors. Few women rose to any positions of authority in government, in the Party, or in management. The only women who ever attained anything approaching a leadership post were relatives of the Kim family, and none of them held a top spot. Women were still expected to cook for their husbands; in fact, working women were allowed to go home early so they could get supper ready. The role of women as mothers was also given great importance in official indoctrination; of course, their primary duty was to raise revolutionary children dedicated to the regime, with unquestioning loyalty to the Great Leader. Most women wore simple clothes in traditional style. When Kim Il Sung got tired of looking at the drab dress of his female compatriots he ordered women to wear more colorful clothes, and they complied, often donning Western skirts and blouses. But then he warned them not to go too far and reveal too much. Men, incidentally, almost always wore simple Western clothes, with a suit and tie for special occasions.

As in the old Korea, everyone was expected to marry. Marriage ceremonies tended to be simple, and included bowing before a portrait of the Great Leader and pledging loyalty to him as well as to one another—and, starting in the 1980s, to Kim Jong Il as well. Those who married were not kids—the minimum marriage age was twenty-eight for women and thirty for men, the highest legal age in the world. This was to limit population growth, which was quite high after the war. When, after a generation, the birth rate started dropping, coming close to replacement level by the late 1980s, the marriage-age restrictions were relaxed. But it was still difficult for most men, at least, to marry young, since they spent so many years in military service. Divorce had been made easy in 1946 with the Law of Equality Between the Sexes, but then in the mid-1950s it became more difficult again.

The 1972 constitution declared that "families are the cell of society." All families—so the propaganda organs proclaimed—had to be bound by unfailing devotion to the Great Leader as well as to each other. Loyalty between parent and child and the love of one's parents were praised, and family-related terms were used in propaganda. Even the Great Leader was the *eobeoui suryeong*, or "fatherly leader" (or, more correctly, the "parently leader," since the Korean term *eobeoui* can mean either fatherly or motherly). Of course, there were some political reasons for this emphasis on family aside from the momentum of tradition. As Kim Il Sung converted his rule into a dynasty, emphasizing the importance of family and bloodlines was a way to promote acceptance of this idea. And it made the nepotism that characterized all the members of elite, as they placed family members in key positions, seem more natural.

No Need for Money: The Command Economy

The Democratic People's Republic of Korea was about as far from a market economy as any modern society has been. People lived in state-owned houses. Most city-dwellers resided in small apartments in grim buildings. They had indoor plumbing, although it was common for several families to share a bathroom. They had electricity, although it was not always on. Few had elevators, so apartments on the lower floors were more desirable. Rents were nominal, meaning housing was essentially free. A public distribution system rationed food and other basic goods. Each family received coupons for a certain quantity of rice, cooking oil, clothes, etc., which they exchanged at a distribution center. On the birthday of the Great Leader or some other special event, they might receive some Korean liquor for the adults, candy for the children, and meat for everyone. These were gifts from the Leader to the people he so loved. There were no private markets. Salaries were very small, but it didn't matter much, since there was little to buy. Most people got by with the basic necessities.

There was little money to spend and few places to spend it, and little time to shop anyway. Most people worked long hours, for in addition to the eight-hour-a-day, forty-hour week mandated by law, they were required to arrive early and stay after for political meetings, discussions of the day's tasks, instructions from the authorities, and discussion of the daily news. On weekends there were "voluntary" work days. Then there were constant campaigns for additional volunteer hours or participation in mass rallies. Nor was there anyplace to go in one's free time—no churches, temples, private clubs, or organizations were permitted. All leisure time was spent at home with family or taken up in state-managed organizations. Universal education through middle school was achieved by the 1970s, but for secondary students, much of the school time was spent volunteering on public projects, from road construction to harvesting crops. Basic healthcare was available, and an immunization program reduced the death rates so that by the 1980s North Koreans had life expectancies closer to those in the first world than those in other poor states. All basic needs were largely met, even if at a very no-frills level.

Entertainment and art were forms of indoctrination. Literary works were always about the heroic deeds of those who had fought for the revolution and their devotion to the leadership, or about the atrocities committed by foreigners—usually Japanese or Americans. Stories began with quotes from the Great Leader, and later, his son. Art, music, cinema, and theater followed the same types of story lines. Newspapers contained little that would pass for actual news. Mention of foreign events was limited to items such as "Members of the Juche Study Club of Khartoum met today to study the works of the Great Leader Kim Il Sung." Or there were reports of their fellow Koreans in the South, who led miserable lives under the heel of the South Korean military clique and their "American imperialist puppet masters," waiting to be reunited under the Great Leader Kim Il Sung. Occasionally the regime carried out campaigns to donate food or clothing for their suffering southern compatriots.

Life in the cities, as grim as it might appear to outsiders, was probably better than on the farm. Farmers worked under detailed instructions from the center. They were permitted only tiny private plots, big enough to grow chili peppers and some other vegetables, and like everyone else were allotted specific quantities of food, clothing, and other necessities. Farms were self-sufficient, with their own schools, distribution centers, and medical centers. As a result, there was no need to leave the farm; in fact, it was forbidden to do so without permission, making farmers virtual prisoners on the land they worked.

Knowing Every Chopstick and Spoon: The Surveillance Society
North Koreans were told, and children's songs proclaimed, that they were living in a paradise on earth where "we have nothing to envy in the world." Yet this was a strange paradise. In fact, by the 1970s, when Kim Il Sung's political system was fully functioning, the DPRK had become as close to George Orwell's *1984* as any society ever had. Nazi Germany and the Soviet Union are characterized as totalitarian societies, but the term is even more apt for Kim's state. Koreans in the North were told where to work and where to live, and were under almost constant surveillance. Each neighborhood or apartment building formed an *inminban* headed by an *inminbanjang*, usually a middle-aged woman whose job was to know everything about everyone—"every chopstick and spoon," as the saying went. Visitors to a home were noted, and permission was required for them to stay overnight. Homes were subject to unannounced inspection by special security units, and to the midnight home check by the *inminbanjang*. No foreign literature of any kind was permitted, not even from other communist countries. Radios and televi-

sions were fixed so that they could only be tuned to state channels, and were checked during security inspections to see they had not been tampered with. Special travel permits were required to buy a train or bus ticket or to go to another city or town. For residents outside the capital, permission to visit Pyongyang was difficult to obtain; when granted, it was considered the chance of a lifetime to see this wondrous place with its famous monuments.

The "Safety Bureau" kept track of all citizens and all Party and state officials. Everyone was subjected to constant indoctrination. All workers had to attend regular self-criticism sessions at their factory, office, or farm. At these, they had to take turns confessing to not living up to the expectations of the revolution and its Great Leader, promising to study his works and follow his instructions with greater diligence. Each citizen had to memorize and adhere to a set of guidelines—the Ten Principles for the Establishment of the Monolithic Ideological System. The first stated, "We must devote ourselves completely to the struggle to unify the entire society with the revolutionary ideology of Great Leader Kim Il Sung." The rest were pledges of absolute loyalty and obedience to the Great Leader, to follow his instructions unhesitatingly, to learn from him, etc. Failing to adhere to these guidelines was punishable by imprisonment.

For those who fell afoul of the authorities, there was a hierarchy of prison camps. Some were only temporary detention centers for minor infractions; other were grim long-term labor camps. The worst were the ones political prisoners were sent to, the *gwalliso*—North Korea's archipelago of labor camps, its version of Stalin's gulags, but worse, and also a bit stranger. Most were located in remote mountain valleys and resembled a string of villages rather than a conventional prison camp. The biggest covered a large area—a whole valley in some cases. They were sometimes divided into "revolutionization zones" and "total control zones." The first involved not only hard labor, but many hours of memorizing the works of the Great and Dear Leaders. Although the conditions in revolutionization zones were appalling, there was hope for rehabilitation and release. For the less fortunate, the "total control zones" were truly hell. Like Dante's Inferno, whose gate had a sign that stated, "Abandon all hope all ye who enter here," there was no hope for inmates. They were simply worked to death.

The strangest aspect of the *gwalliso* was the practice of imprisoning entire families. This often encompassed three generations: a convicted political prisoner could be joined by his children and his parents, or his parents and grandparents. This odd practice was a revival of the traditional Korean practice of collective responsibility, in which parents were responsible for the crimes of their children, elder brothers for the crimes of their younger siblings. Family members were encouraged to inform on one another; and whatever solace there was in having loved ones nearby was offset by the horror of seeing them tortured, starved, and worked to death. This was also a consideration for those who defected, as doing so could result in their loved ones being sent off to a *gwalliso*. Spouses, not being blood relatives, could sometimes avoid being imprisoned, but it required both denouncing their marital partner and getting a divorce. Over time the prisons were consolidated into a smaller number, each with as many as 50,000 inmates.

The Socialist Paradise

The handful of foreign visitors who made their way to North Korea in the '70s and '80s were often impressed by the order, the cleanliness, the lack of extreme poverty, and the progress the country had made in industrialization and education. Yet even the more sympathetic guests could be uncomfortable with the extreme cult of Kim Il Sung and his family, and the isolation of the people who had little contact with or knowledge about the outside world. What did most North Koreans really think of their society? It is hard to know, but most seemed to accept that they were very lucky to be living in this socialist paradise and to have such a wise and compassionate leader.

CHAPTER 7

A STRUGGLING NORTH KOREA: STAGNATION, CRISIS, AND SURVIVAL

From Great Leap to Slow Crawl: The Economic Slowdown

October is a beautiful month in Korea. The skies are deep blue, the air is cool but not chilly, and the leaves are turning bright colors. It was at this time of year in 1980 that the Korean Workers' Party held its sixth party congress. The highlight of the congress was the main address by the Supreme Leader Kim Il Sung; he stood before the delegates for several hours, reviewing his regime's achievements. He had much to be proud of: in less than three decades the country had recovered from the appalling destruction of the Korean War to become the second most urbanized and industrialized nation in Asia. It had virtually wiped out illiteracy, created a powerful military force, and skillfully carved out a position of independence from its two giant communist neighbors, China and the Soviet Union, while receiving aid and support from both. The nation was still divided, but Kim was confident that history was on his side and that the reunification of the peninsula under Pyongyang was inevitable.

Kim may not have been fully aware of it, but the achievements of North Korea's revolution were largely behind him. Economic growth was coming to a halt, and the prospects for reuniting the country under North Korea's leadership were slipping away. It was falling behind its southern rival in terms of industrial output and standard of living. In fact, things were about to go very wrong for the DPRK. South Korea's economy would continue booming, as it was about to embark on a path to democratization and international respectability, while the North was to enter a period of economic decline and isolation. In a decade, its very survival would be uncertain.

Economic growth rates up to the early 1970s were high—in fact, very high—but then they began to flag. When the regime launched its six-year plan for 1971–76, it decided to emulate the five-year plan of 1957 by completing it ahead of schedule—by October 10, 1975, the thirtieth anniversary of the founding of the KWP. To spur production, the regime relied on its method of throwing masses of people on projects, having them work extra "volunteer" hours, and bombarding them with exhortations to further the revolution by meeting production targets. Millions toiled in "speed battles" and days of extra labor to meet that goal. When the big anniversary came in October 1975, sure enough, the regime declared a complete success: all targets had been met by the projected date; it was another heroic victory of the revolution. In reality, however, the plan had fallen far short of its goals. Never admitting failure, the state urged workers to meet the same targets in 1976, despite the fact that it had been announced they had already been met. Then it added an extra year in 1977 to meet the same targets again. Then a new seven-year plan was announced that quietly incorporated some of the old targets. Clearly, there were problems.

By the early 1980s, the economy was barely growing at all; this was particularly alarming since its southern rival was performing so well. Sadly for the patient, hard-working people of North Korea, the only solution the regime came up with was the application of more labor. Everyone was put to work; schools frequently closed so that students could take part in projects; the huge prison population was put to work; and soldiers worked on construction sites and helped with harvesting crops. On Fridays, most offices were closed so staff could be sent out to perform manual labor. Yet the state was achieving diminishing returns—really, virtually no returns—on all this investment in extra effort.

Obtaining foreign currency became a central problem. North Korea needed foreign exchange to buy foreign technology to replace its outdated equipment and to provide a few luxuries for the elite. It didn't produce much that the rest of the world wanted; its industrial goods were so shoddy that even its communist allies didn't want them. Kim Jong Il, even more concerned with this than his father, created Room 39, a special office whose mission was to find ways to obtain precious foreign currency—by any means possible. And eventually almost every means (other than actually reforming the economy) was employed. Much of it involved criminal enterprises: North Korean diplomats smuggled heroin and other drugs; the country produced counterfeit cigarettes, amphetamines, and eventually counterfeit US bills.

It was bad enough that Kim Il Sung relied on old methods that were no longer working, but he also wasted precious capital and the labor of his people on ill-conceived schemes. Like so many dictators, Kim loved grandiose projects. An example was the West Sea Barrage, an eight-kilometer (five-mile) long system of dams and locks essentially blocking off the mouth of the mighty Daedong River from the Yellow Sea. North Koreans are still proud of this project, the longest such structure in world, and love showing it off to foreigners, but it was an enormous mistake. Intended to create hundreds of square kilometers of fertile farmland, it produced only some mudflats too salty for any use while backing up all the filth and sewage of the river, turning the surrounding land into a giant cesspool.

And then there were the show projects to impress visitors or North Korea's own citizens. These included the Pyongyang-Kaesong Express Highway, which was so little used one could take a nap on it without too much worry, and the Ryugyeong Hotel. The latter, begun in 1987, was to be the highest hotel in the world, a 105-story structure containing 3,000 rooms and multiple revolving restaurants. Besides the fact that such a monstrous construction was hardly needed in a city that received so few visitors, the work was halted in 1992, as it neared completion, due to structural and financial problems. It remained unopened, a strange elongated pyramid shape that loomed over the city—an ugly, unavoidable presence that symbolized failure rather than progress.

Reducing the vast military would have helped somewhat. Since the equal-emphasis policy of the 1960s, Pyongyang had attempted to develop both the economy and the military simultaneously. It constructed an entire "second economy" devoted to making military vehicles instead of tractors, and weapons instead of civilian goods. Its vast armed forces swallowed up much of its labor force, as well as its limited resources. Determined to more than match South Korea's military despite having half that country's population, Kim created an incredibly large army. By 1990, more than one million—out of a population of only twenty million—men and some women served in the military. Another seven million were in the reserves. All men had to serve for as many as thirteen years of active duty, with seven or eight being the norm. The DPRK was perhaps the most militarized nation on earth.

For a while, it appeared Pyongyang might learn from China and reform its economy. All signs indicated that Kim Il Sung's regime was at least flirting with the idea. Instead, rather than following the Chinese path, Kim looked to Moscow for help. The Soviet Union had long provided valuable economic assistance by exporting petroleum and other products to North Korea at nominal prices, as well as by supplying military equipment. In the early 1980s the Kremlin decided that it needed to offer more assistance in order to prevent the DPRK from falling into Beijing's orbit. It stepped up its aid and sent in experts to assist on development projects. This helped keep things afloat for a few years, but even with Moscow's support, the economy was stagnating.

Waiting for the Revolutionary Forces: The Threat from the South
In 1980, Kim Il Sung's hope of seeing the South brought under his leadership was not yet a fantasy. He could find many promising signs that the people of the ROK would rise up against their government. In fact, 1980 was a terrible year for the ROK. The assassination of Park Chung Hee in 1979 led to a year of political unrest; the economy tanked; a bloody uprising against the military government took

place in the city of Gwangju; and there was serious labor unrest. Meanwhile, some radical youths and leftist intellectuals expressed admiration for the DPRK. Even the long-term US commitment to defend the South was uncertain. President Carter had called for the withdrawal of troops in 1977, although the Soviet invasion of Afghanistan in 1979 and the increase in East-West tension that followed made that unlikely in the immediate future. Under these circumstances, it was easy for Kim to imagine his three-part strategy coming to fruition.

However, the geopolitical situation soon turned against Pyongyang. In 1981, the political order in the South stabilized, and the hardline anti-communist administration of US president Reagan reaffirmed its commitment to defend the ROK. But the biggest challenge was the rise of the ROK on the world stage. By 1980, South Korea had already surpassed the North in industrial output and living standards by a considerable margin. In 1981 it resumed its roaring economic growth, which continued unabated for the next decade—a sharp contrast to the DPRK. And the world was taking notice: starting in the early 1980s, developing countries, which Pyongyang considered its playground, were turning their interest toward the South, which had more to offer in aid and as an example of successful development. Even the DPRK's friends in the Non-Aligned Movement were busy opening relations with the ROK, having become uncomfortable with Kim's over-the-top cult, his acts of terrorism against the South, and his diplomats' involvement in smuggling.

The awarding of the 1988 summer Olympics to Seoul, a manifestation of the rising respectability of the ROK, had a profound effect on the relationship between the two Koreas. It granted a kind of international legitimacy to a country that had previously been seen as war-torn US client-state. It was the South's opportunity to show the world its economic miracle, to step out of the shadows and build bridges to China, the Soviet Union, and other countries that had previously ignored it or treated it with hostility. And the South Korean government made the most of it. Even Beijing and Moscow, Pyongyang's main allies, sent athletes for training in South Korea and began reporting on the country more favorably.

For Kim Il Sung, this was bad news. He responded by starting a campaign to have the Olympics moved, then lobbied to have the Games co-hosted by Pyongyang. He sent his foreign minister, Kim Nam Won, to dissuade his allies from participating, but with no success. Then he tried to scare people away with reports of a raging AIDS epidemic. When this failed, Kim turned to acts of terror. He tried to blow up South Korean president Chun Doo Hwan during a visit to Burma in October 1983, missing him but killing four members of Chun's cabinet. His agents planted a bomb in Seoul's international airport in 1986 and blew up a Korean Air passenger plane heading for Seoul, killing all aboard. When none of these succeeded in deterring the Olympics, Pyongyang tried an international boycott. This was a pathetic failure—only Cuba, Albania, Madagascar, and the Seychelles joined the embargo; everyone else came. The Olympics were a great success for the South: the world was duly impressed by the big, modern, clean city it saw, and China and the Soviet Union opened trade offices in Seoul—an unthinkable outcome for the North. The Games were also accompanied by South Korea's successful and mostly bloodless transition to democracy. The days of chronic political instability and political repression in the South were coming to an end.

Nothing could be more threatening to the DPRK than the rise of South Korea. The entire rationale for the North Korean regime was that it was the true vehicle by which all Koreans could achieve their dream of a unified, prosperous, strong, respected, independent state. To keep this idea alive, Pyongyang depicted South Korea as a true hell on earth—actually, hell would probably be an improvement over what the southerners supposedly endured. News reports, even textbooks, told of the hunger and physical deprivation of the people of the South, the cruel barbarity they suffered at the hands of the fiendish American "wolf-bastards" and the collaborators. Farmers were driven off the land needed for military bases, workers were boiled alive in chemical vats in American-owned pharmaceutical plants—the stories outdid each other. What kept the people from hanging themselves, in this telling, was the hope that they would someday be liberated by the North and live under the great leader Kim Il

Sung. But by the end of the 1980s, even Kim must have understood that the South was not on the verge of collapse, and that his state was falling hopelessly behind it in economic development.

Innumerable Crises

By the late 1980s the international situation for North Korea had gone from unfavorable to really bad. Only a decade after Kim Il Sung reviewed his achievements with pride and confidence in his hours-long speech, the ground was shifting under his feet. In Eastern Europe, Pyongyang's communist allies were collapsing, with the overthrow of Kim's friend and admirer the Romanian dictator Nicolae Ceausescu in late 1989 coming as a particular shock. Then there was China, which was establishing friendlier relations with the US as well as with the ROK, and abandoning the Maoist model for a mixed market-socialist economy. But at least the Tiananmen Massacre in 1989 showed the limits of China's reform.

Even worse for Pyongyang were the changes in Moscow, which opened formal relations with Seoul in 1990. In 1989, the reform-minded government of Gorbachev was no longer interested in propping up Pyongyang's economy. In 1990 it announced the suspension of most aid projects, and began to insist that the North begin paying market prices for its petroleum and other exports. This had to be done with foreign currency that Pyongyang didn't have. The result was an immediate economic contraction and severe energy shortages. North Korea had relied on generous supplies of cheap petroleum for the massive amounts of fertilizers it used on its fields, for powering its trains and tractors and generating its electricity, so the loss of Soviet petroleum was a particularly hard blow. The contraction of the economy was so severe that Kim Il Sung himself, in his annual New Year's address, admitted that there were problems. It was a startling thing for him to do, since officially everything was always going well in the Democratic People's Republic as it continued on its revolutionary path. Failures were almost never admitted. The economic hardships, including food shortages, worsened; the regular food rations people received had already been reduced in 1987, and were now being reduced further, causing real hunger.

Then there was the nuclear crisis. Pyongyang had been working on developing nuclear weapons, as well as missiles, since the 1970s. By 1990, American satellites showed the North Korean program was large enough to actually produce an atomic bomb; this, along with their testing of explosives used for detonating a nuclear device, raised concerns. The US lobbied for Pyongyang to admit international inspectors; instead, in 1993 North Korea announced its intention to withdraw from the Non-Proliferation Treaty it had previously signed. The ensuing crisis was so serious that the US began plans for a possible military strike, calling it USFK-OpPlan 502716. Nobody wanted war; of course, Kim would lose, but not without wreaking destruction on the South. He had more than 8,000 artillery buried in the mountainsides on the DPRK side of the DMZ, capable of carrying out a devastating retaliatory blow on Seoul, which was just forty kilometers (twenty-five miles) from the border. Fortunately, former US president Jimmy Carter arrived in Pyongyang in June 1994 and signed an agreement with Kim Il Sung, averting possible conflict. Under this pact, known as the Agreed Framework, the DPRK would open its nuclear program to inspection in exchange for the construction of two nuclear power plants by South Korea, to be financed by the US and Japan. Kim also agreed to a summit meeting with the South Korean president. It proved only a temporary respite in ongoing tensions with the US over the nuclear issue.

The summit conference between Kim Il Sung and his South Korean counterpart never took place, as Kim died several weeks after the agreement. His sudden death was still another crisis for the regime. At eighty-two, Kim was a physically vigorous man who showed no obvious signs of ill health. The forty-six years of Kim's rule—even more, if his emergence under the Soviet occupation is counted—was so long that most North Koreans had known no other leader. He set the record for the longest dictatorship in history, broken only by Fidel Castro, who ruled one year longer before stepping down in 2006. During that time, Kim dominated his country in a way that no other modern leader had. It was hard to imagine the DPRK without him.

The Son Becomes the Sun: North Korea under Kim Jong Il

Many observers expected the death of Kim Il Sung would lead to a crisis. How could the regime continue without the person who had dominated it so completely? Unlike most modern dictators, however, Kim had prepared for his succession carefully. By the time he died, his eldest son, Kim Jong Il, controlled all key Party offices, had placed his loyalists in top bureaucratic positions, and was the commander of the Korean People's Army. That is to say, he held almost every lever of power. As a result, the transition went smoothly with no major purges.

Short, with his elevated shoes and his bouffant hairdo, Kim Jong Il hardly looked like a leader, nor did he sound like one. It wasn't that his voice or manner of speaking was strange; rather, he almost never spoke in public at all. When he became leader in 1994, despite being seen everywhere on TV and on posters and even appearing with his father on the badges people wore in public, he had never given a public address. It was rumored that he had a speech impediment, but foreigners who met him found him witty and a good conversationalist. After coming to power, he continued his practice of being seen but not heard by the general public. Nonetheless, the eccentricity of his appearance—and sometimes his behavior—aside, Kim Jong Il was a skilled political operative who had more than twenty years' experience at the center of power before his father's death. He needed all these skills, because soon after he came to power, he had to guide the country through its greatest crisis: the famine.

The Horror of North Korea's Famine

On June 26, 1995, it started raining in North Korea. This was not unusual; late June normally marks the arrival of the summer monsoons, when the peninsula gets much of its rainfall. That year, however, it rained continually for ten days, accumulating a total of sixty centimeters (twenty-three inches). Floods occurred over much of the country, inundating many of the nation's rice paddies and destroying a sizable portion of the crop. As a result, the country, already facing a serious food shortage, was now swept by a famine that would continue for the next four years. It is difficult to say how many people died prematurely due to food shortages. Famines are usually accompanied by confusion, so deaths can be overlooked; people move about, and it is difficult to separate starvation and malnutrition from other causes of death. In North Korea, calculating the death toll was made more challenging by the closed nature of the regime, which treated even routine statistics as state secrets. It is not surprising, then, that estimates vary so wildly. Some experts and outside groups reported up to three million of the nation's twenty million people perished. That's at the high end of the credible estimates; low-end estimates are about a tenth of that number. Even a mid-range estimate of one million is still a terrible number.

The heavy rains were just the tipping point in a country where famine-like conditions had already been underway. North Korea had never been able to feed itself adequately. The challenges of mountainous terrain, a short growing season, and a population that increased rapidly after 1953, doubling in a generation, were compounded by what could only be described as terribly shortsighted agricultural practices. Socialist farming was never successful anywhere, but to compensate for its inadequacies, most communist states allotted farm families small private plots to grow food to sell at markets. A substantial portion of the food consumed in the Soviet Union and Vietnam, for example, came from such plots. In North Korea, however, the only private plots were too tiny to produce anything other than some chili peppers and a few supplementary vegetables for a family; private markets were extremely restricted and could not include grain.

Being unable to go grocery shopping, the North Korean people were dependent on the food distribution system, which supplied everyone with the basics. The most important staple was grain, which was allotted to families based on the number of members. Soldiers, government officials, and men in heavy industry got the most; those in light industry less. Working women received more than housewives; old people and children received the least. The amount was barely adequate for basic needs. What all Koreans wanted was rice, but there was never enough, so it was supplemented with other, less desirable grains—mostly corn. The ratio of rice to corn depended on social status. For most, the percentage of rice declined in the 1980s and 1990s, as corn was a bit easier to grow, if not as tasty or nutritious. Food rations were cut when there was a harvest shortfall; this happened regularly from the late 1980s on. When the flow of Soviet aid and petroleum for fertilizer and fuel stopped, the results were catastrophic; hunger became widespread. Then, starting in 1995, the entire public distribution system broke down and millions received no food at all. One solution would have been to import food, but the regime needed what little foreign funds it had for weapons components and extravagances for the elite.

All famines are horrific events, but this one was unusual. Unlike most famines, which hit rural areas hardest, this one affected urban dwellers. Millions of city folk suffered from severe hunger; many died at home, while others collapsed in the streets. Train stations and other public places were filled with abandoned children, who were called "swallows," begging and scrounging for food, their parents either dead or too weak to assist them. Factories stopped operating, since most of the employees were out foraging in the hillsides or searching for food. Classrooms were empty because children were too hungry or weak to attend, and the teachers were out looking for food or were themselves too weak to show up. The hardest-hit region was the northeast; the cities there began to look like ghost towns with empty streets, since people had left in search of food or were too weak to leave home. Everything that could be eaten was consumed. Dogs and livestock disappeared. People made "green porridge" out of leaves, grass, and twigs, which provided the illusion of food but only caused diarrhea. Malnutrition took a particularly heavy toll on the children, with many suffering from severely stunted growth. Foreigners commented on how small and young they looked for their age.

The nation's industrial plants stopped functioning, and managers and employees stripped them of their machinery for scrap metal. Smugglers conducted a large illegal cross-border trade in scrap metal and anything else that could be sold in China. Crossing over to China became increasingly easy as border guards, often hungry themselves, were bribed to look the other way. The old system of internal control over travel broke down as hundreds of thousands took to the road looking for food or work. Even soldiers and government office workers wandered off in search of food.

Kim Jong Il openly called for international assistance. The World Food Program responded, as did the UN International Children's Emergency Fund. They were joined by food relief assistance from some European countries, Japan, South Korea, and even the United States. A number of private agencies also provided assistance. By 1997, two out of five North Koreans were being fed by the international community. Pyongyang, so secretive, could hardly have been thrilled about the large number of foreigners witnessing its economic failure. Relief workers complained that they were not given direct access to victims, that they were being denied entry into many areas of the country, that they were uncertain whether the food aid was reaching its intended targets, or—as rumor had it—was being diverted to the military. Some aid agencies and governments, frustrated with the restrictions under which they were being forced to operate, pulled out.

Yet it is surprising that international relief workers were permitted entry at all. That such an isolated, secretive country, so concerned about its people finding out the reality behind the wildly distorted depiction of the outside world they had been given, and so concerned about self-reliance, could open itself to foreign aid teams was certainly remarkable. This was a contrast to China's famine in the late 1950s and early 1960s, when Mao's government refused to so much as admit there was a famine, even as many millions perished. But the risk for Kim Jong Il and his government paid off. By the year 2000, the worst of the famine was over. Food assistance, most of it coming from South Korea and the US, continued for a few more years. And the regime managed to survive intact.

Marketization from Below: The Transformation of North Korea in the Wake of Famine

The entire totalitarian system Kim Il Sung and his comrades had constructed appeared to be unraveling. Many outside observers saw a country and a regime on the verge of collapse. Faced with the loss of its Soviet patron and economic decline, and with its people starving; internationally isolated, with its legitimacy threatened by the rise of South Korea, the North Korean state appeared to be doomed. Remarkably, however, the regime managed to avoid the fate of Albania, Romania, and others among its communist allies by adjusting its economy and modifying its ideology.

Adjustments in the economic system took place from the top and—perhaps more profoundly—from below. The near-total command economy that had provided for every citizen's needs broke down. The old institutions remained intact, and the state continued to call itself socialist, but in reality, it was being replaced by a kind of improvised system, half socialist and half entrepreneurial. No longer able to rely on the state to provide for them, ordinary people looked to the informal economy. All kinds of small businesses arose, and markets sprang up everywhere. Government organizations became involved in businesses as well; many engaged in the export of commodities to China, or made deals with Chinese firms interested in the country's mineral wealth. Others exported seafood, coal, and iron. Members of government agencies and the military who had access to vehicles hired them out or ran transport services that replaced the decrepit rail service as the main way to transport goods and people. Agricultural produce and goods imported from China were sold freely. Items that would have been unimaginable previously, such as used Chinese VCRs, became commonplace in the country, along with pirated South Korean TV shows and music videos.

All this presented an enormous challenge to the state and its control over society. And in fact, it did lose a measure of control. It could no longer prevent people from moving or traveling, and cracks in the information cordon that had almost completely cut off the population from any knowledge of the outside world appeared. Rather than stopping the shift to a more mobile population and market-oriented economy, or promoting it, the Kim Jong Il regime chose a middle ground: to control, contain, and also to adjust to a market economy. Government agencies had always been on the lookout for ways to obtain foreign exchange; now they were encouraged to obtain a large portion of funding through entrepreneurial activity. Realizing that the society was becoming a money economy, Kim Jong Il decided to facilitate that process. He shifted the country to a more money-based economy, legalized private markets, and permitted farmers to sell some of their products. He allowed a variety of consumer products, including imports from China, to be sold openly. The government issued travel permits to merchants to go to China and trade. People were allowed to own bicycles and even automobiles, if they had the money to buy them. Almost anything could be purchased on the open market.

Modest reforms continued after his death. In 2012 and 2014, changes in agricultural policies increased the percentage of the crops farmers could keep for themselves or sell; work units were reduced to the size of family units, and the private plots allotted to farm families expanded from 100 square meters (1,076 square feet) to 3,300 (32,292 square feet). Factory managers were given independence to buy and sell materials and products, to hire workers, and to set wages. More and more private restaurants and shops opened. None of these measures were revolutionary, but they worked just well enough to keep the economy afloat, mitigate the worst poverty and give the state just enough revenues to import parts for its military and luxury goods to keep the elite happy.

An interesting part of the country's economic pragmatism was its trade with South Korea. If ordinary people came into too much contact with their southerner compatriots and learned just how prosperous and free they were, it would be a serious threat to the regime. But the DPRK needed the economic aid and foreign currency the South could provide. So for a decade, until relations soured and North Korea's economy had recovered somewhat, it accepted large amounts of rice, cooking oil, fuel oil, and other aid from the ROK. It also permitted South Korean tourists to visit the famed Diamond Mountains just north of the border near the east coast. A resort built by the Hyundai Corporation accommodated southern tourists, allowing them to spend their money and vacation in the mountains without coming into any contact with North Korean people. An even more ambitious project was the Kaesong Industrial Complex built in the city just a few miles north of the DMZ. Over a hundred South Korean firms eventually opened up plants there, taking advantage of North Korea's cheap labor. At one point, 40,000 North Koreans worked for these firms. Again, however, contact between northerners and southerners was kept at a minimum.

The Racial-Nationalist State: From Marxism–Leninism to Ultra-Nationalism

Adjusting its economy to deal with changing realities helped to insure the survival of the Kim dynastic state, but it still faced threats to its legitimacy. How could the regime maintain its credibility when it could no longer claim it was leading the Korean people down the road to prosperity and progress? How could it deal with the collapse of communist systems elsewhere? How could it pretend it was a paradise on earth when obviously well-fed foreigners were distributing food aid? How could it maintain the myth that the impoverished, oppressed masses in South Korea were looking to the North for liberation when the people could see a very different reality on the pirated videos that became so popular?

To deal with these challenges, the North Korean regime had to refashion the official story it told to its people about itself and its place in the world. Because *juche* thought had largely replaced Marxism–Leninism as the ideological foundation of society, it was insulated from the collapse of communist regimes elsewhere. The wonderful thing about *juche* thought was that it was so vacuous that it could be interpreted to mean anything the authorities wanted it to mean. But this was not enough to deal with the changing reality of the world around it, so state propaganda organs turned to a more extreme blood-and-soil ultranationalism. In the early 1990s there was greater emphasis on celebrating the country's unique heritage. Traditional holidays such as the lunar New Year's celebration and the Chuseok autumn festival were revived. But the state went far beyond this in linking itself to an ancient and unique historical past.

Following suggestions by the Great Leader, archaeologists discovered an ancient and probably fictitious Daedong civilization, adding to the nation's antiquity. In 1993, even more amazingly, archaeologists discovered the grave of Dangun, who had previously been dismissed in DPRK texts as an ancient myth. It was now announced that he was a real person who had lived five thousand years ago. Korea was an original civilization, as old if not older than China, Egypt, or any other—and Pyongyang had been the center of it since the distant past. The grave of "King Dangun" was made into a tourist site. DPRK authorities didn't stop there: they proclaimed that Korea not only had a unique, independently developed culture, but the Korean people belonged to a distinctive race. It turned out they were direct descendants of Pithecanthropus, an early human that lived in the Daedong basin of North Korea one million years ago. Not even the Nazis had gone so far as to assert that Germans had evolved separately from other races.

Koreans, in this new reinterpretation of history, were a special, pure, unmixed race, a glorious, virtuous people—but one that was always threatened by foreigners. Foreigners sought to subjugate Korea and violate its purity. Fortunately for Koreans today, they had this brilliant, loving Kim family who provided the leadership needed to keep outsiders at bay, preventing them from blocking the Korean people in their path of progress. The Americans, the Japanese, and others lorded over half the Korean people and were trying to subjugate the free half in the DPRK. The wise leadership and the heroic, powerful Korean People's Army were foiling these efforts.

Economic problems, including the famine, were blamed on the foreign imperialists who used economic sanctions and other methods to bring about the DPRK's economic collapse, although the regime could force them to supply some aid. North Koreans were going through an "arduous march"—a term used to refer to the long journey Kim Il Sung had taken to escape the pursuing Japanese army in the late 1930s. In the early 2000s, references to South Korean poverty were replaced by reports of the humiliation they endured under the thumb of the imperialists and their lackeys. They weren't starving, but they lacked something more important: freedom from foreign oppression. North Korea, the birthplace of Korea, was the last great bastion of Korean independence and ethnic-racial purity.

Besides moving the ideology in a more racial-nationalist, antiforeign direction, there was a greater emphasis on the military. The regime had boasted of its progress in making the country prosperous and powerful; in the 1990s the emphasis shifted from "prosperous" to "powerful." In 1998, Kim Jong Il began his "military first" policy, indicating that strengthening the DPRK military would take priority. The nation might suffer economically, but as long as it was militarily strong it would be free.

How effective was this new ideological evolution? Outsiders wondered how much of all this most North Korean people believed. Cut off from much knowledge of the larger world, they seemed to accept a good deal of it—least most people did—although there was also widespread cynicism. Still, there was no sign of open dissent, and most people were busy just struggling to get by. Some did leave; at first just a few, but by 2010, thousands were crossing over to China. Most were just trying to earn money to bring back to their families. It was a risky move: the illegal North Korean population in China, numbering perhaps a quarter million, had to dodge Chinese authorities who would deport them. Those that got caught either had to pay hefty bribes or suffer imprisonment. Occasionally people who crossed illegally into China were shot when they returned.

Some North Koreans—mostly those who lived near the border and had greater access to news about the outside world—tried to defect to South Korea. This was extremely difficult, as it usually involved not only crossing the border but making one's way across China to either Mongolia or Laos. By the early 2010s about 20,000 North Korean refugees were living in the South. A few managed to pay smugglers to bring family members out as well.

The Politics of Survival: North Korea and the Rest of the World
In its new form, the story created to justify the regime and give meaning to the sacrifices of its people required three things: maintaining a constant flow of international crises and confrontations; keeping restrictions on contact with foreigners, especially with South Koreans; and demonstrating the DPRK's military strength and progress. Kim Jong Il's relations with the rest of the world were based on these three requirements, as well as the need to acquire foreign

currency—whether by aid, trade, or other means—to import weapon parts and luxuries for the elite.

The trickiest aspect of the DPRK's foreign policy was its relationship with South Korea. ROK president Kim Dae Jung, who had been democratically elected in 1998, was keen on improving relations with his "Sunshine Policy," a strategy derived from Aesop's fable about a contest between the wind and the sun over who could get a man to take off his coat. The wind blew furiously, but this only made the man wrap his coat more tightly around him, whereas the sun succeeded just by shining and bringing warmth. Kim Dae Jung tried easing tensions by offering a hand of friendship. In 2000, he traveled to Pyongyang, met with Kim Jong Il, and promised the North more aid. They agreed to open a rail link, to allow reunions of divided families, and to carry out cultural exchanges. But Kim Jong Il, happy to get the aid, could not afford to provide either peace or too much in-person contact. There were token gestures, such as having the two nations march together at the Sidney Olympics in 2000, but most of the cultural exchanges and family reunions that were promised never took place. Kim Jong Il held another summit meeting with Kim Dae Jung's successor, Roh Moo-hyun, in 2007, but again promises of further exchanges were not carried out.

Instead, Kim Jong Il pursued a policy of obtaining whatever foreign aid and foreign currency he could—accepting aid packages from the South, allowing some tourists in the Diamond Mountains, opening the Kaesong Industrial Complex—but restricted any meaningful contact between his people and their compatriots south of the DMZ. Meanwhile, he continued his policy of military confrontation. In 1999 he sent naval vessels into what had been accepted as ROK territorial waters, leading to a clash between the two countries' ships. In 2001, he moved missiles near the border. Aid, trade, and tourist dollars from the South were welcome, but not at the cost of undermining the myth of a hostile South being used as a base for imperialist designs on the DPRK. In 2008, on the very day the new president in Seoul was presenting his plan to help the North develop its economy, a South Korean tourist was shot at the Diamond Mountain resort. Kim refused to apologize, and the resort was closed; the

North confiscated it without compensation. Seoul responded by suspending all aid. By then, Pyongyang had decided to live without it and get by with trade with China. In March of 2010, the North Koreans sank an ROK destroyer with a torpedo, killing fifty South Korean sailors. In November of that year, the DPRK artillery shelled the South Korean island of Yeonpyeong, killing four people and causing popular outrage in the South.

North Korea pursued a similar strategy with the United States, occasionally offering gestures to improve relations in return for aid while also setting off confrontations and creating crises. In 2002, relations with the US worsened when it appeared the North was cheating on its promise to suspend nuclear weapons development. The Agreed Framework, under which Pyongyang promised to halt its nuclear weapons program in exchange for the construction of two peaceful nuclear reactors, came to an end. In 2003 Pyongyang announced it was withdrawing from the Non-Proliferation Treaty of Nuclear Weapons, the second time since 1993 it had done so. But then it agreed to a series of six-party talks with the US, South Korea, China, Russia, and Japan about its nuclear program, although no progress was ever made.

All the while, the DPRK was busy figuring out how to build a nuclear bomb. They succeeded in detonating a small one in 2006, which was followed by a return to negotiations; in 2007, Pyongyang agreed to open to allow International Atomic Energy Agency inspectors in and shut down its nuclear reactor at Yeongbyon. It even destroyed a facility in 2008. But giving in to US demands that the North surrender its nuclear weapons was not a serious option for a regime intent on demonstrating its military progress to its people while also protecting itself from foreign intervention. The US invasion of Iraq in 2003—one of the three countries that President Bush labeled the "axis of evil," along with Iran and North Korea—only made the acquisition of atomic bombs more urgent.

By 2009, Pyongyang was willing to lose all US aid in order to step up its weapons program. It detonated a larger atomic bomb that year, and continued its missile development with the aim of building an intercontinental ballistic missile that could reach the US.

North Korea's nuclear weapons program was troubling to all the powers, including its only ally, China. The Chinese supported UN sanctions against the regime following the 2009 test. But the regime was willing to risk international condemnation to continue with its program. Washington tried many ways of putting pressure on the regime. It froze North Korean assets in a Macau bank that was being used to launder money and interfered with its efforts to export weapons. None of these succeeded in crippling the economy, however; trade with China was increasing enough to both keep the economy afloat and obtain enough foreign currency to buy parts for weapons development and purchase BMWs and cognac for the ruling elite. Efforts by the international community, led by the US, to halt North Korea's development of weapons of mass destruction were largely futile, since the regime regarded these arms as essential for protecting itself and impressing its people.

Beijing could have stopped trade, but feared that doing so would precipitate an economic collapse in North Korea. The great fear was that if the regime collapsed, a flood of refugees would come across the Manchurian border, and South Korea would take over the North. Besides the concern of chaos next door was the worry of having a united, democratic Korea, allied with the US and with Japan on its border. Additionally, the fall of a communist ally, even a rather disgusting one, could be interpreted by its own people as weakness, or even worse, embolden those discontented with the Chinese communist regime. China therefore made token gestures in support of sanctions. It wanted Pyongyang to stop developing atomic bombs, fearing it would go too far in provoking South Korea and the US; yet at the same time it allowed trade to flourish. Exports of coal, iron, rare earths, and other minerals to China made up most of its international trade. Chinese businesses even contracted out textile production to low-cost North Korea; the goods were then reimported and tagged with a "Made in China" label. The Manchurian border city of Dandong, across the Yalu River from Shinuiju, boomed with the cross-border trade.

Meanwhile, Pyongyang employed all kinds of means for earning foreign exchange. Despite sanctions, it sold weapons to various governments from Egypt to Myanmar. It operated a chain of restaurants in Asia; it continued to sell knockoff brand-name cigarettes and narcotics; and it also engaged in insurance fraud, bilking Lloyd's of London out of millions in false maritime claims. It sent laborers to toil in logging camps in Siberia, where they lived under prison-like security, and dispatched workers to countries from Poland to Zimbabwe. It abandoned its attempt to present itself as a progressive model of development to the Third World, and more or less accepted its status as an international pariah, although it could never admit its fallen place in the world to its own people.

Kim Il Sung Reincarnated: Kim Jong Un's Succession to the Throne

In 2008, Kim Jong Il had a stroke. This was never publicly announced, but after an absence, he appeared on TV looking thin, weak, and ill. It might have been a subtle way of preparing the people for the next succession. The regime was so closely linked to the cult of the Kim family that it was inconceivable that anyone other than a member of the family could succeed him. The Korean people needed to be protected by this line of the noblest, wisest members of the purest of races—so Kim looked to his three sons for a successor. The eldest, Kim Jong Nam, would normally have been expected to be the anointed leader, since by tradition the eldest son took on the family business. But Kim Jong Nam had disgraced himself when he was arrested by the Japanese for trying to enter the country on a false passport. His admitted purpose, embarrassingly enough, was to visit Tokyo Disneyland. A fun-loving man, fond of drinking, gambling, and women, he just wasn't leadership material. The second son, Kim Jong Chul, was too soft, so the young Kim Jong Un was finally selected as his father's successor.

In 2010 Kim Jong Un began to appear alongside his father at public functions, and was shown in state media accompanying his father for on-the-spot guidance trips. The problem was that the youngest son was only in his late twenties, and had little experience in governance. There, was, however, no time for the long apprenticeship Kim Jong Il had undergone; the whole process was sped up, with Kim Jong Un receiving regular promotions in Party and military rank. There was even less time than Kim Jong Il probably thought, for the Dear Leader died of a stroke in December 2011. The son immediately assumed command.

CHAPTER 8

AN EMERGING SOUTH KOREA: WAR, AUTHORITARIANISM, AND ECONOMIC DEVELOPMENT

An Unpromising Start: South Korea under Syngman Rhee

When *New York Times* reporter A. M. Rosenthal visited South Korea in early 1961 for a series on the country, he found it still mired in poverty, unemployment, corruption, and political instability. Despite being one of the world's largest recipients of US aid, it had managed to achieve only a modest recovery from the destruction of the Korean War that had ended eight years earlier. So grim did he find the prospects for the country's future that at the end of the series he recommended mass emigration from the crowded country, and called for generous assistance from the West, which he thought would be needed for generations.

Rosenthal's observations were typical of outsiders, who generally came away with bleak assessments of South Korea's prospects. Yet he wrote his series of reports on the eve of one of the most rapid periods of sustained economic growth ever seen. In a little more than a generation, the country would become a wealthy democratic nation noted for its technological sophistication.

Indeed, South Korea's transformation was often labeled a "miracle," yet it was no miracle for the people who endured the many failures, frustrations, and hardships on the road to building a modern developed nation. In fact, the first years of South Korea, from 1945 to the early 1960s, were characterized by mass displacement, hunger, war, and frustrated hopes for a reunited fatherland. The 1960s and 1970s saw rapid industrial growth under the authoritarian regime of Park Chung Hee. But growth was achieved at the cost of political repression, harsh working conditions, and often wrenching social change, while the threat of renewed conflict remained ever present.

South Korea in the 1950s was hardly a very promising society. Already poor, it had suffered a level of destruction that, while not as great as that experienced by the North, was still appalling. Millions had been dislocated during the war, thousands of homes and buildings destroyed. Almost every family had lost someone during the war—they'd either been killed or marched off to the North.

Over this devastation presided the government of President Syngman Rhee. It was authoritarian, corrupt, and seemingly incompetent. Rhee himself, in his late seventies at the end of the Korean War, was energetic, intelligent, and politically shrewd, but primarily interested in maintaining his position as president and lacking any vision of how to pull his nation out of poverty. His Liberal Party was mainly an instrument to keep him and his supporters in power; it had no real ideology or program for development. In contrast to North Korea, the economy under his direction made only a modest recovery. Once an agricultural breadbasket, South Korea now relied on American food aid, exporting almost nothing.

Much of its economy was based on US aid, its chief source of foreign exchange, and Rhee's administration skimmed off as much of this as possible for its own purposes. There was a small business sector, but it worked closely with the Liberal Party. The case of Lee Byung Chull was illustrative: Rhee's government would hoard US aid dollars; then it would provide Lee with a license to exchange the overvalued official currency, the *hwan*, for those dollars. Lee would use the money to buy sugar, which his Number One Sugar Company would then sell at an enormous profit—a percentage of which would

JAPANESE GENERAL GOVERNMENT BUILDING This building in downtown Seoul was the headquarters of the Japanese colonial administration. Designed by a German architect, it was shaped like the Chinese character for Japan and was situated in front of the main royal palace, blocking its view. Despite the objections of historical preservationists, the South Korean government tore it down in the 1990s, regarding it as a symbol of colonial repression. *Photo: Wikimedia Commons* © 門田房太郎.

SYNGMAN RHEE The longtime exiled nationalist leader and first president of the Republic of Korea, Syngman Rhee, who was educated in the United States and received a PhD from Princeton University, lived the majority of his life in the United States. As president he governed in an authoritarian manner until he was ousted in a 1960 student-led uprising. *Photo: Wikimedia Commons.*

CROSSING THE 38TH PARALLEL United Nations forces cross the 38th parallel in 1950, the first year of the Korean War. This original border ran in a straight line, cutting through provinces, valleys, and villages. The current border represents the cease-fire line of 1953, running southwest to northeast. *Photo: National Archives and Records Administration.*

SOUTH KOREAN SOLDIERS South Korean soldiers at the evacuation of Suwon Airfield in 1950. Outnumbered, with inferior weaponry and caught by surprise, the ROK army was forced to withdraw to the southern part of the country, where they were joined by US and UN forces. *Photo: National Archives and Records Administration.*

FIGHTING IN SEOUL American M26 Pershing tanks enter downtown Seoul, South Korea, in the Second Battle of Seoul during the Korean War. In the foreground, United Nations troops round up North Korean prisoners-of-war. *Photo: Naval Historical Center.*

KOREAN WAR REFUGEES In this famous photo, a young Korean girl carries her baby brother by an M26 tank during the Korean War. Millions of Koreans became refugees during the war. Hundreds of thousands of families became separated, especially during the chaotic first year when cities and towns changed hands multiple times. Many were never reunited. *Photo: National Archives and Records Administration.*

ROH MOO-HYUN A former human rights lawyer and political dissident under the military government, Roh Moo-hyun served as president of South Korea from 2003 to 2008. His election in 2002 came as a surprise since his candidacy was not taken seriously by the political establishment. Roh led what may have been the first internet-based national political campaign in history, funding it with small online donations. *Photo: Megapixl © Markwaters.*

STUDENT DEMONSTRATION Student anti-government demonstration at Konkuk University in 1987. Student demonstrations spearheaded the democratization of South Korea, helping bring down the authoritarian rule of Syngman Rhee in 1960 and contributing to the public pressure that led to the military carrying out democratic reforms in the late 1980s. *Photo: Bigstock.*

1988 SEOUL OLYMPICS The lighting of the Olympic torch at the 1988 Olympic Games in Seoul. The successful games were a signal to the international community that South Korea was emerging as a dynamic modern state. The event helped to dispel the popular image of the regime as an impoverished, war-torn land. The games also provided a useful means for the ROK to enter into diplomatic and trade relations with China and the Soviet Union. *Photo: US Department of Defense.*

STATUE OF PEACE The Statue of Peace, popularly called Peace Girl, was erected in honor of the "comfort women" who served as Japanese sex slaves during World War II. The comfort women have become both an example of the brutal nature of Japanese rule and a metaphor for the subjugation of the Korean people. Japan's failure to fully acknowledge responsibility has been an ongoing issue in Tokyo-Seoul relations. *Photo: Wikimedia Commons © YunHo Lee.*

PYONGYANG The Pyongyang skyline with the 1,080-foot-tall, unfinished Ryugyong Hotel in the background. Under the Kim dynasty, Pyongyang has been made a display city dominated by monuments and official buildings, and living there is considered a privilege. For most North Koreans, a visit to the capital is a rare and precious opportunity. *Photo: Megapixl © Chrispyphoto.*

GUARDING THE DMZ South Korean soldiers on duty at the DMZ, the most heavily fortified border in the world. Flare-ups involving exchange of fire and casualties were common in the 1960s and 1970s, but became less common later. In 2018 the leaders of North and South Korea met at the DMZ for the first time to ease tensions. *Photo: Megapixl © Vacclav.*

PRAYER RIBBONS Prayer ribbons are tied to a fence at the Freedom Bridge near the DMZ. The division of Korea left several million family members divided. With all communication between the two Koreas cut off, they did not even know their relatives' whereabouts or whether they were alive or not. *Photo: Megapixl © Loeskieboom.*

KIM IL SUNG AND KIM JONG IL Official painting of the "Great Leader" Kim Il Sung and his son and successor the "Dear Leader" Kim Jong Il. From 1982, father and son were often depicted together. This reinforced the idea that Kim Jong Il was his father's rightful and natural successor and prepared the way for his smooth assumption of leadership in 1994. *Photo: Megapixl © Linqong.*

NORTH KOREAN MILITARY PARADE Members of the Korean People's Army perform their famous goose step at a Pyongyang military parade celebrating the sixtieth anniversary of the end of the Korean War in 2013. Military parades allow the regime to show off new weaponry and impress its people with the country's military strength and resolve. *Photo: Megapixl © Gordeev20.*

PROPAGANDA POSTERS Shown here are two propaganda posters on the streets of the North Korean capital, Pyongyang. Nowhere else are people as subjected to constant political indoctrination as the North Koreans. Nearly all literature, music, art, and education is centered on promoting political propaganda. *Photo: Megapixl © Nyiragongo70.*

REUNIFICATION MONUMENT The Reunification Monument in Pyongyang represents the hope for the reunification of Korea. Almost every Korean considers the division of the country after 1945, a division imposed by outside powers, to be a great tragedy and believes that eventual reunification was inevitable. *Photo: Megapixl © Nyiragongo70.*

NORTH KOREAN YOUTH A North Korean girl wearing the red scarf and white blouse of the Kim Il Sung Socialist Youth League. This is part of the regimentation and organization of almost all life in North Korea. Most young people become members when they enter their teens; it is a major milestone for them. However, membership is denied to children from families of bad *seongbun. Photo: Megapixl © Linqong.*

PYONGYANG COMPUTER LAB A computer room at the Grand People's Study House in Pyongyang, North Korea. The computers give access to a North Korean intranet, not the Internet. In 2019, North Korea was the world's only country not connected to the Worldwide Web. *Photo: Wikimedia Commons © Bjørn Christian Tørrissen.*

PARTY MONUMENT Monument in Pyongyang of the symbol of the Korean Workers' Party of North Korea: the hammer, the sickle, and the writing brush. Formed in 1946, the KWP remained the ruling party of the Democratic People's Republic of Korea. Though it continued to call itself socialist, all references to Marxism-Leninism disappeared after the 1970s. *Photo: Megapixl © Linqong.*

KAESONG CITY STREETS A traffic officer with little traffic in Kaesong, the old capital of Goryeo, now located in North Korea just eleven kilometers (seven miles) from the DMZ. Outside the city are tombs of the Goryeo kings, North Korea's only UNESCO World Heritage site. *Photo: Wikimedia Commons © Kok Leng Yeo.*

BUSAN Long the main port for trade with Japan, Busan has become the second-largest Korean city, a metropolitan area of about eight million people in 2019. With mountains on its outskirts and fine beaches, Busan is one of South Korea's most livable cities. *Photo: Megapixl © Pukpao5559.*

AIR POLLUTION IN SEOUL Seoul, with more than twenty million people, suffers from terrible air pollution. Most of it is the product of the ten million vehicles on the roads and the coal-burning power plants, but smog drifting in from northern China also contributes. *Photo: Adobe Stock © Savvapanf Photo.*

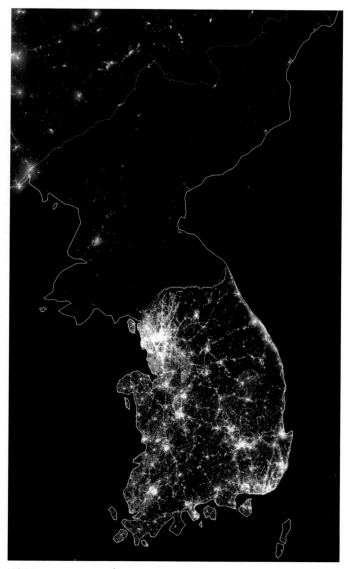

KOREA AT NIGHT This 2012 NASA satellite photo of the Korean peninsula at night dramatically contrasts the two Koreas. South Korea is seen filled with light while North Korea is in darkness; only a dim spot of light marks the capital, Pyongyang. By the 2010s, the gap in living standards between the two Koreas was the greatest of any two bordering countries in the world. *Photo: NASA.*

SEOUL A view of the Seoul skyline from Bongeunsa Temple in the Gangnam district. As a result of urban sprawl, this Buddhist temple, once located in the countryside, now finds itself in the midst of one of the country's most modern and fashionable areas. Today about one third of all South Koreans identify as Buddhist and about one third as Christian. *Photo: Megapixl © Sepavo.*

SEOUL NIGHTLIFE A typical night street scene in the Myong-dong shopping and entertainment district of Seoul. By the 2010s, South Korea had achieved Western living standards and had become a brand-conscious consumer society. The young people in this street did not experience the grim poverty their parents and grandparents endured. *Photo: Megapixl © Asiantraveler.*

GANGNAM STYLE Korean rapper Psy performs "Gangnam Style," part of the "Korean Wave" of entertainment. South Korea emerged as a center of popular culture in the early 2000s with its TV dramas and movies. By the late 2010s, Korean entertainment, especially K-Pop, had a global audience. *Photo: Wikimedia Commons © Korean Culture and Information Service.*

TRADITIONAL WEDDING A couple in traditional Korean wedding dress. In South Korean weddings, it is common for the bride and groom to perform the wedding ceremony in Western clothes and then change to traditional Korean dress for a photo opportunity. This is just one way contemporary South Korea combines the new with the traditional. *Photo: Megapixl © Tofudevil.*

APRIL 2018 INTER-KOREAN SUMMIT In 2018, South Korean president Moon Jae-in and North Korean leader Kim Jong Un attended three unprecedented summit meetings, which raised hopes for an easing of tensions between the two Koreas. All previous efforts at improved relations had ended in failure. *Photo: WIkimedia Commons © Cheongwadae / Blue House.*

SECOND US–NORTH KOREA SUMMIT President Trump is greeted by Kim Jong Un at their second summit meeting held in Hanoi, Vietnam, on February 27, 2019. North Korea insisted that the US end its support of economic sanctions against the DPRK, while the US insisted that North Korea had to first give up its nuclear weapons. As a result of this standoff, the summit was unsuccessful. *Photo: The White House.*

go to the Liberal Party. In this way he became Korea's richest man. And he was only one of a number of business leaders to operate in this cycle of buying cheap dollars and recycling some of the profits to the ruling party. Thus the small business sector was not only unproductive, but it was tarnished by its ties to a corrupt and increasingly discredited regime.

One way out of poverty would have been to reestablish ties with Japan. This made perfect sense to the Americans, who wanted Seoul to establish diplomatic relations with Tokyo; then it could sell rice, seaweed, and seafood to the Japanese in return for manufactured goods, rather than relying on aid money for almost all its foreign exchange. But Rhee, who was almost pathologically anti-Japanese, would have none of it. He refused to even normalize diplomatic relations with Tokyo. Instead, from time to time he seized Japanese fishing boats just to stir up tension, claiming the former colonial rulers were still violating the country's sovereignty. This frustrated the Americans—yet Rhee was not just being a difficult old man; he and many Koreans were dead set against reverting back to the colonial times when Korea functioned as a source of cheap food for an industrial, dominant Japan.

On paper, the country was democratic, with free elections and opposition parties, but Rhee and his Liberal Party made full use of the government apparatus to intimidate voters and manipulate the election procedures. Rural voters were sometimes simply brought to the polls by local officials and told who to vote for. Still, the Party was only able to maintain a bare majority in the 1954 National Assembly elections. The new Assembly then voted to change the constitution so Rhee could run for a third term in 1956—which, of course, he did. He was challenged by the Democratic Party, which had been created in 1955 by a merger of smaller opposition parties. This new party, dominated by conservatives, offered not a radical alternative vision but simply a cleaner, more competent government. The Democratic Party nominated Shin Ikhui, another aging political veteran, to run against Rhee; however, Shin, who had serious health problems, died weeks before the elections. The only other choice for voters was a more left-leaning third-party candidate, Cho Bongam, a socialist who had been the principal architect of the country's recent land reform. Rhee won easily, but about a third of the voters—mostly in urban areas—voted for Cho. After the election, Rhee had Cho arrested on charges of treason and executed. Even so, the trends did not look good for Rhee: the urban and middle classes, fed up with his corruption and incompetence, were turning against him, and these were the groups that were growing as education and urbanization expanded.

In 1960, Rhee ran again despite being eighty-five years old. The Democratic Party, which seemed to have learned nothing from its earlier experience, nominated another older conservative with health problems, Cho Byeongok, who also died just before the election. There was no foul play involved with either Shin's or Cho Beongok's death, just extraordinarily poor choices and bad luck for the party. The focus of the election then turned to the competitive race for vice president, a race that took on great significance because few expected the aging president, who now had no opposition, to live out his four-year term. The Democratic candidate was a mild-mannered Catholic, Chang Myon, who faced Liberal Party candidate Yi Kibung. Yi had been adopted by the childless Rhee and his wife as their son, but was widely unpopular. This time the government took no chances, and blatantly manipulated the election results so that the extremely unpopular Yi won by an enormous landslide. No one believed his election had been legitimate.

This proved too much for the public. Anti-government demonstrations broke out, first in the southern port city of Masan and then throughout the country. When, on April 19, 1960, tens of thousands of students paraded in the streets of Seoul toward the presidential mansion, the police fired on them, killing many. When the demonstrations continued over the following days, the military commander in Seoul refused to use force to stop them, and Rhee was finished. He resigned under US pressure, and the Americans spirited him away to exile in his former home of Hawaii. Yi Kibung and his wife committed suicide.

The overthrow of Rhee was followed by an experiment in democracy, which, unfortunately, did not go well. From 1960 to 1961,

South Korea tried a parliamentary system with the ruling Democratic Party prime minister Chang Myon. Chang and many members of his cabinet were sincere believers in a Western-style democracy and made plans for a comprehensive program of economic development. Had there been time, perhaps they would have succeeded in guiding the country out of poverty. During their brief administration, however, all the pent-up frustrations of ordinary citizens came to the fore. Workers organized real unions, not the government-controlled official ones; students organized almost daily demonstrations; schoolteachers went on strike. Seoul was often paralyzed by strikes and protests. Then there was North Korea, which, seeing an opportunity, sent feelers out to the protesters calling for a peaceful reunification. When a group of students decided to meet their Northern counterparts at Panmunjom on the DMZ, it alarmed conservative anti-communist elements. The military, disgusted with civilian incompetence and concerned about national security, carried out a coup under General Park Chung Hee.

Looking back, it is easy to dismiss this sad decade. But several positive developments did take place that laid the foundations for South Korea's "economic miracle." One major change was land reform. On the eve of the Korean War, the Rhee regime had finally capitulated to peasant demands, US pressure, and the fear of a communist revolution and carried out a land reform. The process, which was completed over the next several years, limited landholding to just 7.5 acres (3 hectares). Unlike in the North, landowners were compensated by farmers, who had to make payments over a number of years, but high inflation quickly reduced these to nominal amounts. This land reform also differed from the North's in that the land was not taken away by the state; rather, it turned the country's farmers into small agricultural entrepreneurs.

Many former landlords took their modest compensation and invested it in educational institutions; in this way, land reform contributed to perhaps the most fundamental change the country experienced at this time—the expansion of education. From the late 1940s to 1961, primary-school attendance tripled to become nearly universal for all boys and girls; enrollment in secondary schools increased by a factor of eight and in higher education by a factor of ten. Adult literacy campaigns taught millions how to read and write, while teacher-training programs enabled the schools to maintain a fairly high level of instruction, even during rapid expansion. As a result, Korea in 1961 may have been extremely poor, but it had the best-educated population of any very poor country. At the same time, a steady stream of South Koreans was entering the US for advanced training, returning with prestigious degrees and creating a core of competent technocrats. By the end of these 1950s, these technocrats were already meeting and drawing up long-range development plans, although they had not yet been implemented when the military took over.

Given the fundamental changes that were underway, would the civilians who were trying to create a democratic system in 1961 have succeeded in bringing about the economic miracle? Could South Koreans have been spared the brutality and oppression of the military dictatorship that frog-marched the country into an industrialized society and still have become prosperous? Of course, we will never know.

Park Chung Hee's Forced March to Economic Development

Park Chung Hee, the new leader of the ROK, was the youngest of seven children from a poor peasant family in Gyeongsang, a region of southeast Korea that was the homeland of the ancient Silla state. A bright pupil, he won a competitive scholarship to a teacher-training institution and became a schoolteacher. Although he only taught for three years, there remained something of the stern schoolmaster about him. Park graduated from the Manchukuo Military Academy in 1944 and was commissioned as a second lieutenant in the Japanese Imperial Army. After the war he served in the ROK army, but was implicated in the Yeosu rebellion; he barely escaped execution and was dismissed. His brother was involved in leftist politics, but it is not clear whether Park flirted with communism. When the Korean War broke out, he was reinstated and served with distinction. Park was a small, slender man, not very physically imposing or charismatic; however, he had a reputation for being intelligent, well-disciplined, and uncorrupt, and he was well respected by younger officers. He would dominate the country for the next eighteen years.

For Park, especially, economic development was the most urgent task. There were several reasons for this. One was the humiliation of being so dependent on the US, which supplied over half the government's revenue. As Park stated it, the US had a "52 percent share" in the state, which meant that the ROK could hardly call itself an independent country. At the same time, much of the desire to find a path to economic development was driven by the rivalry with North Korea. With Pyongyang's industrialization roaring ahead, the task seemed urgent. Not only was it a military threat, but the stagnation of the South as the North surged ahead in the march to progress only undermined Seoul's claim to be the "true" representative of the Korean nation. Furthermore, South Korea wanted to emulate Japan.

Then there was the poverty that pervaded the nation. Park, who had spent a year in the US for military training, was only too aware of the sad plight of his country, which was among the poorest in the world—its per capita income was about the same as Haiti's. The streets of Seoul were filled with beggars and children selling gum; much of the countryside was at the subsistence level, with homes lacking electricity or running water, connected to cities and towns by rough, unpaved roads winding through the mountains. There were few jobs even for the growing number of secondary-school and university graduates. The task of pulling the country out of poverty seemed so daunting that even foreign-aid advisors tended to be rather pessimistic about the country's prospects. Yet Park was determined to make it happen.

Park and most of the other military leaders were clear about where they wanted to go, but unsure how to get there. Their advantage was that they were pragmatic, flexible, and willing to take advice. After an initial period of mixed and confusing policies, the junta followed a development path that copied Japan's state-led model, but with the South Korean state playing an even bigger role in supervising the economy. Its first big economic move was to nationalize the banks and cancel all rural debt. With control of the nation's lending, it could direct money toward the investments it saw as productive. The junta then drew up a five-year economic development plan for 1962 to 1966 that directed state efforts toward specific economic targets.

At first, leading members of the business community were charged with corruption and arrested or fined. Early on, however, the junta realized that they needed the entrepreneurial skills of the country's business community. Charges against the top two dozen businessmen were dropped after they pledged to donate all of their property to the state if it was needed for national reconstruction. Lee Byung Chull, who was hiding in Japan—the very symbol of all that the military men had despised about the old regime—was allowed to return. The junta created the Promotional Committee for Economic Reconstruction with Lee as the chair, and a new partnership between the business community and the state was forged; this one proved highly productive.

The five-year plan was a huge success. Its target was 7.1 percent economic growth based on light industry, which some foreign advisors had considered a bit too optimistic. In fact, however, growth over the next five years averaged almost 9 percent; exports grew by 29 percent a year and manufacturing by 15 percent a year. South Korea had only one resource—cheap labor—and this was utilized for low-cost, labor-intensive industries: textiles, footwear, wigs. South Korea opened itself to foreign investment, which supplied the capital and technology it needed to industrialize. Incentives were offered to encourage foreign investment: investors could benefit from low taxes, the ease of getting the profits out of the country, and a government willing to provide the infrastructure and other assistance they needed. Korean workers were cheap and willing to work long hours, and if they caused trouble, the government would crack down on them. South Korea was careful to include technology transfer agreements linking local firms with foreign ones. In this way, Kia and Hyundai made car parts for Detroit while simultaneously learning how to make the cars that would compete with it. The state also stepped up technical education and training, creating the Korean Institute for Science and Technology in 1966 and staffing it with PhDs in science and engineering from some of the best schools in the world.

Looking for foreign investors, Park turned to Japan. In the 1960s and 1970s, the Japanese needed places to invest their vast profits, as well as somewhere to offshore their manufacturing as labor costs rose. There was South Korea, right next door, sharing the same time zone, with a business community that in most cases could speak their language. South Korea needed capital and technical know-how, so it was a natural match. There was a problem, however: lingering hatred prevented Seoul from opening up diplomatic relations, and any attempt to do so would raise accusations of treason. Park himself was compromised by his past service in the Imperial Army, and there were genuine fears that little South Korea could find itself becoming a de facto economic dependent of Japan. Nonetheless, Park ignored the massive demonstrations against normalizing relations and signed the Peace Treaty in 1965. Tokyo offered a modest $800 million in reparations, but the treaty resulted in a flood of Japanese investments.

In the 1970s, the Park regime focused more attention on rural development and on shifting from light to heavy industry. The transformation of the countryside came swiftly and rather heavy-handedly. In 1971 Park launched the New Village Movement, which mobilized the rural population in an effort at forced modernization. Farmers were ordered to remove their picturesque—but to Park's mind, backward—thatched roofs for tile ones; poor families had to settle for corrugated metal roofs. Family-planning programs were vigorously carried out to bring down the birth rate. Industrial development refocused from textiles to heavy and chemical industries. Despite the skepticism of many American advisors, the shift to heavy industry was mostly successful. By the 1980s, South Korea was becoming one of the world's largest exporters of steel and its second-largest shipbuilder. The symbol of its success was the enormous Pohang Iron and Steel complex, the largest and most modern of its kind—and also a rarity, being a profitable state-owned and -managed enterprise, although it was eventually privatized.

From Lucky Strike to LG: The Rise of South Korea's *Chaebol*

A signature feature of South Korea's economic development was that it centered around large *chaebol*. Derived from the Japanese term *zaibatsu*, the *chaebol* were family-owned conglomerates; some became enormous in size. Since the state owned the banks, it could lend money on generous terms to companies that it favored; it also gave them all kinds of special preferential treatment, such as exemptions from import duties on capital goods and special rates on utilities and railroads—both of which the state also owned. Furthermore, the state-owned banks would lend capital at favorable rates. An important element of this relationship—and the reason it worked—was that favored businesses had to prove themselves through performance. State aid went to the most efficient ones. The *chaebol*, it is worth pointing out, were not the products of the state; they were the creations of dynamic, talented entrepreneurs, many of whom predated the Park era. It was the Park regime's support that allowed them to flourish, and some grew to be among the world's largest privately owned companies.

Who were these talented entrepreneurs? One of the oldest was Koo In-hwoi, who in 1947 founded the Lucky Chemical Company, which became the country's largest toothpaste manufacturer. The name Lucky was popularized by American Lucky Strike cigarettes, a hot black-market item in Korea—one of the many products from the US military's PX supply stores that somehow found their way to street vendors. Park's government, attracted to Koo's business acumen, lent him money for an export item—electric fans made under the label Goldstar (Geumseong in Korean). Koo now called his company Lucky-Goldstar. Koo passed away in 1969 just as Goldstar was taking off. His family continued to expand the company, which was renamed LG in 1995 and became one of the world's largest manufacturers of consumer electronics.

Another early entrepreneur, Kim Sung Kon, founded the Ssangyong (Twin Dragons) textile company in 1939. In the 1950s, he got involved in an import-license agreement with the Rhee government to import cement. Despite his connections with the Rhee regime, he turned out to be a resourceful, go-getting entrepreneur. With government support, he branched out into construction, trading, and automobile production. Ssangyong became one of the largest of the *chaebol*.

Few *chaebol* founders could match Chung Ju Yung for energy, ambition, and entrepreneurial skill. A man from a humble rural background in Kwangwon province in what later became North Korea, Chung had gotten his start back in the colonial time. Having little taste for farming, he stole a cow, sold it, and went to Seoul, where he started an auto-repair business. During the Korean War he did contract work for the US and ROK armies. When the Park regime gave him a contract to build a bridge over the Han River, Chung completed it ahead of schedule in 1965; the government, duly impressed, gave him all kinds of additional construction contracts. Chung developed a reputation for completing projects with lightning speed, and built many facilities in Vietnam for the American and Korean forces. In the 1970s he won many lucrative contracts in newly rich oil-exporting countries which were anxious to convert their new oil wealth into visible infrastructure as quickly as possible. Chung famously got into shipbuilding by signing a contract with a shipping company to build vessels. He then started a dockyard from scratch and built the ships on time. When the government decided to develop an auto industry, Chung's Hyundai (the Korean word for "modern") Car Company was born.

Then there was Lee Byung Chull, the notorious crony capitalist who flourished under the Rhee regime. He differed from Chung in that he came from a wealthy *yangban* background, but was more attracted to industry than landowning. Lee started the Samsung (Three Stars) company in the 1960s. Starting in the late 1960s, he focused on electronics, for which his company became internationally known, but he got into other things as well, from appliances to automobiles.

Although the *chaebol* had modern-looking corporate structures, and eventually developed state-of-the-art research labs and training centers, they remained family businesses. The top managerial positions were almost always held by family members. Chung Ju Yung's vast Hyundai group was run by his eight sons (the "eight princes," as they were known). Stocks might be publicly traded, but the family always kept a controlling share. Samsung, for example, became the world's largest family-owned enterprise in the twenty-first century. The next managerial tier was run by high-school and college classmates of the founder and his sons, followed by those from the same hometown. Thus there was something very traditionally Korean about these modern enterprises.

Moon Villages and Flyers: The Social Cost of Industrialization

While Park and the *chaebol* heads are often praised for their part in South Korea's economic development, it was done at great cost. Workers went home to slums known as "moon villages," which sprang up on the hillsides of cities. Working conditions were often horrible: Korean workers put in longer hours than those in any other industrial country, averaging nearly fifty-five hours a week in the 1980s—and many worked far longer. This was more than the notoriously workaholic Japanese worker; twelve-hour days were common, and the six-day work week was the norm, with many men and women receiving only every other Sunday off. Scant regard was given to safety, and South Korean industries had among the world's worst safety records. Tired workers at shipyards became "flyers" as they fell to their deaths from the high scaffolding; construction workers being driven to complete projects ahead of schedule suffered terribly frequent accidents. In the 1970s, a Korean was fifteen times more likely to be injured at work than his Japanese counterpart. Especially appalling were the conditions under which women, who made up about a third of labor force—especially in the garment industry—lived. Female factory workers, mostly country girls earning money to send home to their families, worked in dingy, noisy sweatshops. They were housed in "beehives," grim company buildings so nicknamed for their warrens of tiny rooms. Often they were locked in at night. Many had short hair, since they cut it periodically to sell for wigs.

Korean industrialists used Confucian terminology of paternalism, loyalty, and harmony to create a sense of the company as a big family. Management was the benevolent parent figure looking out for the workers, who repaid this generosity with loyalty and hard work. The workers didn't buy it, though: labor unrest was common, as were attempts to form independent labor unions. In theory, workers were represented by Korean Federation of Trade Unions, a government-controlled institution created to keep control of labor, but they despised it. Harmony was maintained with the help of riot police, who were called in not infrequently to break strikes and demonstrations. Companies hired their own gangs of thugs to beat up and intimidate troublesome employees. Initially, workers had the legal right to collective bargaining and collective action, even if in practice it was met with brutal retaliation, but in 1971, the state suspended this right, making any kind of labor protest cause for police intervention. Employers also hired their own corps of enforcers to beat up labor organizers.

Government and company measures were effective enough to give the illusion to foreign investors that Koreans were hardworking (which they were) and happy to toil endlessly for modest wages (which they were not). The long hours and docile nature of the labor force were selling points that were promoted by the state, employers, and foreign investors.

All this was too much for young labor activist Jeon Dae-il, a worker in the Pyeonghwa Market, a hideous block-long, four-story complex of small garment factories and clothing shops employing 20,000 workers. He witnessed workers suffering from tuberculosis and respiratory ailments from laboring in cramped workshops lacking proper ventilation. Workers were given amphetamines to keep them awake during the long hours they put in. He sent complaints to government officials about the worst abuses he saw, only to be told he was being "unpatriotic." Frustrated, one day he set himself on fire and went running through the streets of downtown Seoul, shouting, "We are not machines! Enforce the labor code," before dying. Jeon's actions were not anomalous; violent labor protests broke out occasionally. Women took part in or even initiated some of these, such as the protest at the Dongil Textile Company in 1972, and another at the Y.H. Trading Company in Busan in 1979. But under Park, state repression and corporate thuggery largely succeeded in containing labor unrest.

Near Dictatorship: The Authoritarian System of Park Chung Hee
Park Chung Hee was right about South Korea not being fully independent; it still relied on US aid and protection, and so Park was forced to comply with American pressure to restore the government to civilian rule. He did this by taking off his military uniform, donning a suit and tie, and running for president in 1963 as the head of his own Democratic Republican Party. The election was at least partially fair, and he legitimately won, while his party captured control of the National Assembly. It was not a landslide, and there was real opposition, but not enough to keep him and his party from power. He was reelected in 1967, and in 1969, the National Assembly used rather dubious methods to amend the constitution so he could run for a third term.

By 1971, Park was pretty confident that his system was doing well and that he had the grateful support of his people. Evidence of growing prosperity was everywhere; even the ordinary people were seeing their living standards improve, and the future looked bright. But in spite of the decade of spectacular economic expansion, there was more opposition to him than he seemed to have realized. When he ran for a third term, his main opponent was a young lawyer from Jeolla province in the southwest named Kim Dae Jung. Kim, who like Park was a self-made man from humble origins, proved a good campaigner and did surprisingly well, even though all the power and patronage of the state was against him. He was outspoken in his criticism of the authoritarian nature of the regime and the exploitation of labor. Although Park won 51 percent to 44 percent, the closeness of the election shocked him. Not only had he failed to win in a landslide as he expected, but he had not carried the cities—a bad sign for a rapidly urbanizing society. In fact, he may not have won the popular vote at all, since there was a lot of voter manipulation in the rural areas. Park did well among farmers, the elderly, and anticommunist conservatives, but fared badly among the young, the educated, and the rising middle class—all the demographic groups that were likely to dominate the future.

In addition to weakening domestic support, there other signs of trouble. The US was placing protectionist pressure against South

Korean textiles, the country's biggest export. More worrisome, in the early 1970s the United States was disengaging from its commitment to defend South Vietnam, and there was concern that a withdrawal from South Korea would be next. Furthermore, in 1972 Nixon visited North Korea's ally, China. Then there was uncertainty over where the talks with North Korea that took place in 1972 were leading. Worried about internal opposition and labor unrest, feeling internationally insecure, and wanting to strengthen his hand in negotiating with Pyongyang, Park decided to give up the game of playing at a semi-democracy and go for more absolute power.

On October 17, 1972, he proclaimed martial law; he dissolved the National Assembly, banned all political parties, placed restrictions on free speech, and expanded the authority of police to arrest subversive elements. He had a new constitution written, known as the Yushin ("revitalization") Constitution. This allowed for a rather toothless National Assembly and gave the president near-dictatorial powers. Unwilling to risk another direct election, he was to be elected by the National Unification Board, a body that he appointed—which meant that Park essentially elected himself. Not surprisingly, he won.

Not content with his new constitution, Park issued a series of emergency decrees that further strengthened his authority. The most notorious was Emergency Measure No. 9, in 1975, which made any criticism of the president a crime. A wave of political repression placed many politicians, writers, artists, intellectuals, and journalists in jail. Dissidents living abroad were kidnapped by the Korean Central Intelligence Agency (KCIA) and brought back home to be imprisoned. The KCIA itself was a vast secret-police organization which had nearly a million informants. A notorious incident involving the KCIA was its abduction of Kim Dae Jung. Park sought revenge against his former political opponent, who had fled to the US and secured a position at Harvard. While Kim was visiting Tokyo, Park had his agents abduct him from his hotel room. They placed him in a boat on the open sea, tied and blindfolded him, and prepared to dump him into the ocean. His aides, suspecting Park was behind Kim's sudden disappearance, alerted Washington. Realizing that he had to act quickly, a resourceful American diplomat contacted the office of President Park and pretended to be speaking on behalf of the US president as he demanded Kim's release. The bluff worked, and Park had Kim Dae Jung, still blindfolded, dumped on the street in front of his house in Korea. He then was allowed to return to the US. While Kim's high profile helped save him, other dissidents were less fortunate.

Many Revolutions: South Korea's Society in Rapid Change

Under the years of military rule, South Korea became more urban, more literate, and more Christian. Cities swelled in size. In 1950, South Korea was an overwhelmingly rural society, but by the 1980s it had become a mostly urban one. The population of most rural areas began shrinking after 1960 as people left for the cities. All the older cities grew and new ones emerged, such as the industrial cities of Masan and Gumi. Nothing, however, approached the size of Seoul, which grew into a megacity. From less than a million it was approaching eight million by the late 1980s, or about the size of New York or London. It was the country's leading industrial center, its cultural and entertainment center, and its educational center—all the top universities were located there—while also being, of course, the seat of government. So central was Seoul to the country that all trains either were labeled as going "up" (toward it) or "down" (away from it).

The speed of South Korea's urbanization was matched by the growth in literacy rates. Every child went to school, and almost all graduated. This is particularly surprising because education wasn't cheap. Rather than pour scarce resources into schools, the state shifted much of the cost onto parents, who had to pay all sorts of fees even for so-called "free" public primary schools. And no matter how poor they were, almost all of them managed to come up with the money. Classes were enormous, with 100 students in a single classroom; teachers sometimes taught two classes—one in the morning and another in the afternoon. After 1960, when primary education became universal, educational development focused on secondary schooling. Fewer than one in three young people matriculated into both middle and high school in the early 1960s, but by the late 1980s over 90 percent did so. By that time, enrollment rates in schools at all levels were already approaching those of advanced nations like Japan, Western Europe, and the US. Extensive in-service training kept teaching competence high, and teacher-training programs were continuously improved.

If one went out at night in Seoul or any other city in South Korea in the 1980s, another major change in the country would become apparent in the lighted crosses, which were ubiquitous. South Korea was not only becoming more urban and literate; it was becoming more Christian—the growth of that religion after 1950 was phenomenal. Christianity had a long history in the country, but despite the early growth of Catholicism and the prominent role Protestant missionaries had played in Korea in the late nineteenth and early twentieth centuries by building churches, schools, and hospitals, in 1945 only a small percentage of Koreans were Christian, and the majority of those were in the North, not the South. But then the religion took off. With their world shaken by the upheaval of the Korean War and the rapid industrialization and urbanization of society, Koreans were looking for something to provide them certainty, meaning, and solace. Many found it in church. Furthermore, Christianity was associated with modernization and progress. By the late 1980s, nearly a third of South Koreans were Christian—many of them very fervent—making it the second most Christian nation in Asia after the Philippines, although Christians never outnumbered Buddhists.

How did the South Korean Economy Grow so Fast?

Both Koreas experienced spectacular economic growth, but the patterns were very different. In the North, the economic boom happened a decade earlier, in the 1950s, and then slowed to a halt after twenty years. The South started in the 1960s and saw three decades of very rapid growth; though it slowed down in the early 1990s, the economy continued to expand and incomes continued to rise steadily for another generation. By the early twenty-first century, the country had become one of the first third-world countries to achieve first-world status.

How did South Korea achieve this?

Both Koreans and some foreigners attributed South Korea's economic success to its Confucian heritage. In the 1980s, the term "Confucian ethos" was bandied about as a key to understanding the rapid economic and social modernization of South Korea, as well as the rest of the "four little tigers": Taiwan, Hong Kong, and Singapore. This term suggests that the success of the "four little tigers" had deep cultural-historical roots. Confucianism taught respect for education, hard work, willingness to delay gratification (thus encouraging a high savings rate), and government by merit. The last meant that states managed to attract talented civil servants, helping to make government both respected and effective in carrying out policies.

None of this was necessarily wrong, but it did not explain why South Korea made so little progress before 1961, or why North Korea, with the same heritage, had such a different trajectory. In fact, many Koreans, in both North and South, cited their Confucian heritage—its veneration of tradition over innovation, its rigid ideas of hierarchy, its patriarchy, its contempt for technical and military skills, and its resistance to change—as an obstacle to progress. This view was shared by most Westerners before the 1960s. Given this state of affairs, it's not hard to understand why historians are wary of cultural explanations: not only are they poor predictors of future trends, but they tend to simplify and stereotype too much, and reinforce prejudices. Yet one cultural factor that worked to Korea's advantage was its respect for learning and the fact that it equated education with social status. This contributed to the drive for schooling that created a literate, numerate, and disciplined workforce. The school system might have been an unenviable pressure cooker, but it produced, at minimum, workers who could read instructions; and at best, workers who were competitive, quick to learn, and unafraid of challenges.

Much of the credit for South Korea's "economic miracle" goes less to culture than policy. The government hit upon a successful formula: export-led growth that combined both state planning and promotion of industrial development with private ownership and the profit motive. Much like North Korea, the state could mobilize credit and resources for development, only these were implemented through the private market. Furthermore, the ROK state in directing development was pragmatic and flexible, rather than being tied to a rigid set of ideas as the DPRK was. This flexibility—along with the focus on consumer products and the openness to foreign ideas, technologies, and investors—was a great advantage the North did not have. And while the North modeled itself in part on the historical dead-ends of Stalinism and Maoism, the South looked to the more dynamic US, Western Europe, and especially Japan for inspiration. Furthermore, there was one other factor it inherited from the miserable years of Japanese rule: a powerful authoritarian state that could impose policies overriding special interests.

Another explanation is that South Korea had the help of the United States. American aid does not seem to have done much to promote growth, but American universities trained thousands of bright young people in administration, economics, education, science, and technology. The US military presence acted as a guarantor of stability to reassure foreign investors, so that South Korea, while devoting considerable resources to the military, did not have to do so to the same degree as the North did. America's largely open market was also a great advantage, as it absorbed the bulk of the country's exports in its early years. Having Japan next door helped, too; it provided foreign investment, technical transfers, and—perhaps most important of all—a model of how a culturally related people could build a prosperous, modern society.

Park Chung Hee's Last, Bad Years

Park Chung Hee's authoritarian tendencies were on full display in the 1970s, and he seemed to be making the country into an outright one-man-rule police state. But his reliance on the United States was an obstacle. For all his talk of autonomy, he still depended on the US—not so much for aid anymore, but for its commitment to defending the country. Park could never completely suppress all his opponents if he wanted to keep dealing with the US. For the most part, American officials disliked Park; they found him difficult to work with and were often sympathetic to the opposition elements, so they were not averse to pressuring Park to restrain himself from cracking down on them. Park only alienated the US further when he sent KCIA agents to kidnap and harass Korean-Americans. Then there was the Koreagate scandal in 1975, in which Tongsun Park, a Korean businessman acting on behalf of the South Korean government, was involved in bribing US congressmen. All this led to greater sympathy for the opposition.

An even greater obstacle to Park's complete consolidation of power was the resistance from the South Korean public, which never accepted his dictatorial ambitions. Throughout the 1970s there were constant protests and demonstrations by political opposition groups, Christian organizations, labor activists, students, and intellectuals. These people endured dismissal from jobs, expulsion from school, beatings by government thugs, arrest, and torture, and yet still kept resisting his rule. In the late 1970s, unrest appeared to be growing despite the country's economic boom, and in the summer of 1979, brutal treatment of group of women workers at a textile plant set off a new round of protests aimed at the Park regime. At this time an emerging political leader in the largely powerless National Assembly, Kim Young Sam, called the president a dictator and was ousted from parliament. Opposition members of the Assembly walked out, which intensified the protests—they were centered in the area around Busan, Kim's home base. As the situation became more chaotic, Park's security chief, KCIA director Kim Jaegyu, suggested a compromise with the opposition. Park, who was increasingly isolated and stubborn, instead indicated he was going to use the military to suppress the protesters. Kim Jaegyu met with Park for dinner at a KCIA compound near the Blue House. Park was accompanied by a young college coed, a habit had he acquired since the assassination of his wife. At the dinner table, Kim shot Park and his bodyguard, killing both instantly and bringing an era to an end.

As a side note, Kim Jaegyu did not appear to have any real plan other than to kill Park. He seemed to expect to be treated as a national savior for terminating the rule of a man who, for all his gifts and achievements, had acquired too much power and hung on for too long. Instead, he was arrested and executed.

Park had so dominated South Korea that his death created a crisis—but it was also an opportunity for a more open society. From late 1979 through May of 1980, South Korea went through a brief "Seoul Spring" while a caretaker government led by President Choi Kyu Hah, a professional bureaucrat who had served as Park's vice president, presided over the country. Politicians, journals, intellectuals, and students lobbied for a new, more democratic constitution and debated over its contents. Kim Dae Jung and Kim Young Sam emerged as the two major leaders at this time. But even as the public enjoyed its new freedom of expression, the military still held real power.

In Korea, classmate bonds are strong and last a lifetime. The eighth graduating class of the Korean Military Academy had formed a clique that had put Park in power; the eleventh class put his successor, two-star general Chun Doo Hwan, into power. On the night of December 12, Chun and his classmates seized control of the army. Unlike Park's coup, it was not bloodless; there was an exchange of fire as the plotters attempted to arrest much of the high command. Some fled to the nearby US military compound. After gaining control of the army, the new military group took control of the government step by step. In mid-May, Chun seized full command of the government, banning all demonstrations, labor strikes, and political activity. A number of leading opposition politicians were arrested, including Kim Dae Jung. Chun was now the new military leader of South Korea.

Kim Dae Jung's home area of Jeolla in the southwest had been a stronghold of the opposition to Park. Once part of ancient Baekje, this region was neglected by Park in favor of his home region, which became the industrial heartland of the country. Jeolla, once a prosperous agricultural area, was now the poorest part of the country with the least developed infrastructure and the fewest modern industries. The announcement of the arrest of the local hero resulted in a spontaneous uprising in the main urban center of South Jeolla province, Gwangju. Students, joined by ordinary citizens, seized control of some armories and took over the city. For nearly ten days, Gwangju was the center of the opposition—until Chun sent paratroopers into the city and slaughtered the poorly armed protesters. Officially 200 were killed, but the real figure was much higher.

The shocking Gwangju Incident was not forgotten, and from the beginning of his government, Chun Doo Hwan was deeply resented—even hated—by many South Koreans. Nonetheless, he went on to write a new constitution, and after disqualifying almost everyone else, he ran for president. Underground satirists reported that he was considering entering his dog in the race so he would have an opponent, but was afraid he might lose. Choosing not to take such a chance, he ran uncontested and was elected president for a seven-year term. Chun might have not been popular, but he had the apparent blessing of the US, partly because of its willingness to tolerate another brutal military strongman as long as he was anti-communist. Thus the rise of Chun led to the rise of anti-Americanism in South Korea. But the Americans found him as charmless and unappealing as most of his fellow citizens did, and kept a frosty distance while quietly supporting the democratic opposition.

The Fifth Republic: The Last Dictator
Chun Doo Hwan's period in power, from 1980 to 1988, was in many respects a continuation of the Park Chung Hee era. While it was a different military clique, it held the same policies, and the same technocrats were drawing up and implementing plans. There were some similarities between the two leaders: Chun, like Park, came from a poor rural background and had chosen a military career as a way out of poverty. Once in power, he focused on economic development, listening to his experts as he did so. Yet there were differences. Park was not a lovable character, but he was respected by many; Chun, by contrast, was viewed with contempt by the majority of the public. The bloody way he seized power, the stain of the Gwangju Incident, the personal corruption associated with his wife and his in-laws, and his complete lack of personal charisma contributed to this. He was mockingly dismissed as an octopus-headed thug in private ("octopus-headed" was a reference to his baldness); he was the butt of jokes—also told in private, of course—making him appear ignorant and stupid. Most of all, his administration was resented by many citizens who were tired of military rule and the restrictions on their personal freedom, and who had felt robbed of the

chance to select a new leader on their own in 1980.

Chun attempted to overcome this resentment with token gestures of liberalization. The nightly curfew and the ritual of standing at attention at 5 pm ended; schoolkids no longer had to wear military uniforms; and censorship eased up a bit. By the mid-1980s, most banned politicians were allowed to return to public life, and semi-free Assembly elections were permitted. Chun's administration scored many successes; it won the bid for the Olympics, and the economy hummed along quite nicely after 1981. Yet his administration was not popular, and political unrest gradually grew.

Then South Korea underwent another transformation—one that took place with the same unexpected swiftness of its economic transformation: it became a democracy.

CHAPTER 9

PROSPEROUS SOUTH KOREA: DEMOCRATIZATION AND FIRST-WORLD STATUS

South Korea Wins a Gold Medal: The Great Coming-Out Party

W hen Kang Song Hee was a young girl in the 1950s, she would leave her home early to line up and collect food aid for her family; her older siblings were busy trying to earn money by doing odd jobs. Sometimes on cold winter days she had to stay inside because her clothes were not warm enough. Two decades later, by the 1970s, the country she lived in was undergoing impressive economic growth, and there was no need to line up for food aid. But daily existence for her and most others was still hard. South Koreans had among the world's longest working hours; companies employed armed thugs to intimidate disgruntled employees; the state harassed and arrested its political opponents. Young factory girls were virtual prisoners, kept locked in their company dorms at night. Air-raid drills and nightly curfews reminded citizens that their country was still at war with their northern neighbor, a conflict that was used by the government to label all forms of dissent treason. There were improvements: the standard of living was rising, the educational system had expanded, and people were healthier, better fed, and better housed than in the recent past, but many South Koreans still sought to improve their lives by emigrating abroad.

Then things changed in the 1980s, as working conditions improved and wages rose sharply, the authoritarian regime broke down, and the country became freer and more democratic. The successful hosting of the Olympics in 1988 and the lifting of travel restrictions in the same year brought the world to South Korea and South Koreans to the world. By the end of the century, the country had officially graduated to "developed" status; the large majority of the population identified as middle class, and their concerns had shifted from economic growth to quality-of-life improvements. Living in a prosperous, open society, Song Hee's grandchildren could hardly imagine the hardships their grandmother had experienced as a young girl.

Most South Koreans were genuinely excited about hosting the Olympics. This was understandable; it was a great coming-out party, a chance to demonstrate to the world that their country had climbed out of poverty and was emerging from the shadow of the US. The Chun Doo Hwan regime used it to promote infrastructure projects such as its construction of the Seoul subway system, which became the largest in the world. Mass campaigns, such as those promoting clean toilets and lobbying for the removal of dog- and snake-meat restaurants from the main streets, were all part of creating a new, internationally respectable image. But rather than garnishing support for the regime, the Olympics became a point of pressure, as opposition groups demanded democratic reform. There was a rise in violent anti-government student demonstrations, which grew so frequent that the smell of tear gas became just part of city living. Labor unions—not the official ones that were tools of the state, but the illegal ones organized by the workers themselves—carried out more frequent strikes. Some of these turned violent as increasingly militant industrial employees resisted the police. Politicians and journalists became bolder in criticizing the regime.

Rising tensions came to a head on April 13, 1987. Chun Doo Hwan had promised, after electing himself president, that he would serve only one seven-year term. This became important, because most South Koreans could console themselves that they wouldn't have to suffer him any longer than that. Most people assumed that at the end of his term there would be open elections. However, Chun had different plans: he decided that his former military academy classmate and coup plotter, Roh Tae Woo, would be his successor. On that April day, his administration announced that there would be no popular election; instead, the National Council for Unification, a body of Chun appointees, would select the next president. Everyone knew they would follow instructions and pick Roh. And in fact, Roh Tae Woo was not without qualifications: he had served competently as the person in charge of the Olympic games, and he was liked and respected by foreigners. Most of the public, however, was outraged that they would have no choice in the matter. Demonstrations now began daily, spearheaded by university students, but often encouraged by crowds of ordinary citizens, and became more massive. Office workers in their standardized white shirts, shopkeepers, even old grannies selling noodles—all joined in or shouted their support for the demonstrators, yelling at the police to leave them alone.

By June of 1987, Seoul and other cities were paralyzed by anti-government protests so severe that the International Olympic Committee was considering relocating the Games. Then, on June 29, Roh, the heir apparent to the presidency, issued a declaration that the ruling party would consider a new constitution and a freely contested election. Over the next few months, most political prisoners were released and censorship was lifted. The first fully free election in nearly three decades took place; yet the opposition was split between Kim Dae Jung and Kim Young Sam, who each had their regional supporters and personal followers. Kim Jong Pil, the founder of the KCIA under Park Chung Hee, also ran, this time as a reform candidate and committed democrat. With the opposition divided, Roh won with 37 percent of the vote—mostly older, conservative, and rural voters. Shortly afterward, the opposition parties gained an overwhelming majority in the National Assembly, a body that now wielded real power. Thus Roh served as a weakened leader who had to negotiate with the opposition. This he did rather successfully, proving to be an able if not especially popular president who functioned as a transitional leader to fully democratic civilian rule. That shift took place in the presidential race of 1992, when former political dissident Kim Young Sam defeated his rival former political dissident Kim Dae Jung; no one from the military participated.

Meanwhile, in 1988 the Seoul Olympics went ahead successfully. South Koreans did well, winning many gold and silver medals. But the biggest gold medal was the games themselves, which were not only a great advertisement for the country's export industry, but also represented an opportunity to build bridges with former communist adversaries China and the Soviet Union. Full diplomatic and trade relations with both countries eventually followed, isolating North Korea. The fall of communism in Eastern Europe and the Soviet Union from 1989 to 1991 made the international situation even more favorable to the South and created an economic crisis in the North. President Roh tried a more conciliatory policy toward the weakened DPRK, but little came of his efforts.

Life was becoming better for most South Koreans. A wave of labor strikes and union organizing from 1987 on led to sharp wage increases and improved working conditions. The reduction of most censorship stimulated the arts and intellectual life. College professors, no longer worried about police spies in their classes, could lecture more freely. In 1988, restrictions on traveling abroad were removed. These restrictions had primarily been an effort to prevent foreign exchange from leaving the country, but they had the effect of limiting people's exposure to the outside world. Now free to travel, South Koreans made up for lost time; soon millions were taking annual vacations abroad, which opened their eyes and contributed to a greater acceptance of foreign cultures and peoples.

How were the South Koreans able to shake off centuries of authoritarian rule so easily? For one, it was not that easy, and the situation in the late 1980s was uncertain; still, it managed to do so. A major reason was that society had changed so much. Most South Koreans, even those of fairly humble means, began considering themselves middle class. They were no longer willing to be ordered around and hectored; they wanted to have an active say in how they were governed. Being well-educated people, they were aware that governments in Japan, the United States, and Western Europe—the societies they aspired to be identified with—had open societies where the political leaders were directly accountable to ordinary citizens. Most South Koreans wanted no less than this themselves.

Students played an important role: following in the honored tradition of the righteous scholar, they expressed criticisms of the regime that many others silently agreed with. Militant labor groups also were important in pointing out the inequities of South Korea's authoritarian march to industrialization. Christian churches provided an institutional basis for political opposition. Most churches were not centers of social and political activism—more often they preached the gospel of material success—but some were active in the political protest and labor movements. The Young Catholic organization and the Protestant-sponsored Urban Industrial Mission were important in supporting labor unions. Cardinal Stephen Kim (Kim Suhwan), the Catholic archbishop of Seoul, was a key voice in the moderate opposition to government oppression and to the social injustices caused by the country's rapid industrialization. Kang Won Young, a Presbyterian minister, used his Christian Academy as a safe meeting ground for intellectuals and political activists. The fact that churches had international links meant they had some ability to offer protection to political dissidents.

The US also contributed to South Korea's democratization. Its role was complicated, because Washington was willing to tolerate all manner of tyrants if they were anti-communist, including military strongmen in Seoul. Yet the United States also protected dissidents and promoted democratic government with projects such as the US Leadership Program, which brought prominent Koreans to the US to observe the American political and economic systems. Both Kim Young Sam and Kim Dae Jung were graduates of the program. But most influential of all was the model of a modern, progressive, successful nation that the US, along with its Western allies, presented to the Korean people; a model South Koreans wanted their country to emulate.

Democratic Pains

In 1992, when Kim Young Sam was elected president, the transfer of power from the last military-linked president, Roh Tae Woo, went smoothly. The only thing remarkable about the election was that it was unremarkable. Just five years after the massive demonstrations against the authoritarian military regime had threatened to plunge the country into chaos, the election between two former political dissidents seemed routine. Military intervention appeared unthinkable, and the results of the election were accepted by all parties. Kim Young Sam aligned his party with political allies of the old regime. Yet once in power, one of first things he did was to purge the military of anyone who had previously been involved in politics, effectively reducing the armed forces to technocratic servants of the civilian-led state.

In 1995, President Kim went after the two former presidents, Chun and Roh. Investigations found both had amassed large fortunes in secret money to both enrich and protect themselves. Everyone expected this to some extent, but the quantity of money they had stolen, amounting to hundreds of millions of dollars, was a surprise. Both were placed on trial and sent to prison. Kim then pursued his anti-corruption campaign, but was undermined in this effort when his own administration became enmeshed in the Hanbo scandal. A number of his close associates were found to be receiving payments from the Hanbo Iron and Steel Company in exchange for keeping the heavily indebted company from bankruptcy. Furthermore, Kim's second son was convicted on charges of influence peddling. Kim, although not personally implicated, lost credibility as an effective reformer when he failed to control corruption among his family members and close associates. At the same time there was a resurgence of labor and student unrest, only adding to the feeling that his administration was not as capable as had been hoped.

When Kim Young Sam's five-year term was up, his party nominated a conservative, Lee Hoi Chang, as its candidate in the December 1997 election. Lee's opponent was Kim Dae Jung, who was making his fourth try at the office. Kim had narrowly lost the presidency in 1971 and was hated by the military and distrusted by many conservatives, who felt among other things that he was soft on North Korea and perhaps secretly sympathetic to the communists. This was hardly true—Kim was a devout Catholic, and while a champion of the working poor and often skeptical of the power of business interests, he was very much pro-American and committed to a vision of South Korea as a Western-style liberal democratic society. He was also a champion for his home region of Jeolla, which had fallen behind the rest of the country in economic development. In 1997, already in his seventies, he was still energetic, and ran a vigorous campaign. Although he won in a close contest, the results were accepted by all and he took office in 1998 without incident.

South Korea was becoming democratic in many other ways, with much of the democratization coming from below. Labor unions, once instruments of state control, had become truly representative of their members, and citizens formed hundreds of NGOs of all kinds. Some proved to be effective government watchdogs, promoting government transparency, the rights of women and the handicapped, environmental concerns, and other issues. The press and broadcast media vigorously scrutinized the government. There were limits to freedom of expression, however; under the National Security Law, any activity that was determined to be pro–North Korean was a state crime. Still, on the whole South Koreans were demonstrating a commitment to accountable government, transparency, and the rule of law.

The economy continued to chug along at about a 7 percent growth rate, slower than in the past but still impressive. Wages continued rising, and signs of greater prosperity were everywhere. The ROK began opening its protected domestic markets to foreign goods, a requirement for joining the new World Trade Organization. Although this threatened some businesses, it also meant that Korean consumers now had access to a greater variety and quality of goods. Once-rare imported items such as wine, brand-name clothes and German luxury cars were available to those who could afford them, and even the less affluent could find a wider range of goods and eat at international fast-food chains or order a pizza from Domino's. Additionally, restrictions on automobile ownership and foreign travel ended. Streets were becoming clogged with traffic, while chain restaurants, international department stores, and designer clothes were now becoming part of the Korean scene.

In 1996, South Korea became a member of the Organisation for Economic Cooperation and Development (OECD), a thirty-member group of developed nations—that is, a kind of club of mostly rich nations. At this time it was reclassified by the World Bank as a developed economy. This meant that it was no longer considered a poor third-world country that received preferential development loans, but one that should be giving, rather than receiving, foreign aid. It was one of the first countries after World War II to officially "graduate" from the third world to the first.

Troubled Tiger: Financial Crisis and Recovery

South Korea was democratizing fast, yet one basic feature of the bad old days remained unchanged. Its economic development was still based on the link between government and big business—what was sometimes called the government-*chaebol* axis. At times they seemed so close that they could be called Korea, Inc. The *chaebol* continued to expand into all manner of enterprises. So accustomed were they to moving into new business lines and investing in new plants that they overinvested, which led to wasteful and unnecessary competition. Most accumulated massive debts, as state-owned banks kept lending them money and government regulators did little to stop them. In the past, the state had exercised some control over these family-owned conglomerates by stopping the flow of credit; however, by the 1990s they had gotten "too big to fail," as a bankrupt or contracting *chaebol* could bring the entire economy down with it. Furthermore, the *chaebol* used their money to provide slush funds, campaign contributions, and secret payments to politicians. Thus, even as firms continued piling up mountains of bad debt, they could count on more favorable loans to keep on growing. Economists pointed out the need for reform, but there was no political will to tamper with a system that so many profited from. Something dramatic was needed to break the bonds that tied the state to the *chaebol* and prevented effective reform.

That dramatic event took place in the summer of 1997, when Thailand went into a financial meltdown and ran out of foreign reserves. This set off a chain reaction throughout Asia; Hong Kong, Indonesia, and South Korea were hit hard. In the late fall, Seoul's stock market crashed and there was a run on the won, causing it to lose nearly two-thirds of its value. Fast running out of money, the South Korean government had to ask the International Monetary Fund for emergency help. A $57 billion package of loans was put together to stave off default—the largest such package that had ever been assembled. With the banks out of cash and the IMF pressuring the country to restructure its economy, the time for reform had come.

The hubris, corruption, and problems of the *chaebol* were dramatically illustrated by the story of Kim Woo-jung and Daewoo. Kim Woo-jung was among the most colorful of the *chaebol* founders. Born in 1936, he was only nine when colonial rule ended, and was still a teenager at the end of the Korean War, making him much younger than most other founders—a product of the postwar generation. Kim was the son of a provincial governor and attended the best schools; at an earlier time, he might have become a civil servant, but instead he became part of Park Chung Hee's drive for industrialization. He founded the Daewoo Company, a clothing and textile firm, in 1967 (the name, which means "Great Universe," is symbolic of the founder's expansive ambitions). Impressed with Kim's efficiency, Park had him take over a small auto firm that was failing. The renamed Daewoo Motors began making parts for General Motors and then started manufacturing its own cars. Not content to stop there, Kim took over a failing shipbuilder, and also went into the construction of oil rigs, machine tools, defense equipment, helicopters, and electronics. In fact, it seemed there was no industry that Daewoo wasn't involved with.

Kim Woo-jung became a kind of hero to the younger generation of Koreans, much the way Steven Jobs later did to many ambitious young Americans. He famously worked 100-hour weeks, never taking a day off—although he did take one morning off to attend his daughter's wedding. His autobiography, *Every Street is Paved with Gold*, sold a million copies in five months, a phenomenal number for a relatively small country. Kim Woo-jung's industrial empire continued to expand in the 1990s. Determined to make Daewoo Motors one the world's largest automakers, he built huge auto plants in Asia and Europe and hired a top European auto designer to create attractive vehicles—all this while entering other new and unrelated manufacturing businesses. Yet his vast conglomerate—the second largest in the country by the late 1990s—never made a profit, and was built on debt. He made full use of secret payments, including to presidents Chun and Roh, as well as a string of officials who prevented a close examination of his companies' books.

And then it all came to a crashing end with the financial crisis, and his businesses entered bankruptcy. Like other *chaebol*, Daewoo had so doctored its financial statements that it was difficult to distinguish between good loans and bad. Yet the degree to which the firm had falsified its reports went beyond most others—seven top company officers were arrested. Kim fled to Vietnam in 1999, heading for the Daewoo Hanoi, a plush hotel opened by his wife three years earlier (the opening had had three thousand guests from around the world, including future Russian president Vladimir Putin). Kim then fled to Europe, even as unemployed former Daewoo employees were hanging up wanted posters featuring his image. In 2005 the now-aging CEO, the object of an Interpol search, returned to Korea, where he was charged and convicted of fraud and embezzlement and forced to turn over billions of dollars of his personal fortune. Still well connected, he was pardoned after a year in prison and went into quiet retirement. Daewoo Motors was sold to GM for a pittance, its plants converted to the production of Chevrolets or shut down altogether. Many of the other subsidiaries closed, but some, including the shipbuilding and electronics companies, survived as independent firms. Kim Woo-jung, whose career had inspired so many young Koreans, was now a cautionary tale.

The fall of Daewoo was just part of the big shake-up caused by the Asian financial crisis. In return for the loans, the IMF required reforms, giving the administration of Kim Dae Jung an opportunity to carry them out despite the knowledge that it would cause considerable hardship. Indeed, Koreans came to call the entire period the "IMF Crisis." Banks were forced to merge or close; *chaebol* were required to sell off many of their subsidiaries and concentrate on their core businesses; and many competing firms were required to merge in order to avoid unnecessary duplication. Foreign companies were allowed to take over some Korean companies—a particularly bold move, since Koreans north and south had a fear of foreigners penetrating and dominating their economies. Companies with bad debt could no longer expect a bailout, and some, like Daewoo, were allowed to fail. Labor lost some of its protections in a bid to make the labor market more flexible. The reforms were painful not just for businesses, but for many ordinary Koreans. In fact, it was the workers and the salaried employees that suffered most, not the new business elite. Many Koreans lost their jobs; others lost the guaranteed lifetime employment they once had. Unemployment, which had been virtually zero for a generation, rose to 8 percent. Being unemployed carried such a stigma that many workers still pretended to go work every day, and suicides rose.

What happened next was rather surprising. The economy contracted by nearly 6 percent in 1998 for the first time since the awful year of 1980. Lenders expected a long, slow recovery and repayment, but instead, helped by a weak won that made South Korean exports a bargain, the economy roared back, growing 10 percent in 1999 and 9 percent in 2000. Within a short time, South Korea was able to pay back its emergency loans; beyond that, it began to accumulate massive trade surpluses and within a few years moved from its chronic indebtedness to being a creditor nation with a large stockpile of dollars. But in some ways, the swift recovery was unfortunate, since it made it easier to avoid continuing to implement the kinds of reforms that would have further broken down the business-government axis, promoted transparency, limited corruption, and made the economy less dominated by a few large family-controlled firms.

In the years after 2000, the economy continued to grow, albeit at a slower rate, until the 2008 international financial crisis. However, many ordinary people no longer benefitted. Wages for many workers increased more modestly than in the past. The "IMF Reforms" did little to stop the surviving *chaebol* from dominating the national economy, and the families and the managers that ran them became wealthier than ever. The workforce found itself divided into those who had managed to get secure jobs in large firms and others who worked at small private firms, and then subcontractors who had little job security and few fringe benefits.

Domestic Politics

Though Kim Dae Jung was accused of being a radical by his political opponents, he proved to be a moderate, pragmatic leader who was willing to compromise. He even formed an alliance with Kim Jong Pil, an architect of the very Park regime that had tried to murder him. His administration followed a pattern similar to that of Kim Young Sam, enjoying enormous popularity initially, as even those who had voted for his opponent pinned their hopes on him for a better future. The honeymoon would inevitably come to an end when the public realized that there would be no radical changes and some scandals would take place within his entourage. This happened with Kim Dae Jung, as close confidantes were implicated in insider trading, embezzlement, and stock manipulation scandals. All three of his sons were involved in some financial irregularities; one was sentenced to four years' imprisonment. Old habits of doing business and influence-peddling proved stubbornly difficult to eradicate. Other problems Kim Dae Jung had to deal with were the rise of labor unrest after a period of voluntary restraint during the financial crisis; his failures to improve the country's inadequate social welfare system; and popular disappointment with the modest results of his engagement with North Korea.

Limited to a single five-year term by the constitution, Kim Dae Jung was succeeded by another former dissident, Roh Moo-hyun. Roh, who was from a poor farming family near Busan, had often missed school to help on the farm, but managed to become class president in elementary school. He went on to become a lawyer, but did so in a very unusual way: unlike the vast majority in his profession, he never attended university, but took the law exam and passed. A human rights lawyer, he defended student dissidents and workers. At one point he was arrested after being involved in a case concerning a Daewoo Shipyard worker killed by police while on strike. Although Roh was elected to the National Assembly, he was an improbable candidate, on the margins of politics; nonetheless, when the liberal party decided to hold a national primary, he ran, and his candidacy took off.

Younger voters were excited by this honest, uncorrupted, courageous champion of the poor and oppressed. His supporters used the internet to gain support and raise money. Some went around with piggy banks to collect small donations. Regarded as unsophisticated because he lacked a university degree, little traveled because he had never been outside his small country, Roh was not taken very seriously by the political establishment. To their surprise and dismay, however, he won the primary and the nomination. And then he went on to narrowly defeat his opponent from the conservative Grand National Party.

Roh's presidency was as unconventional as his rise to office. In a country impressed by prestigious degrees, he appointed people without them, including many former dissidents. Unfortunately, his inexperience and that of his administration became increasingly apparent, and he quickly became an unpopular president. Despite some enthusiasm among younger supporters, many Koreans found him amateurish and embarrassing. In 2007, voters went for the conservative candidate Lee Myung-bak, a former Hyundai executive who was the popular mayor of Seoul. Roh left office with most of his popularity gone, and found himself and some members of his administration under investigation, although few thought him personally corrupt. He retired to the region he had grown up in and ran a duck farm there. One day in 2009, he climbed up a cliff behind his home and jumped off. A suicide note left on his PC stated, "There are too many people suffering because of me." It was a sad end to a good, decent man who had neither the experience nor the temperament to serve as president.

One of Roh Moo-hyun's accomplishments—and a sign of a maturing democracy—was the effort to try to deal more honestly with South Korea's past. In 2005, his government created a Truth and Reconciliation Commission patterned on the one established in

South Africa after the end of apartheid. With fifteen commissioners and a staff of more than two hundred, it investigated the political movements under Japanese colonial rule and all acts of political violence, incidents of terrorism, and human rights violations committed in Korea from 1945 through the democratization of the country in the late 1980s. A major focus was dealing with the mass murders that had taken place during the Korean War. It uncovered more than a thousand executions, including hundreds committed by US troops, the most notable of which was the massacre at No Gun Ri, in which US forces killed a large group of South Korean refugees. Other parts of the recent past were investigated as well; for example, Kim Dae Jung's 1973 kidnapping was revealed to have been ordered by President Park. There was a political aspect to this, as investigations into the crimes of the Park regime served the liberal party. Conservatives began feeling nostalgia for Park Chung Hee's regime, and his daughter, Park Geun-hye, emerged as a leader in the conservative party. Still, the attempt to deal more openly with the past had a lasting effect.

Sunshine and Lots of Clouds: South Korea's Foreign Policy

South Korea's great foreign-policy challenge was dealing with North Korea. By the 1990s, the DPRK was becoming less of a rival than a problem—a dangerous one. The "Sunshine Policy" of Kim Dae Jung tried to deal with the North by offering aid, trade, and friendly exchange. It seemed at first to be successful in gradually improving relations and slowly bringing the two Koreas closer together. In the summer of 2000, Kim Dae Jung arranged a summit conference and went to North Korea to meet Kim Jong Il. The unprecedented visit, accompanied by a team of southern journalists, excited the South Korean public. But there was general disappointment when Pyongyang failed to follow through with its agreements on the reunification of separated families, cultural exchanges, and the reopening of the rail link between the two countries. Furthermore, the entire event was later tarnished when it was revealed that Kim Dae Jung had paid Kim Jong Il a half-billion dollars to meet with him. The South Korean president regarded the secret payment as being worth the opportunity, but it looked suspiciously like a bribe, and when the ROK got little in return, many of the public were upset.

Roh Moo-hyun continued the same Sunshine Policy, but North Korea didn't make it easy for him. The DPRK's detonation of a nuclear device in 2006 was met with anger and angst, not least because it was a blatant violation of the Joint Declaration on Denuclearization that the two countries had agreed to in 1992. The ROK had asked the US to withdraw its nuclear weapons, which it had done; furthermore, South Korea had agreed not to pursue its own nuclear weapons in return for Pyongyang's promise to refrain as well. When the DPRK violated its agreement, the ROK responded by supporting the UN sanctions; nonetheless, the reaction to North Korea's nuclear weapons was not as strong as might have been expected. The "Sunshine Policy" still had a lot of public support in the South. Tired of years of tension, South Koreans often blamed their own government's former hardline anti-communist stance for preventing a thaw in relations. Most wanted desperately to bring about some sort of peaceful reconciliation leading to a future reunification.

This became one of the divides in South Korean politics, with the younger and more progressive-minded supporting reconciliation, while older and conservative people remained totally distrustful of the northern regime and felt the negotiations were a trap to achieve the withdrawal of US troops and the reduction of the ROK's defenses. Older voters had vivid memories of the 1950 invasion and of the terrorist attacks carried out by the North, whereas younger voters tended to see North Koreans as their poor cousins in need of assistance. The family reunion issue was still a sharp emotional hurdle for the older generation, who remained bitter and sad about it while still hoping to meet with their lost family members. Although it was a fading issue for the younger generation, almost all Koreans still hoped to see reunification someday.

Besides dealing with North Korea, the other main focus of South Korea's foreign policy was grappling with the rise of China. Trade with China from the early nineties had grown steadily, finally surpassing trade with the US in 2004. China's rapid industrial and infrastructure development, resembling that of the South a bit earlier, brought a seemingly unlimited demand for steel, capital equipment, and other products. Increasingly wealthy Chinese consumers bought Korean cars and electronics, as well as movie tickets to Korean films. Additionally, as South Korean wages rose, companies began moving their manufacturing to China. By the 2010s, millions of Chinese were visiting the nearby peninsular state, igniting a tourist boom. Unlike much of the developed world, South Korea ran a trade surplus with China, contributing to their own country's economic well-being. Koreans had always admired China, and after decades of no relations at all, they enthusiastically welcomed a new, profitable relationship with it.

Only gradually did South Koreans begin to see a dark side to the rise of China, as their imposing neighbor was becoming more nationalistic and assertive. The first real troubling sign was the Northeast History Project. This was a government-funded program to support archaeological and historical research in Manchuria, which sounded harmless enough, but had implications that were deeply distressing to Korean national sentiment. Concerned about the ethnic minorities that lived along the border regions of the country, China sought to create an official history that suggested all the areas that lay outside the traditional Chinese heartland—Tibet, Inner Mongolia, the northwest region, Manchuria, etc.—had always been associated with China. The Chinese government went as far as to label Goguryeo a Chinese state in its history textbooks. That not only offended some Korean nationalists, who felt a vague claim to southern Manchuria based on the boundaries of Goguryeo, but even suggested that northern Korea itself was historically part of China. Did that signal a possible plan to annex North Korea someday?

Then there was the Chinese policy of claiming most of the South China Sea, even building up and fortifying tiny islands in what were recognized by all other nations as international waters. South Korea had no claim there, but much of its foreign shipping went through this area. In 2013, Beijing declared a large area south of the ROK as an air-defense identification zone, and demanded that all planes flying through identify themselves to the Chinese defense forces—a clear violation of international law. Most of South Korea's commercial and passenger air traffic passed through this zone, and Seoul refused to comply. Still, the growing dependency on the Chinese market and the influence China had on Pyongyang meant that, once again, Koreans found their cherished desire for autonomy from outsiders compromised by geopolitical realities. Beijing, for its part, still sought good relations with the South. In 2014, Xi Jinping became the first Chinese leader to visit South Korea—in fact, it was the first time any Chinese ruler had come to the peninsula.

With the shared threats of North Korea and an aggressive China, Japan was a natural ally and partner. Interpersonal relations improved as South Korea grew more confident in dealing with Japan and could openly admire aspects of its culture, and Japanese began to acquire a taste for Korean popular culture and for its food. Older Japanese attitudes of contempt for Koreans as inferior, backward cousins diminished, although they did not disappear entirely. But resentments from the colonial times lingered, and were played up in South Korean textbooks and by movies that still treated colonial Japanese as heartless villains. Japan's unwillingness to deal with its imperialist past didn't help, either; for example, Japanese history textbooks failed to acknowledge the harsh policies Tokyo had inflicted on the Koreans. The most emotionally laden issue concerned the comfort women. By the early 2000s, a few of these now-aging women began to speak out on the horrors they had suffered, and their heart-wrenching testimonies drew international attention. The Japanese government responded by at various times denying the existence of comfort women, rejecting responsibility, or claiming they had been volunteers. Although Tokyo eventually offered compensation, by that time most of the women were dead; in any case, most survivors found it inadequate.

Another nagging issue with Japan was over the island of Dokdo—or, as the Japanese called it, Takeshima. Little more than a rocky outcropping in the midst of the Sea of Japan, it was held by the ROK, which stationed a few troops on the island to make good its claim. They were the only inhabitants. Nationalistic leaders in Japan reasserted their claim to the island from time to time, causing much outrage in South Korea. Furthermore, the Sea of Japan itself was a source of friction: South Korea insisted on calling it by the Korean name—the East Sea—and pressured international organizations, governments, and cartographers to do so as well. Trying to avoid angering either Seoul or Tokyo, mapmakers and governments began simply using both names, with one in parentheses.

Although South Korea had troubles with its three immediate neighbors, relations with the US were generally good. South Korea supported the US on most international issues, including the invasions of Afghanistan and Iraq; it sent 3,600 troops to Iraq—the third-largest contingent of any country—despite public opposition to the war. Of course, issues arose; Americans complained about the chronic trade deficit they had with South Korea, and about the country's restrictions on its agricultural exports. It actually made good sense to import American rice and beef rather than subsidizing overpriced local products. But the famers, while dwindling in numbers, still made up a formidable voting bloc that politicians ignored at their peril. A free-trade agreement was eventually worked out in 2007, easing these trade tensions somewhat. ROK and US forces continued their annual joint military exercises and maintained good working relations with each other. Meanwhile, the anti-American sentiment that had been common among young people and intellectuals in the 1980s declined.

Rice Maker No More: A Society Undergoing Social Change

South Korean society was operating in fast motion, and even a few years' absence would return you to a neighborhood or community almost unrecognizably changed. From the 1960s to the early twenty-first century, the most ubiquitous sign was "Under Construction." Indeed, the whole country did seem to be under construction.

No less profound but much slower were the changes related to gender and family. Under South Korea's Family Law, compiled in the 1950s, husbands headed households, eldest sons were favored in inheritance, and men usually received custody of children in the case of divorce, which was uncommon. It was a surprisingly unprogressive document, something that the Confucianists of the Joseon dynasty would not have felt entirely uncomfortable with. Thus, South Korean women lagged behind their sisters in the North in almost every measure of gender equality except representation in top leadership positions—both Koreas were politically dominated by men. But not all South Korean women accepted this, nor were they passive little "rice makers," as they were sometimes jokingly referred to by their husbands. Women were active in the labor movement, in church organizations, and increasingly in political movements. Some sought to actively reform the Family Law.

Few contributed more to overturning the patriarchal nature of society than Lee Tai-young (Yi T'ae-yŏng, 1914–95). Lee, born in what became North Korea, was the daughter of a gold miner; she married a Methodist minister who was later imprisoned by the Japanese. She supported her four children by working as a seamstress and taking in laundry. Somehow, she managed to enter the top-ranking Seoul National University, the first woman to do so, and became Korea's first female lawyer in 1952. The obstacles she had to overcome to get that far are staggering to ponder. Lee later founded the Korea Legal Aid Center for Family Relations, which provided assistance to poor, uneducated women. She was arrested by the Park regime in 1976 for calling for democracy; her main focus, however, was on reforming the laws that kept the country's patriarchal structure intact, and on empowering women.

The efforts of Lee Tai-young and others resulted in the revision of the Family Law in 1977. This gave women greater rights in marriage, divorce, inheritance, and child custody, but still fell far short of establishing gender equality. With a surge of activism in 1987, women founded the Korean Women's Association, and in 1989 managed to pass a new revision of the Family Law. The eldest son was no longer automatically expected to succeed as the head of the household, and inheritance was made more equal. By the 1990s, women were allowed to head households, inherit property, and divorce their spouses. Still, South Korean women lagged behind other developed nations in their rate of representation in the professions—in fact, in almost all measures of equality—well into the early twenty-first century. Most female college students majored in home economics, English, fine arts, or other subjects that prepared them for a suitable marriage, not for a profession.

Under pressure from women's groups, the Kim Dae Jung administration created a Ministry of Gender Equality in 2001. By the early 2000s, the number of women in universities exceeded that of men; in 2010 they comprised nearly half of the students in all master's degree programs and about a third of all doctoral candidates. Women were also beginning to raise previously taboo subjects like spousal abuse and sexual harassment. They campaigned against the country's large sex industry, which encompassed traditions such as the room salons where men went for drinking and sex. Despite this, the older Korean ways stubbornly held fast. By most measures, women in South Korea held fewer high posts in government and the corporate world than those in almost any other modern industrialized country except perhaps Japan. They suffered from one of the world's widest gender gaps in pay. It is unfortunate that when a woman, Park Geun-hye, was elected president in 2013 (see next chapter) her administration was plagued with scandal and incompetence, and she was removed from office.

Few changes in society were more shocking from a traditional Confucian point of view than the rising divorce rate. Before 1990, divorce was still rare, and brought shame upon a family. Then, like so many things in Korea, it changed dramatically, tripling in just one decade between 1995 and 2005. By 2010 it was higher than that of Japan or the European Union, although still lower than the US, with about one in three Korean marriages ending in divorce. More shocking to traditionalists was the fact that some women didn't want to get married at all. Staying single, while still not common, was no longer unthinkable. Many young women expressed their reluctance to live a life where their principal role was to cook and clean for a man and raise his children.

For all the social changes, family bonds and many of the Confucian values associated with them were still strong. During the period of rapid development, families worked together as a unit to promote their members' welfare. Parents, in particular, made enormous sacrifices to insure a better life for their children. Nowhere was this more evident than in education. No matter how poor, every family managed to scrape together the money needed for school fees that were far from nominal. As the country became more prosperous, the cost of education went up, since most parents sent their sons and daughters to after-class cram schools or hired tutors to assist them. The ultimate goal was to pass the college entry examination, which by the twenty-first century was taken by more than half of all young people. Those with the highest scores could go on to SKY—Seoul National, Koryo, or Yonsei universities—the three most prestigious schools. Those who did not do well on the exam often spent the next year studying full-time to take it again.

The national obsession with education brought startling results. By the 2010s, South Korea had one of the highest rates of entry into higher education in the world, and its secondary students tested among the highest of any nation in international assessments of math, science, and reading—a remarkable achievement for a country where, two generations earlier, most adults had no formal schooling at all. But what a pressure cooker education was! Young South Koreans spent more time studying than anything else. After regular school was over, most attended cram schools and private study halls well into the evening on weekdays, and also on weekends and during school vacations. Just as South Korean workers once had the longest hours in the world, surveys showed that South Korean schoolkids spent more hours per week studying than students anywhere. All this placed a heavy psychological burden on young people and a heavy financial burden on their parents. Since supervising studying as well as selecting cram schools could be a full-time job for a mother, this state of affairs hindered women from entering the workplace.

Yet there was rationality to this obsession with exam preparation. South Korea remained a society that was very status-conscious; the most effective way for anyone to preserve or improve their status was through educational attainment. For all its social change, South Korea was still, as it had been in the past, a highly rank-conscious society that associated learning with merit, used competitive exams to assign status, and viewed the family as a collective unit, with parents making sacrifices for their children.

Like North Korea, the South Korean government promoted its

cultural heritage. It sponsored archaeology projects and the restoration of ancient sites, and fostered the preservation of artistic and crafts traditions by designating certain persons as "living cultural treasures," encouraging them to pass on their skills. Unfortunately, in its rush for development, the ROK did not preserve much of its physical heritage. Traditional neighborhoods, with their twisting warrens of tiled-roof houses, each with a little courtyard in the center, were torn down as fast as possible. These were replaced with ugly blocks of high-rise apartments looking so much alike that huge numbers had to be painted on their sides to distinguish one from another. For most Koreans, living in a modern apartment with all the conveniences was a big step up in the world, and they saw no need to preserve reminders of their former poverty. Only in the twenty-first century was there an effort to protect a few remaining traditional urban neighborhoods and villages from destruction by making them into living museums.

The social changes and the challenges of recent Korean history were captured by writers who flourished despite censorship during the years of military rule. An example was the satirical and critical poetry of Kim Jiha, one of the most widely read writers in the country. He wrote of the corrupt collusion between favored businessmen and the bureaucratic patrons, and of a government that trampled on human rights and dignity in its rush toward development. Koreans love poetry—books of poetry sometimes top the bestseller lists—so the voice of a poet like Kim could have considerable influence in shaping the country's consciousness. Novelists wrote about the hardship of slum dwellers and the dislocations caused by sudden change. In the early 2000s, however, literature moved away from political and social themes and toward fantasy and playful reimagination of the country's past. Social themes were often directed at more international scenarios and the plight of peoples outside the country. All this reflected the transition from being a country striving to catch up with the rest of the world and seeking a path toward economic prosperity and political freedom to a more complacent one—still with plenty of anxieties, but the anxieties of the rich and comfortable, not the poor and struggling.

CHAPTER 10

CHALLENGES IN EVERY DIRECTION: KOREA TODAY

North Korea under the Grandson

I n the second decade of the twenty-first century, South Korea was becoming a center of high-tech industry and pop culture, with customers and audiences throughout the globe. It was a rapidly changing society experiencing the implications of a gender revolution and the challenges of an aging population. It had one of the most democratic, if contentious, political systems in Asia; and a globe-trotting sophisticated citizenry that was open to new ideas and experiences while treasuring much of their cultural heritage. But this newly dynamic, prosperous Korea had to deal with the other Korea, with its impoverished and oppressed population, its militarized government, and its unpredictable leadership prone to bouts of open hostility. What had happened to the peninsula was historically unique: one of the world's oldest, most ethnically homogenous lands had in a couple generations evolved into two radically different societies. Indeed, the boundary between them was not only the most fortified and dangerous in the world; it also marked the sharpest contrast in living standards, lifestyles, and political systems between two adjacent states anywhere.

In North Korea, the regime was determined to keep itself in power at all costs while the general population managed to somehow muddle through. Economically, it stagnated; diplomatically, it grew more isolated. Despite being called the Democratic People's Republic of Korea, it was the least democratic country in the world, paying little heed to its people outside of a small group of elites. In fact, it wasn't even a republic, but a monarchy—now ruled by the third-generation head of the Kim dynasty, Kim Jong Un.

The grandson of the Kim Il Sung and the son of Kim Jong Il, Kim Jong Un was surrounded by people of his father's generation. Some outside observers even thought that he might become their puppet, but this assumption was mistaken. The young Kim showed a ruthlessness that took many by surprise. In late 2013 he had Jang Song Taek, his uncle-in-law, who was widely regarded as the second most powerful figure in the country, arrested. Jang's humiliating arrest at a Party meeting where he was dragged away was shown dramatically on TV. A few days later he was executed. It was the first public announcement of the purging and execution of a top-ranking official in half a century, and the first known execution of one so closely related to the Kim family. Rumor had it that Jang and other victims of the purge were executed by anti-aircraft guns, while other officials watched the bodies explode into tiny pieces. These pieces were then fed to dogs. That last detail was perhaps an imaginative flourish, but it did convey the mercilessness the new leader showed to anyone who posed as a possible threat to his power.

Young Kim removed many of his high military commanders. Most were not purged, but simply demoted or forced into retirement. Overall, the scale of the actual purges was small but high-profile, signaling that there could be no challenge to his authority. One possible threat was his half-brother Kim Jong Nam, who, as Kim Jong Il's eldest son, could have had a good claim on the succession. Kim Jong Nam, however, had discredited himself with his irresponsible behavior; he lived in exile in China, where he spent half his time in Macau. By all accounts he was a fun-loving, apolitical man fond of gambling and women, and was not considered a serious contender for power; besides, he was living under Chinese protection. It came as a surprise, then, when Kim Jong Un had him assassinated. The older Kim was traveling outside of China, walking through the Kuala

Lumpur airport, when two attractive Southeast Asian women, recruited by North Korean intelligence, approached him and shoved a handkerchief smeared with a deadly toxin in his face. He died within minutes. This brazen, bizarre act sent a clear message: no potential rival was safe, even one under Beijing's protection.

Since he had been educated in Switzerland and had greater experience of the world than his father, it was widely expected that Kim Jong Un would be more open to change, more liberal-minded. This was not the case. There were a few cosmetic differences; for example, he was shown in the media with his wife, a popular singer who wore fashionable clothes, attending entertainments and laughing together—something that his father had never done. Also unlike his reclusive father, he spoke in public, and addressed the people of the DPRK directly on television. His outgoing personality resembled his grandfather's. His physical resemblance to his grandfather was so great that rumors in South Korea claimed he had had plastic surgery to enhance the similarities.

In fact, Kim Jong Un made his grandfather, rather than his father, the reference point of his administration. He revived some of the old institutions; for example, in 2016, he held the first party congress since 1980. His father had never bothered to hold one. In form and content, the event was very much a throwback to the days of Kim Il Sung, even referring to a new five-year plan, which would be the first central plan since the early 1990s. Some institutions were given back their older names. At the congress, Kim announced that the "grim struggle" of recent years was over, that the country would progress ahead economically and militarily. This twin goal of military and economic progress, which he dubbed *byungjin*, was in fact a revival of his grandfather's "equal emphasis" policy.

However, there was really no equal emphasis at all; rather, the emphasis was on the military, not the economy. Kim was single-mindedly focused on developing the country as a nuclear state, conducting the nation's third nuclear weapons test on February 12, 2013—then another on January 6, 2016, and a larger one on September 9, 2016. The sixth nuclear test, on September 3, 2017, was far larger than previous ones, causing earth tremors in adjacent regions of China and Russia. North Korea claimed, plausibly, that it was a hydrogen bomb; and indeed, the test site of the bomb, Mount Mantap in the northeast, was visibly transformed by the powerful denotation. He continued with his missile development, testing far more of them than his father had. On August 29 and again on September 15, 2017, he fired missiles over northern Japan, creating enormous alarm in that country. Attempts to develop a multi-stage intercontinental ballistic missile were unsuccessful at first, but then progress accelerated. On July 4, 2017, he provocatively launched a missile capable of reaching Alaska. A second successful test of a missile capable of reaching the continental US took place three weeks later, on July 28. The next, in November, was capable of reaching Washington, DC. The speed with which North Korea's weapons program progressed caught the US, South Korea, Japan, and the international community by surprise, and alarmed them greatly.

Rather than easing international tensions, Kim Jong Un was bent on creating them. In the spring of 2013 he denounced the US and South Korea during their annual joint military exercises. Of course, those exercises had been taking place since 1976, and every year Pyongyang claimed they were part of fervent preparations for a military invasion, rattling its sabers in response. But this time was different. The vitriol and threats issued by Pyongyang went beyond anything previously seen, with a declaration that it would turn Seoul into a "sea of fire" and propaganda images showing DPRK missiles destroying Washington, DC. North Korea declared the 2013 Military Armistice void, and decreed all agreements with the ROK, including the Joint Declaration of Denuclearization of the Korean Peninsula, to be terminated as well. Ominously, most channels of communication with the ROK were severed, and even the Kaesong Industrial Complex was closed. Yet there was no sign that the country was preparing for war. It was unclear what Kim was trying to accomplish. Was he trying to demonstrate to his military and people that this pampered princeling who had never served in the military was a tough and able commander? Was he trying to test the preparedness of his military? Or was he just trying to create a state of military tension to justify his focus on military spending and to rally the public behind his regime? Perhaps he was trying to achieve all these objectives.

The United Nations passed a series of resolutions imposing economic sanctions on the DPRK. Most were targeted at the export of military goods and imports of materials that could be used for weapons programs and luxuries for the elite. With the missile launches and nuclear tests in 2017, the sanctions were expanded to target many of North Korea's basic exports. But even though China had voted for the sanctions, it enforced them selectively or minimally. Since nearly 90 percent of North Korea's trade was with China or passed through it, it was the one country that could make these sanctions effective. The Chinese, however, were unwilling to risk seeing the regime collapse. It feared chaos on its borders, a flood of refugees, loose nukes. Furthermore, if South Korea annexed the North, it would place a democratic society allied to the US and Japan on China's border; China was also uncomfortable with the domestic repercussions of having an ally fall, and a communist one at that. Still, the Chinese were clearly unhappy with the regime. For the first six years of Kim Jong Un's rule, no Chinese leader or foreign minister visited Pyongyang, even as they managed to make it to Seoul; nor did Kim Jong Un and his top lieutenants visit China.

An exchange of intemperate remarks between Kim Jong Un and US president Trump in the summer of 2017 gave the world jitters, since it made the threat of nuclear war seem real. And it wasn't just nuclear weapons and a missile delivery system that Pyongyang was working on—the regime was engaged in cyber warfare. Specially trained agents used servers abroad to carry out attacks. In late 2014, they hacked the computer systems of Sony Pictures Entertainment in retaliation for the movie *The Interview*, a rather crude comedy about the (fictitious) assassination of Kim Jong Un. The attack damaged the company and scared off movie theaters from showing the film, although it was aired online. This was the tip of the iceberg: North Korea repeatedly attempted to hack into South Korea's utilities, nuclear plants, and government agencies; it hacked into banks and stole funds, and was suspected of letting loose internationally disruptive computer viruses. Then there was the country's chemical and biological weapons program, which included the use of VX—the internationally banned, very dangerous toxin that had been deployed to kill Kim Jong Nam. North Korea seemed unwilling to play by any international rules, becoming a true outlaw nation.

Besides its concerns about an unlikely US attack, North Korea faced real threats from its neighbors, China and South Korea. South Korea's very freedom and prosperity was an existential threat: if Northern citizens realized just how much they had been deceived by their government, the impact would be devastating. It was therefore central to its security to keep the public misinformed about the South. This meant perpetuating the lie that South Koreans were living under foreign occupation, waiting for the North to liberate them. Refugees, to the extent that they believed any of this, were soon set straight when they encountered mainly contempt for the North—or even worse, disinterest—among southerners.

China posed a very different existential threat. North Korea, for all its vaunted self-reliance, had become economically dependent on its giant neighbor, which had absorbed almost all the country's exports after the sanctions took effect. This gave it enormous leverage over North Korea. The greater long-term threat was that China would intervene in its affairs or even annex the country. Some in South Korea, seeing how important China was to the DPRK, began calling it the "fourth province of Manchuria." By this they meant that China was preparing to either economically or politically absorb the country into its huge northeast region, which was divided into three provinces.

North Korea under Kim Jong Un carried out a few modest reforms, but mostly the regime simply let the semi-marketization of the economy continue. There was some economic growth, but it was modest and started from a low level; much of it was directed at improving the lives of the elite—the bureaucrats, party officials, military and security officials, and key scientists and technicians needed for its weapons programs. These were the people that mattered to the regime, and for them, life did get better. There were more luxury vehicles; private restaurants and shops selling imported goods opened; and the state created amusement parks for the children, golf courses and a ski resort for the adults. There was a visible housing mini-boom in the mid-2010s, as luxury apartment buildings—at least, luxury by North Korean standards—went up. There were just enough visible projects in the capital to demonstrate to foreigners, and perhaps their own people, that the country was making economic progress.

The lives of the non-elite, however, improved only slightly. In 2018, the WHO estimated that 40 percent of the population suffered from malnutrition. Contrary to the expectations of some in the West, Kim Jong Un carried out no liberalization; in fact, security was actually tightened. A flourishing market in illegal Chinese cell phones, some of which could pick up signals from China, had provided a window to the outside world, as did the booming market in videocassettes and DVDs of South Korean dramas and movies. Kim's regime reduced these little windows to the outside by developing its own cell phones that could not pick up Chinese signals, and by becoming more efficient in cracking down on smuggled foreign entertainment. There was less tolerance of illegal border crossings, and defection became more difficult.

The world largely ignored the plight of ordinary North Koreans. There were no famous dissidents on the world stage; no Hollywood celebrities championed their cause; and isolation and language barriers made it difficult for their voices to be heard. A number of refugees, such as Shin Dong-hyuk, whose extraordinary life and escape from the Camp 14 political prison became the basis of an international bestseller, attracted the world's attention. Yet North Koreans in general were often viewed by the outside world as strange automatons goose-stepping to the tune of the Great Leader, rather than a people suffering from a humanitarian crisis. Nonetheless, there were exceptions. In early 2014, the UN Human Rights Council issued a report by three leading international jurists that found the violations of human rights in North Korea so extreme as to constitute a crime against humanity. While this drew attention to the odious nature of the regime, it had no impact on its behavior or the lives of its people.

Was North Korea at a dead end? It seemed to have no plan but to survive. There was no realistic vision of a path forward. Even in a good year its economy grew only modestly, and less than most of its neighbors. Once one of the most developed countries in Asia, it now was one of the poorest—and the gap grew yearly. By marshaling its meager resources, it was able to build up weapons of mass destruction. Yet even its conventional armed forces were falling behind those of other countries. Its military vehicles were old and lacked enough fuel to do much training; its air force was becoming a museum of ancient planes; and its soldiers were shorter, skinnier, and more poorly equipped than their counterparts in the South. Only its missiles; its nuclear, biological, and chemical weapons; and its cyber warfare units made it a significant threat. But this appeared sufficient for the regime to protect itself from invasion and perhaps keep itself in power.

The End of Miracles in South Korea

If North Korea only became more isolated in the second decade of the twenty-first century, South Korea became even more global, economically and culturally. However, the economic miracle was now over. Having leaped to middle-income status, it found reaching the top tier of high-income countries was a slower slog. Yet its capacity for change had not slowed; its culture and society continued to evolve at a pace and in ways that were often unexpected.

Politics revolved around swings from more conservative to more left-leaning governments. Lee Myung-bak, the conservative candidate who was elected president in 2007, gained office partly due to the unpopularity of his liberal predecessor Roh Moo-hyun and partly for his promise to resume the country's high economic growth rate. Lee's failure to achieve his unrealistic goals and his sometimes authoritarian style resulted in strong opposition to his policies, including candle-lit demonstrations that became a more or less regular feature of South Korean life. His popularity plummeted.

Lee was succeeded by his rival within the conservative Grand National party, Park Geun-hye. In December 2012, she defeated the liberal opposition candidate Moon Jae-in, Roh Moo-hyun's former chief of staff. The divide was in large part generational: Park won overwhelmingly among those over fifty, but did poorly among younger voters.

The eldest daughter of Park Chung Hee, Park Geun-hye was studying at a private school in Europe when her mother was shot and killed in an attempted assassination of her father in 1974; she then returned to Korea. During the next few years she took on the role of first lady, and was an object of sympathy for much of the public, representing the human side of the austere Park Chung Hee. Only five years into this role, her father was assassinated, and she withdrew from public life. She never married or had children, which was rather unusual for a Korean woman of her generation. In 1998 she entered politics and was elected to the National Assembly, becoming an active member of the conservative party. She lost the presidential nomination to Lee Myung-bak in 2007, successfully gaining it five years later.

She was a polarizing figure. For many older Koreans, she triggered nostalgia for the days of her father, when the country was proudly lifting itself up by its bootstraps. But for others she was an embarrassing reminder of that past, and of her father's political repression, his crude anti-communism, the exploitation of workers and the human-rights violations. Indeed, her candidacy was as much about dealing with the ROK's recent history as it was about specific issues. Interestingly, her gender was not controversial. This was not so much because Koreans had arrived at the point where gender no longer mattered—it was still a male-dominated society—but rather that progressives disliked her and dismissed her rise as being due to the fact that she was a surrogate for a former dictator, while her supporters backed her despite her sex.

Park's administration became a national embarrassment. She appeared to have trusted few people, but one she placed her faith in was Choi Soon-sil, the daughter of shamanistic cult leader Choi Tae-min. His was one of the many strange religious cults—some Christian, some hard to characterize—that arose during the unsettling years of the country's post-1945 upheavals and the dislocations caused by its rapid modernization. Choi Tae-min declared himself a Buddha at one point, then appropriated the trappings of Christianity, but he was best characterized as a charlatan who took advantage of the young Park Geun-hye by providing solace to her in the days after her mother's assassination. He then used his influence over her to enrich himself, a practice his daughter Choi Soon-sil continued. Although she held no official position and was not qualified by training or background to do so, Ms. Choi was President Park's closest confidante, and even had access to classified documents. Choi used her position to set up two foundations for culture and sports which were really massive influence-peddling schemes. Prominent businessmen seeking access to the president donated millions of dollars to these foundations, which existed primarily to enrich Choi and her friends.

Choi was unknown to the general public, but South Korean journalists became aware of her influence, and after details of her activities came out in the press, President Park's approval rating began to plunge. While influence-peddling was a common practice, the scale of the scheme and the unsavory nature of those involved caused national outrage. Massive nightly candle-lit demonstrations appeared in Seoul that grew ever larger, becoming the biggest in the country's history. The public grew more outraged by Park's poor handling of the crisis and by the revelation of more unsavory details, such as Choi's maneuverings to get her daughter into the prestigious Ewha Women's University. Tampering with the all-important college admissions process touched a raw nerve among Korean families. President's Park's approval rating fell into the single digits; in fact, in what may have been a record in the history of polling, it fell to 1 percent among younger voters.

Televised hearings before the National Assembly revealed the scale of corruption involved. The old government-*chaebol* axis was revealed in its darkest light; at one point the CEOs of the major *chaebol* sat before the TV cameras looking like a criminal lineup. Each had given generous donations to Choi's foundations in return for political favors. Even the head of the mighty Samsung *chaebol* found himself under investigation and was convicted of bribery. The National Assembly voted to impeach Park, who remained defiant. A new election was held in early 2017, which Moon Jae-in won handily. The whole scandal revealed the pervasive corruption that still characterized business and politics—but it also showed how the country was changing: its free and sometimes combative media; the growing public demand for transparency; its intolerance of corruption. Furthermore, it demonstrated the strength of its democratic institutions.

The Republic of Samsung: The *Chaebol*, the Economy, and Political Conflict

South Korea was so dominated by *chaebol* that it became a matter of concern for those of all political leanings. After the financial crisis of 1997–98, the state had broken up the largest *chaebol* into multiple companies, but in most cases the same families controlled them. Just a handful of giant conglomerates such as Lotte, Ssangyong, Hyundai, and the largest, Samsung, controlled much of the economy. Each was a sort of universe in itself. For example, the huge Lotte group offered consumers everything they could possibly need. A South Korean could live in one of the many Lotte apartment buildings found everywhere throughout the country, finance their home through Lotte's financial services, and buy their insurance from Lotte. They could shop at a Lotte Department Store and buy groceries there, including Lotte food products; they could eat at one of the ubiquitous Lotteria chain restaurants, and see a movie at a Lotte cinema. On the weekend they could go to Lotte World, one of the world's largest entertainment parks, and when traveling they could stay at one of the many Lotte Hotels. Indeed, for some, life could be one large Lotte World.

But the biggest of the *chaebol* was Samsung. In the 2010s it made up 17 percent of the entire economy. By any measure it was huge. In 2016, Samsung Electronics was the world's second-largest information technology company by sales revenue, close behind Apple. Samsung Heavy Industries was the world's second-largest shipbuilder, Samsung Engineering the world's thirteenth-largest construction company, Samsung Life the fourteenth-largest insurance company—and there were other Samsung companies making cars and appliances and running amusement parks. So big and influential had it become that the country was sometimes called the Republic of Samsung. Since the Lee family still held control over the group, it could be regarded as the world's largest family enterprise—a title that might only be challenged by the ibn Saud family, if the kingdom named after them is thought of as another family enterprise.

In early 2017, the forty-nine-year-old head of the Samsung group, Lee Jae Yong, from the third generation of the family, was convicted of bribery in the Park Geun-hye–Choi Soon-sil scandal and sentenced to five years in prison. However, as extraordinary it was that someone from such a powerful family could be sent away to prison, it had little effect on the power and wealth of the *chaebol* and the families that ran them. Since members of the *chaebol* families tended to marry each other, there was a fear that they could become (or had already become) a small social class of their own. If so, it was remarkably similar to the small, intermarried group of elite aristocratic families that had dominated Korea from the Silla period to the end of the Joseon dynasty. And it faintly resembled the small, intermarried ruling elite that had emerged in North Korea. These analogies should not be pushed too far; South Korea was a far more democratic society than either of these, with power more broadly shared. Still, the concentration of wealth among the *chaebol* families made the general public uneasy.

Calls for reining in the power of the *chaebol* were strong, since it was felt by many that they were making it difficult for small start-ups to succeed. South Korea wanted its own Silicon Valley, with its many new creative firms. It also needed to move from manufacturing to a more knowledge-based and service-oriented economy. A symbol of this move was the brand-new city of Songdo, a high-tech, eco-friendly "smart city" located sixty-four kilometers (forty miles) southwest of Seoul near the Incheon International airport. Mostly completed by 2018, it had an imposing skyline and some impressive facilities, but did not quite live up to its intended status as an international business hub. There was also an effort to develop centers away from Seoul, which had become a gigantic megalopolis inhabited by more than twenty million people, or 40 percent of the population. However, efforts to decentralize the country by moving its scientific and technological research facilities to the city of Daejeon and constructing an entirely new central administrative city—Sejong City—had little impact on the continued concentration of people and economic activity in Seoul.

Economic development sometimes clashed with the growing concern over environmental issues. The country had an impressive system of national parks for outdoor recreation, but there were few green spaces in the densely populated urban areas where the majority of the population resided. Some progress was made in cleaning up rivers and streams and preserving wetlands; much less so in dealing with air pollution. Seoul, in particular, was often covered by a sickly haze that made it difficult to even tell whether the weather was sunny or cloudy. On one day in March of 2017, the air quality was rated the second worst in the world. Pollution was frequently blamed on China, which sent its notoriously dirty air over the peninsula. However, the government reported that only 30 to 50 percent of the pollution was external; the rest was self-generated, much of it from the country's coal-burning power plants.

Baby Bust: A Society Undergoing Demographic Change

Of the many changes in South Korean society, none loomed larger than the "baby bust." In the 1960s and '70s, the state vigorously promoted family planning—and was only too successful. By the twenty-first century, it was encouraging women to have more children. The decline in the birthrate was dramatic, and in the early 2000s it fell off the chart. With an average of 1.2 children per woman by late 2010, South Korea was tied with Singapore for the lowest birthrates in the world—lower even than Japan or Italy, with their rapidly aging, shrinking populations. Women married late—typically at twenty-nine—and had their first baby at thirty. Many were not having children at all. As many as 15 percent of young women stated they did not want to get married, and bearing a child out of wedlock was still socially unacceptable and uncommon. Many women saw childbearing as a burden—a life of cooking, cleaning for their husbands, and caring for their child; one in which they no longer had any identity but as their husband's wife and their son's mother. In fact, traditionally, Korean woman were seldom called by their given names once they had a son; instead, they were known as their son's mother. For example, Kyung Hee became known as her son Chulsoo's mother—or, in Korean, Chulsoo-*eomma*.

Even in the 2010s, South Korea was one of the most male-dominated societies in the developed world. Only some Muslim nations and largely preindustrial societies in Africa had a smaller percentage of women represented in political office, in managerial positions, as university presidents, and as CEOs. The very persistence of this paternalism was partly responsible for the lack of interest many women had in marriage, but it wasn't the only reason that women were having so few children. There was also the expense, especially of education: the educational arms race of getting one's child into the best schools kept driving up the cost and burden of schooling.

Not only were Koreans having fewer babies, but as a result of improvements in healthcare, they were also living longer. By the 2010s, South Koreans were among the longest-lived people in the world, despite having higher than average rates of tobacco and alcohol consumption. The compulsory retirement age meant there were fewer older workers in the workforce, and the inadequate social welfare system meant that life was not always very comfortable for senior citizens. Most families living in comfortable but small condominium complexes did not want to share their limited space with their elderly parents, leaving them lonely and isolated. Many elderly people were forced to take part-time jobs to support their meager pensions. The biggest problem was how to support what would become one of the oldest populations in the world by mid-century when there were so few younger people. This was a problem shared by almost all developed countries, but South Korea's case looked to be more extreme than most.

With the looming labor shortage and the prospect of a declining and aging society, many officials suggested immigration as an answer. The problem was that this ran counter to the kind of ethnic-nationalism that characterized modern Korea. Although not as extreme as the blood-and-soil nationalists in the North, South Koreans still thought of themselves in racial terms. They took pride in being a "pure-blooded" nation.

But it simply no longer was. Interracial and interethnic marriages were becoming common, in part due to the shortage of women. When the age-old preference for male children met the sonogram that could determining the sex of a fetus, there was a sharp rise in abortions, and soon far more boys were being born than girls. As is so often the case in South Korea, public attitudes quickly shifted again; daughters became more valued and the ratio of male and female babies returned to normal. But for the generation born in the 1980s, it was too late; men turned to arranged marriages with women from other Asian countries such as Vietnam, the Philippines, Mongolia, and Uzbekistan. The number of bi-ethnic children was growing so fast that, according to some estimates, they would make up a third of all children by the mid-2020s—a truly startling number in such a homogeneous country.

There were also a growing number of immigrants from poorer Asian countries like Bangladesh, Nepal, the Philippines, China, Kirghizstan, and Mongolia, who mostly did the "three-D" jobs—dirty, difficult, and dangerous—that South Koreans increasingly did not want to do. The government did offer employers permits to bring in foreign workers, but this process was so cumbersome that many just brought them in on tourist visas and employed them illegally. The need for immigration resulted in efforts by government officials and academics to promote multiculturalism. Although the idea was intellectually accepted by many, it involved such a redefining of what it meant to be Korean that it was likely to be a hard transition to make.

In any case, as foreigners were moving into Korea, Koreans were moving across the world. Emigration had been little more than a tiny trickle before the 1970s. Few had the money or means to do so, and the government made it difficult, believing that a large population was necessary to compete with the North. In 1970, however, President Park, worried about overpopulation, decided to allow and even encourage emigration abroad. For most emigrants, America was the first choice; those unable to get a US visa often went to Canada, Argentina, Brazil, or Australia, and in smaller numbers to other countries. From the mid-1990s, emigration began falling because of growing prosperity and democratization, as well as the general improvement in living conditions. Yet, if no longer a flood, a steady stream of South Koreans continued to depart for a different life abroad. They emigrated to spare their kids from the pressure cooker of the Korean education system, to try for a second chance if they had failed to get into a prestigious school, for the opportunity to work at a world-class university or research institute, to escape the obligations and expectations of Korean society, to be able to own a large home with a spacious yard—very difficult to do in crowded Korea—or simply to join family members who had already emigrated. Many were students who had found jobs in their host countries and never returned.

By 2018, the South Korean government estimated seven million Koreans and people of Korean descent were living overseas. This included the 2.5 million living in China, mostly clustered in southern Manchuria near the North Korean border, where they formed the Yanbian Autonomous Region. About 900,000 lived in Japan, descendants of those who had voluntarily emigrated or had been shipped off there during colonial times. More than two million lived in the United States. There were 200,000 Koreans or people of Korean descent in Canada; 150,000 in Australia; 80,000 each in the Philippines and Vietnam; 50,000 in Brazil, where they replaced the Jewish community in São Paulo's garment industry; and smaller numbers elsewhere. Most Koreans prospered overseas. An exception was in Japan, where they faced unrelenting discrimination, but even there many ran successful business enterprises—both legitimate and not-so-legitimate. Many Koreans overseas maintained strong family ties in their home country, visited often, and returned to retire or take jobs. All this extended South Korea's influence in the world and contributed to its growing cosmopolitanism.

Gangnam Style: Pop Culture and the Korean Wave

Few developments in South Korea seemed more improbable than its emergence as a global center of pop culture. Korea had been on the periphery of international consciousness, a marginal player on the world stage. In the 1980s, its economic success had begun attracting some attention, but it was never considered a "cool" or "hip" place. Its entertainment was largely imitative of American—and more often, Japanese—movies, comics, TV, popular music, and fashions. The South Korean government took pains to protect its small movie industry, severely restricting the number of foreign films imported each year, mostly Hollywood productions. Cinemas mainly showed local movies, which were much less popular. In fact, most movie companies depended on the profits they earned from gaining licenses to import films. Some Korean singers were very popular, often singing nostalgic songs for older folks, but young people listened to American pop. Television often consisted of American shows dubbed into Korean. Japanese popular culture was strictly prohibited—no movies, songs, books, TV shows, or manga. Then, when the government joined the World Trade Organization in the 1990s, it had to end its restrictions on foreign cultural imports as part of the agreement to open up its markets.

Officials were particularly worried about Japan's slick entertainment industry overwhelming Korea's, just as in the past they had feared that opening trade with Korea's former colonial master would overwhelm it economically. What happened instead was almost the opposite; the flood of Japanese and other cultural imports contributed to a "take-off" of Korea's own entertainment industry, and soon it was the Japanese who were complaining about the Korean cultural invasion. Some of this was due to individual artists who began to experiment and innovate in the freer society of democratic Korea. State policies assisted; the Motion Picture Promotion Law of 1995 provided state subsidies to local filmmakers, and four years later the National Assembly enacted a Basic Law for Cultural Promotion to assist film and television production. Then the *chaebol* became involved: Cheil Jedang, a corporate group associated with Samsung, which had until then been primarily known for food processing, formed the CJ entertainment company.

Though they were initially modeled after Japanese J-pop groups, K-pop groups soon developed their own distinctive style that was enormously popular, not just in Korea but throughout Asia. They sang songs while dancing with almost robotic precision. Almost always young and cute, they winked at their adoring fans and flirted with them while performing constantly. Eventually K-pop groups established fan bases worldwide.

South Korean films also scored big hits, with increasingly slick domestic productions doing better than the now-unrestricted flow of Hollywood films at the box office, and became popular throughout Asia. A few directors, such as Park Chan-wook and Kim Ki Duk, won critical acclaim for their artistic and creative films, but most Korean films were pure entertainment. Even more successful were the Korean dramas that came to dominate television in almost every country along the Asia-Pacific rim. So many were watching them that the governments of China and Vietnam limited the number of hours local broadcasters could devote to Korean programs to protect their own industry. Even in spite of such efforts to restrict them, Korean dramas remained wildly popular. The well-produced shows presented beautiful people dealing with situations that other Asians could identify with. The nice homes and settings, not entirely unrealistic among the large, prosperous middle class of Seoul, presented a reachable modernity that Southeast Asians, Chinese, and others could aspire to. The shows were not only popular in Asia, but had large audiences in the Middle East, Latin America, and even Russia.

In the early 2000s the burst of Korean entertainment across Asia was known as the Korean Wave, or *hallyu* in Korean. In 2012, South Korea had become second only to the US as an exporter of entertainment. That milestone year was symbolically represented by the hit video "Gangnam Style" by Korean rapper Park Jaesang—better known by his stage name "Psy." By this time Korea had become "cool," with young people abroad—especially in neighboring Asian countries—imitating Korean hairstyles, clothing, and other fashions. By 2019, the Korean Wave was becoming truly international with the boy group BTS becoming a global sensation.

Koreans were still importers and adapters of entertainment such as Japanese karaoke—a Korean version of which, *noraebang*, became a standard feature of Korean life. They were avid video gamers, and the "PC bangs"—gaming rooms where young, mostly male gamers hung out—could be found in virtually every city neighborhood. Open 24-7, the PC bangs contributed to a serious video-game addiction problem, and eventually special computer-free clinics were established to treat young people who suffered from this illness. Some traditional cultural forms survived as well, such as the Chinese board game *baduk* (also called by its Japanese name, go). *Baduk* had many avid fans, and South Koreans were often the world champions of the game. Taekwondo, a modern form of traditional martial arts, was popular, along with several other martial forms, and the ancient sport of archery still thrived—South Koreans usually dominated this low-profile Olympic event.

Reunion? Reconciliation? Prospects for the Future

In 2017, the new president, Moon Jae-in, was elected on a platform that emphasized domestic issues: the effort to end government-business collusion, anti-corruption, greater transparency, curbing the power of the *chaebol*, improving the inadequate social welfare safety net, narrowing the growing gap between rich and poor, and promoting equitably distributed economic growth, as well as tackling air pollution. He promised a major jobs creation program to deal with unemployment—a growing if still modest problem. Moon, a former student activist and human rights lawyer from Busan, had been Roh Moo-hyun's chief of staff, and was mainly focused on creating greater social justice. His gestures—wearing more informal attire, keeping his modest home in an ordinary middle-class neighborhood, carrying his papers in a backpack, and being addressed informally—were all well-received. They were a clear break from tradition and symbolized a more democratic, open, equitable society.

Although his agenda was mainly centered on domestic issues, he was almost immediately confronted with foreign policy crises. To the east, Xi Jinping was consolidating power to a degree not seen since Mao, while moving China along an authoritarian and aggressively nationalist path. On the other side of the Pacific, America's new president, Donald Trump, seemed less than fully committed to defending South Korea and threatened to end its most-favored nation status, which would harm Korean exports. Nearer to home, Japanese prime minister Abe was pushing Japan in a more nationalist direction.

The biggest problem was North Korea. At first, Moon, who was a supporter of the Sunshine Policy, had no choice but take a hard line on North Korea, which issued bellicose threats, launched missiles, and tested a nuclear weapon. One reversal was on the issue of THAAD (Terminal High Altitude Area Defense) missiles; aimed at shooting down incoming DPRK rockets, they infuriated Beijing, which saw them as a threat. When the Park Geun-hye government had asked the Americans to install them, the Chinese retaliated by banning Chinese travel agents from sending tours to the ROK, a blow to the Korean tourist industry. Moon had opposed the system's deployment, but now he supported it.

Meanwhile, the Korean public, uncertain of the US commitment to the defense of their country despite attempts by Trump administration officials to reaffirm it, and fearing nuclear blackmail by North Korea, began to support the development of defensive nuclear weapons. A late 2017 poll showed that 60 percent wanted South Korea to develop its own nuclear weapons, and 70 percent wanted the US to redeploy tactical nuclear weapons in the ROK—a radical reversal of opinion. With its twenty-four nuclear reactors, South Korea had a large stockpile of nuclear material—enough to build over 4,000 bombs and the technical expertise to build them. But Moon reiterated his opposition to going nuclear. In 2018, Kim Jong Un took a more conciliatory stance, and Moon seized upon the opportunity, meeting Kim along the DMZ and helping to arrange a summit meeting between the North Korean leader and President Trump in Singapore.

The issue of North Korea pointed to the fact that, for all its achievements, South Korea still faced an intractable problem: the division of the country. Reunification had been the dream of almost all Koreans for two generations, but attitudes began to change after they witnessed the example of Germany's reunification in 1990. The general consensus was that Korea's reunification would be similar— the more populous and much wealthier half of the country, the ROK, would absorb the less populated, poorer half. The enormous costs and difficulties involved in the reunification of Germany were truly sobering. West Germany had four times the population of East Germany, while South Korea was only twice as populous as North Korea, and the economic disparity was much greater. North Korea was far poorer and far more isolated than East Germany, so the cost of bringing them up to a comparable standard of infrastructure and income would be far more challenging. Some estimates stated that the cost could exceed three trillion dollars, a staggering amount even for prosperous South Korea.

Furthermore, North Koreans were so isolated from the rest of the world—far more than the East Germans had been—that the task of integrating them into their society would be daunting. This was borne out by experiences with North Korean refugees who made it to the South. At the government-run Hanawon Institute, they had to be taught what a credit card was, how to use the internet, how to drive a car, how to open a bank account. Of course, such things can be learned, but even the refugees—who represented those who rejected the official culture and were enterprising enough to overcome the many obstacles and make it to the ROK—often had problems adjusting. Employers complained that they lacked initiative and were always waiting for orders. These complaints may have reflected prejudice toward North Koreans; still, they suggested assimilation and integration would not be easy.

By the 2010s, many South Koreans were no longer so eager for unification. Most hoped for it someday, but assumed it would be a long-term process taking one or more generations. Younger people in particular had less interest in dealing with what they considered a strange, alien, and backward culture.

The Two Koreas in Historical Perspective

The two Koreas may have moved in radically different directions, yet they share the same historical heritage. Both Koreas emerged from the same Confucian traditions that still influence their societies. They share the same powerful sense of nationalism. Nationalism is a potent force everywhere, but Korea differs from many states in that this national identity is based on a long history of being a geographically, linguistically, ethnically distinct people living in a single political unit. That sense of a common Korean identity is so deeply rooted that even three generations of isolation and hostility are unlikely to undermine it.

The two Koreas have been shaped by their common history. Both societies are characterized by a strong sense of hierarchy and patriarchy, despite espousing ideas of equality. Family and blood ties remain important to both. In North Korea, social status is determined primarily by family background, as had been the case in Korea from the earliest historical times. And the leadership itself was based on the "Paektu bloodline" of the Kim family. In the South, the family-based hierarchical structure is more fluid and subtle, but still can be seen; it is less obvious in politics than in other areas such as business. In fact, the ROK became unique in having a modern industrial economy dominated by some of the world's largest family enterprises.

Both states carried on their long traditions of centralized, bureaucratic rule. Until the system began to fray in the late 1990s, North Korea was arguably the most centralized society in the world; everything from policy decisions to food distribution was decided from the capital. Even South Korea has had very little local autonomy; the very fact that two of five people live in greater metropolitan Seoul reflects the centralized nature of the state. Both Koreas used the powerful states they inherited from premodern and colonial times to carry out state-directed economic development.

Koreans have always been fast learners, eager to acquire knowledge from abroad. In the past they borrowed heavily from China; later from Japan; more recently from the West. In each case they took what they regarded as the best from others and adapted it to their own society: Buddhism, Confucianism, Chinese literary and artistic styles, and then later Japanese and Western concepts of government, economics, and society. The two Koreas continued this tradition, with the North borrowing from Marxism-Leninism, Stalinism, and Maoism, along with some aspects of the Japanese imperial culture, to create its own version of a progressive society. The South borrowed from the United States, prewar and postwar Japan, and the industrial societies of Western Europe to create its own synthesis—a South Korean–style modern, sophisticated society.

Yet for all their common heritage, the two Koreas evolved into very different societies. The division of Korea has been the nation's great modern tragedy. After more than seven decades, most Koreans still tend to think of themselves as one people. The division of their country is regarded as "unnatural"; still, in the late 2010s, there is no obvious pathway to reunification. Nor is it clear to just what extent the two Koreas have become not only two states, but two cultures.

As of 2019, the prospects for Korean reunification do not seem bright. But then Korean history, especially in modern times, has been filled with unexpected turns. Who before 1945 would have predicted the division of this ancient, culturally and ethnically homogeneous land into two such very different societies? It is unlikely that anyone in 1953 would have foreseen North Korea's evolution into a bizarre family-cult state. South Korea's rise in just sixty years from one of the world's poorest to one of its wealthiest and most technologically advanced societies took almost all observers by surprise. Therefore, the only safe prediction is that whatever Korea's future course may be, it will certainly be shaped by its long historical tradition, and most likely won't be boring.

Further Reading

I f you are interested in learning more about Korea, a good place to start is Kyung Moon Hwang's *A History of Korea*. This book is an episodic rather than narrative history of Korea that is readable and filled with insights. Keith Pratt's *Everlasting Flower: A History of Korea* is a readable general history that emphasizes cultural history. My own *A Concise History of Korea: From Antiquity to the Present* is probably the most comprehensive history of Korea published in English, available in two volumes or one combined volume. *Korean History in Maps: From Prehistory to the Twenty-first Century* by Lee Injae, et al, is a beautifully produced collection of maps along with a guide to Korean history. The two-volume *Sources of Korean Tradition* compiled by Peter Lee is a good introduction to the primary sources.

Most of the material on Korea's early history is on the scholarly side, but still worth checking out if you want to know more about Korea's origins. For the history of Goryeo there is Edward Shultz's *Generals and Scholars: Military Rule in Medieval Korea* and Sem Veermersch's translation *A Chinese Traveler in Medieval Korea: Xu Jing's Illustrated Account of the Xuanhe Embassy to Koryŏ*. The books of the late JaHyun Kim Haboush are great sources to delve into the long Joseon period of Korean history. *A Heritage of Kings: One Man's Monarchy in the Confucian World* is highly recommended, as are her two edited collections of private letters—*Epistolary Korea: Letters* and her translated and the annotated *Memoirs of Lady Hyegyŏng*. A recent work by Don Baker and Franklin Rausch, *Catholics and Anti-Catholicism in Chosŏn Korea*, also contains primary sources and a clear readable narrative account of early Catholicism in Korea. Kichung Kim provides an introduction to premodern Korean literature in his *Classical Korean Literature* and Soyoung Lee to its art in *Korean Painting*. *The Korea Journal* (www.ekoreajournal.net) has many accessible articles on premodern Korean history.

By contrast, one can be easily overwhelmed by the publications available on modern Korean history. Michael Robinson's *Korea's Twentieth-Century Odyssey* is a good introduction, especially on the colonial period. Richard Kim's semiautobiographical [?] novel of growing up under Japanese colonial rule, *Lost Names: Scenes from a Korean Boyhood*, vividly depicts this period as well. Helie Lee's *Still Life with Rice* provides a very engaging account of one woman's effort to survive in the turbulent period from colonial repression to the horror of the Korean War. There are so many books on South Korea that it is hard to single out just a few. Daniel Tudor's *Korea: The Impossible Country* is a readable introduction. A large body of more academic works deal with the country's "economic miracle," its democratization, and with social change. John Lie's *Han Unbound: The Political Economy of South Korea* is a useful introduction to the country's rapid transformation. Two news sources, the *Korea Times* (www.koreatimes.co.kr) and the *Korea Herald* (www.koreaherald.com), are both good for keeping up with current events in South Korea.

For North Korea, it is hard to cut through the many foreign policy/nuclear threat books to get to a real understanding of that nation. There are my *North Korea: A History*, Andrei Lankov's *The Real North Korea: Life and Politics in the Failed Stalinist Utopia*, and Adrian Buzo's *The Guerilla Dynasty*. Daniel Tudor's and James Pearson's *North Korea Confidential: Private Markets, Fashion Trends, Prison Camps, Dissenters and Defectors* is a good account of the recent evolution in North Korea. Lankov's *South of the DMZ* provides a wealth of information on life in North Korea, as does Barbara Demick's *Nothing to Envy: Ordinary Lives in North Korea*. Especially valuable are the published accounts by North Korean refugees such as Kang Chol-Hwan's *The Aquariums of Pyongyang: Ten Years in the North Korean Gulag* and Yeonmi Park's *In Order to Live*. Finally, the websites *38th North* (www.38north.org) and *Daily NK* (www.dailynk.com) are useful for keeping up with events in North Korea.

Bibliography

T his book draws upon years of reading about and studying Korean history. The bibliography below leaves out the work of many good historians, including their published articles in English and Korean. It does include books that have been important in shaping my understanding of Korean history and that contain information and insights that have been incorporated in this book.

Armstrong, Charles K. *The North Korean Revolution, 1945–1950.* Ithaca, NY: Cornell University Press, 2003.

———. *Tyranny of the Weak: North Korea and the World, 1950–1992.* Ithaca, NY: Cornell University Press, 2013.

Baker, Don, and Franklin Rausch. *Catholics and Anti-Catholicism in Chosŏn Korea.* Honolulu: University of Hawaii Press, 2017.

Barnes, Gina L. *State Formation in Korea: Historical Archaeological Perspectives.* Richmond, UK: Curzon Press, 2001.

Best, Johnathan W. *A History of the Early Korean Kingdom of Paekche.* Cambridge, MA: Harvard East Asia Center, 2006.

Brazinsky, Gregg. *Nation Building in South Korea: Koreans, Americans, and the Making of Democracy.* Chapel Hill: University of North Carolina Press, 2007.

Breuker, Remco E. *Establishing a Pluralist Society in Medieval Korea, 918–1170: History, Ideology, and Identity in the Koryo Dynasty.* Leiden, Netherlands: Brill, 2010.

Buswell, Robert E. Jr. *Tracing Back the Radiance: Chinul's Korean Way of Zen.* Honolulu: University of Hawaii Press, 1991.

Buzo, Adrian. *The Guerilla Dynasty: Politics and Leadership in the DPRK 1945–1994.* Sydney: Allen & Unwin, 1999.

Byington, Mark E. *Early Korea: Reconsidering Early Korean History through Archaeology.* Cambridge, MA: Korea Institute, Harvard, 2008.

_____, ed. *Early Korea: The Samhan Period in Korean History*. Honolulu: University of Hawaii Press, 2010.

_____, ed. *Early Korea: The Rediscovery of Kaya in History and Archaeology*. Honolulu: University of Hawaii Press, 2012.

_____, ed. *The Han Commanderies in Early Korean History*. Cambridge, MA: Korea Institute, Harvard University, 2013.

Caprio, Mark. *Japanese Assimilation Policies in Colonial Korea, 1910–1945*. Seattle: University of Washington Press, 2009.

Ch'oe Yong-ho. *The Civil Examinations and the Social Structure in Early Yi Dynasty Korea: 1392–1600*. Seoul: Korean Research Center, 1987.

Chung, Young-Iob. *Korea under Siege, 1876–1945: Capital Formation and Economic Transformation*. New York: Oxford University Press, 2006.

Clark, Donald N. *Living Dangerously in Korea: The Western Experience, 1900–1950*. Norwalk, CT: Eastbridge, 2003.

Cumings, Bruce. *Korea's Place in the Sun: A Modern History*. Updated edition. New York: W.W. Norton and Company, 2005.

_____. *The Origins of the Korean War*. Vol. 1, *Liberation and the Emergence of Separate Regimes, 1945–1947*. Princeton, NJ: Princeton University Press, 1981.

_____. *The Origins of the Korean War*. Vol. 2, *The Roaring of the Cataract, 1947–1950*. Princeton, NJ: Princeton University Press, 1990.

De Bary, William Theodore, and JaHyun Kim Haboush, eds. *The Rise of Neo-Confucianism in Korea*. New York: Columbia University Press, 1985.

Demick, Barbara. *Nothing to Envy: Ordinary Lives in North Korea*. New York: Spiegel & Grau, 2015.

Deuchler, Martina. *The Confucian Transformation of Korea: A Study of Society and Ideology*. Cambridge, MA: Council on East Asian Studies, Harvard University, 1992.

Duncan, John B. *The Origins of the Chosŏn Dynasty*. Seattle: University of Washington Press, 2000.

Eckert, Carter J. *Offspring of Empire: The Koch'ang Kims and the Origins of Korean Capitalism*. Seattle: University of Washington Press, 1991.

Gardiner, Kenneth H. J. *The Early History of Korea: The Historical Development of the Peninsula up to the Introduction of Buddhism in the Fourth Century C.E.* Honolulu: University of Hawaii Press, 1969.

Gradjanzev, Andrew H. *Modern Korea.* New York: Institute of Pacific Relations and John Day Company, 1944.

Gragert, Edwin H. *Landownership under Colonial Rule: Korea's Japanese Experience, 1900–1935.* Honolulu: University of Hawaii Press, 1994.

Griffis, William Eliot. *Corea, the Hermit Nation.* 9th ed. New York: AMS Press, 1971.

Haboush, JaHyun Kim. *A Heritage of Kings: One Man's Monarchy in the Confucian World.* New York: Columbia University Press, 1988.

———. *Epistolary Korea: Letters in the Communicative Space of the Chosŏn, 1392–1910.* New York: Columbia University Press, 2009.

———. *The Memoirs of Lady Hyegyŏng: the Autobiographical Writings of a Crown Princess of Eighteenth-Century Korea.* Translated and with an introduction and annotations by JaHyun Kim Haboush. Berkeley, CA: University of California Press, 1996.

Haboush, JaHyun Kim, and Martina Deuchler, eds. *Culture and the State in Late Chosŏn Korea.* Cambridge, MA: Harvard-Hollym, 1999.

Haggard, Stephan, and Marcus Noland. *Famine in North Korea: Markets, Aid, and Reform.* New York: Columbia University Press, 2007.

Han, Sung-joo. *The Failure of Democracy in South Korea.* Berkeley: University of California Press, 1974.

Henderson, Gregory. *Korea: The Politics of the Vortex.* Cambridge, MA: Harvard University Press, 1968.

Henry, Todd A. *Assimilating Seoul: Japanese Rule and the Politics of Public Space in Colonial Korea, 1910–1945.* Berkeley, CA: University of California Press, 2014.

Heo, Uk, and Terrence Roehig. *South Korea's Rise: Economic Development, Power and Foreign Relations.* Cambridge, UK: Cambridge University Press, 2014.

Henthorn, William E. *A History of Korea.* New York: The Free Press, 1971.

Hulbert, Homer. *The Passing of Korea.* Seoul: Yonsei University Press, 1969.

Hwang, Kyung Moon. *A History of Korea.* New York: Palgrave Macmillan, 2010.

Illyŏn. *Samguk Yusa: Legends and History of the Three Kingdoms of Ancient Korea.* Translated by Tae-Hung Ha and Grafton K. Mintz. Seoul: Yonsei University Press, 1972.

Jeon, Sang-woon. *Science and Technology in Korea: Traditional Instruments and Techniques.* Cambridge, MA: MIT Press, 1974.

Kang, Chol-hwan. *The Aquariums of Pyongyang: Ten Years in the North Korean Gulag.* Yair Reiner, trans. New York: Basic Books, 2001.

Kendall, Laurel. *Shamans, Housewives, and Other Restless Spirits.* Honolulu: University of Hawaii Press, 1985.

Kendall, Laurel and Mark Peterson, eds. *Korean Women: View from the Inner Room.* New Haven, CT: East Rock Press, 1983.

Kim, Alexander Joungwon. *Divided Korea: The Politics of Development 1945–1972.* Cambridge, MA: East Asian Research Center, Harvard University Press, 1975.

Kim, Byung-Kook, Ezra Vogel, and Jorge I. Dominguez, eds., *The Park Chung Hee Era: The Transformation of South Korea.* Cambridge, MA: Harvard University Press, 2011.

Kim, Key-hiuk. *The Last Phase of the East Asian World Order: Korea, Japan, and the Chinese Empire, 1860–1882.* Berkeley: University of California Press, 1980.

Kim, Kichung. *Classical Korean Literature.* Armonk, NY: M.E. Sharpe, 1996.

Kim, Suzy. *Everyday Life in the North Korean Revolution. 1945–1950.* Ithaca, NY: Cornell University Press, 2013.

Kim, Richard. *Lost Names: Scenes from a Korean Boyhood.* New York: Praeger, 1970.

Kim, Youngmin, and Michael J. Pettid, eds. *Women and Confucianism in Chosŏn Korea.* Albany: State University of New York Press, 2011.

Koo, Hagen. *Korean Workers: The Culture and Pattern of Class Formation.* Ithaca, NY: Cornell University Press, 2001.

Lankov, Andrei. *North of the DMZ: Essays on Daily Life in North Korea.* Jefferson, NC: McFarland & Company Inc., 2007.

———. *The Real North Korea: Life and Politics in the Failed Stalinist Utopia.* Oxford: Oxford University Press, 2013.

Larsen, Kirk W. *Tradition, Treaties, and Trade: Qing Imperialism and Chosŏn Korea, 1850–1910.* Cambridge, MA: Harvard University Press, 2008.

Lee, Chong-sik. *Park Chung-Hee: From Poverty to Power.* Palos Verdes, CA: KHU Press, 2012.

Lee, Helie. *Still Life with Rice.* New York: Scribner, 1996.

Lee, Injae, Owen Miller, Jinhoon Park, Yi Hyun-Hae and Michael D. Shin, eds. *Korean History in Maps: From Prehistory to the Twenty-first Century.* Cambridge, UK: Cambridge University Press, 2014.

Lee, Ki-baik. *A New History of Korea.* Translated by Edward W. Wagner with Edward J. Shultz. Cambridge, MA: Harvard University Press, 1984.

Lee, Peter H., ed. *Anthology of Korean Literature: From Early Times to the Nineteenth Century.* Honolulu: University of Hawaii Press, 1981.

Lee, Peter H., ed. *A History of Korean Literature.* Cambridge, UK: Cambridge University Press, 2003.

_____, trans. *Lives of Eminent Korean Monks: The Haedong Kosu'ng Cho'n.* Cambridge, MA: Harvard University Press, 1969.

_____, and William Theodore De Bary, eds. *Sources of Korean Traditions.* Vol. 1, *From Early Times Through the Sixteenth Century.* New York: Columbia University Press, 1997; and Choe, Yong-ho and William Theodore De Bary, eds. *Sources of Korean Traditions.* Vol. 2, *From the Sixteenth to the Twentieth Centuries.* New York: Columbia University Press, 2000.

Lee, Soyoung. *Art of the Korean Renaissance, 1400–1600.* New York: The Metropolitan Museum of Art, 2009.

Lewis, James B., ed. *The East Asian War, 1592–1598: International Relations, Violence, and Memory.* London: Routledge, 2015.

Lett, Denise P. *In Pursuit of Status: The Making of South Korea's "New" Urban Middle Class.* Cambridge, MA: East Asian Research Center, Harvard University Press, 1998.

Lie, John. *Han Unbound: The Political Economy of South Korea.* Stanford, CA: Stanford University Press, 1998.

McBride, Richard, II, ed. *State and Society in Middle Silla.* Honolulu: University of Hawaii Press, 2011.

Myers, Brian. *The Cleanest Race: How North Koreans See Themselves—And Why It Matters.* Brooklyn, NY: Melville House, 2010.

Myers, Ramon H., and Mark R. Peattie, eds. *The Japanese Colonial Empire, 1895–1945.* Princeton, NJ: Princeton University Press, 1984.

Nelson, Laura C. *Measured Excess: Status, Gender, and Consumer Nationalism in South Korea.* New York: Columbia University Press, 2000.

Oberdorfer, Donald. *The Two Koreas: A Contemporary History.* New York: Basic Books, Revised Edition, 2013.

Palais, James B. *Politics and Policy in Traditional Korea.* Cambridge, MA: Harvard University Press, 1975.

_____. *Confucian Statecraft and Korean Institutions: Yu Hyŏngwŏn and the Late Chosŏn Dynasty.* Seattle: University of Washington Press, 1996.

_____. *Views on Korean Social History*. Seoul: Institute for Modern Korean Studies, 1998.

Peterson, Mark A. *Korean Adoption and Inheritance: Case Studies in the Creation of a Classic Confucian Society*. Ithaca, NY: East Asia Program, Cornell University, 1998.

Park,Yeomi. *In Order to Live*. New York: Pengiun, 2015.

Pettid, Michael J. *Unyŏng-Jŏn: A Love Affair at the Royal Palace of Chosŏn Korea*. Berkeley, CA: University of California Press, 2009.

Portal, Jane. *Korea: Art and Archaeology*. London: British Museum, 2000.

Pratt, Keith. *Everlasting Flower: A History of Korea*. London: Reaktion Books, 2006.

Pratt, Keith, and Richard Rutt. *Korea: A Historical and Cultural Dictionary*. Richmond, UK: Curzon Press, 1999.

Robinson, David. *Empire's Twilight: Northeast Asia under the Mongols*. Cambridge, MA: Harvard University Press, 2009.

Robinson, Michael E. *Cultural Nationalism in Colonial Korea, 1920–1925*. Seattle: University of Washington Press, 1988.

Schmid, Andre. *Korea Between Empires, 1895–1919*. New York: Columbia University Press, 2002.

Shaw, William. *Legal Norms in a Confucian State*. Berkeley, CA: Institute of East Asian Studies, University of California, Center for Korean Studies, 1981.

Shin, Gi-wook. *Ethnic Nationalism in Korea: Genealogy, Politics, and Legacy*. Stanford, CA: Stanford University Press, 2006.

Shin, Michael D., et al., eds. *Korean History in Maps: From Prehistory to the Twenty-first Century*. Cambridge, UK: Cambridge University Press, 2014.

Shultz, Edward J. *Generals and Scholars: Military Rule in Medieval Korea*. Honolulu: University of Hawaii Press, 2000.

Soh, C. Sarah. *The Comfort Women: Sexual Violence and Postcolonial Memory in Korea and Japan*. Chicago: University of Chicago Press, 2008.

Suh, Dae-sook. *Kim Il Sung: A Biography*. Honolulu: University of Hawaii Press, 1989.

Suh, Jae-Jung, ed. *Truth and Reconciliation in South Korea: Between the Present and Future of the Korean Wars*. London: Routledge, 2014.

Toby, Ronald P. *State and Diplomacy in Early Modern Japan*. Princeton: Princeton University Press, 1984.

Tudor, Daniel. *Korea: The Impossible Country: South Korea's Amazing Rise from the Ashes*. Rutland. VT: Tuttle, 2018.

Tudor, Daniel, and James Pearson. *North Korea Confidential: Private Markets, Fashion Trends, Prison Camps, Dissenters and Defectors*. Rutland. VT: Tuttle, 2015.

Wada Haruki. *The Korean War: An International History*. Lanham, MD: Rowman & Littlefield, 2014.

Wells, Kenneth M. *New God, New Nation: Protestants and Self-Reconstruction Nationalism in Korea, 1896–1937*. Honolulu: University of Hawaii Press, 1990.

Woo, Jung-en. *Race to the Swift: State and Finance in the Industrialization of Korea*. New York: Columbia University Press, 1991.

Xu Jing. *A Chinese Traveler in Medieval Korea: Xu Jing's Illustrated Account of the Xuanhe Embassy to Koryŏ*. Translated, Annotated and with Introduction by Sem Vermeersch. Honolulu: University of Hawaii Press, 2016.

Yi T'oegye and Michael C. Kalton. *To Become a Sage: the Ten Diagrams on Sage Learning*. New York: Columbia University Press, 1989.

Yoo, Theodore Jun. *The Politics of Gender in Colonial Korea: Education, Labor, and Health, 1910–1945*. Berkeley, CA: University of California Press, 2008.

Young, Carl F. *Eastern Learning and the Heavenly Way: The Tonghak and Ch'ŏndogyo Movements and the Twilight of Korean Independence*. Honolulu: University of Hawaii Press, 2014.

Yu Song-Nong. *Book of Corrections: Reflections on the National Crisis during the Japanese Invasion of Korea, 1592–1598*. Translated by Byonghyon Choi. Berkeley, Cal: University of California Press, 2002.

Zhang, Shu Guang. *Mao's Military Romanticism: China and the Korean War, 1950–1953*. Lawrence: University of Kansas Press, 1995.

Index

agriculture, 15–16, 34, 96–98; in North Korea, 135, 149, 159
Agreed Framework, 160, 171
American missionaries, 84
An Junggeun, 89
"Arduous March." *See* famine
aristocracy. See *yangban*
assimilation policy, 99–101

"baby bust," 233
Baektu Mountain. *See* Paektu Mountain
Baekje, 26, 28, 29, 30, 1–32
Balhae, 39–40, 45
Beop, King, 26
Bone-ranks, 27, 34
Buddhism, 33, 36–37, 47, 50, 242; criticism of, 59–60; introduction into Korea, 25–27
Busan, 122
business community, 95
Buyeo, 21
Byeonghan, 19
byungjin policy, 223

Cairo Conference, 109
Censorate, 60–61, 64
chaebol, 183–186, 206, 208–209, 231–232
Chang Myon, 179
Cheondogyo, 92
China, 10, 28–33; influence on Korea, 10,

18–19; intervention in late Joseon Korea, 84–87; intervention in Korean War, 124–127; relations with Korea, 38, 45, 73–77; relations with North Korea, 137, 170–72; relations with South Korea, 113–15
Cho Bongam, 8
Cho Manshik, 102, 110
Choe Changik, 132
Choe Chiwon, 35, 50
Choe Chungheon, 48–50
Choe U, 492
Choi Soon-sil scandal, 229–30
Chun Doo Hwan, 140, 195–97, 200, 209
Chung Ju Yung, 185
Christianity, 81–82, 85, 191, 242; role in democratization, 203
civil examination system, 44, 60, 62
Classics Mat, 60–61
Colonial period, 99–103; economic development during, 95, 106; end of colonial rule, 108–109; legacy of, 105–106; social change, 95–97; wartime period, 98–103
comfort women, 99
commoners, 36, 44, 71–72
communism, 102–103, 104–105
Confucianism, 33, 35, 47, 242; influence on

North Korea, 142; influence on South Korea, 192. *See also* Neo–Confucianism
core class, 144

Daewongun, 82–83
Daewoo, 207–208
Dangun, 13–15, 168
Demilitarized Zone (DMZ), 129, 139
Democratic People's Republic of Korea (DPRK). *See* North Korea
division of Korea, 107–8
Dokdo dispute, 215
dolmens, 16–17
Donghaks, 87

"eastern barbarians," 18
Eastern Expeditionary Headquarters, 52
education: in North Korea, 112–53; in South Korea, 179–80, 219
Eulji Mundeok, 29–30
exile movements, 103–5

Family Law, 217
famine in North Korea, 161–64, 168

Gabo Reforms, 87
Ganghwa Island, 51, 76, 82; Treaty of, 82
Gapshin Coup, 86
Gaya, 23
gender equality, 146, 217–18, 234

General Sherman, 82, 142
geomancy. See *pungsu*
geography of Korea, 8–10, 1, 3
Gija, 14–15
Goguryeo, 19, 24–25, 28–32
Gojong, King, 82, 83, 88–89
Gojoseon, 17–18
Goryeo, 33, 43–55; founding of, 42–43; legacy of, 55–56
government-*chaebol* axis, 206
Great Han Empire, 88
"Great Leap Forward," 135–36
Gungye, 42
Gwanggaeto, 24
Gwangjong, 44
Gwangju Incident, 195–96
Gwansan, Battle of, 1
gwalliso, 150
gwisin (spirits), 73
Gyeongju, 37
Gyeonhwon, 422

hallyu. See Korean Wave
Han peoples, 19–20
Han'guk (name for Korea), 19
Hangul, 11, 63–64
"Hermit Kingdom," 77–78, 4
Hideyoshi, 74
historians, 81–82
hostile class, 144
Hwabaek, 28
Hwaeom Buddhism, 37
Hwang Jini, 69
Hwarang, 28
Hyundai, 185

Ichadon, 27
"IMF Reforms," 208–9
inminban, 149

Incheon Landing (Korean War), 123
Independence Club, 88
Iryeon, 56
Ito Hirobumi, 89

Jaisohn, Philip. *See* Seo Jaepil
Jang Pogo, 41–42
Jang Song Taek, 222
Jangsu, 24
Japan, 10, 52, 82, 83; colonial rule, *see* colonial period; imperialist intrigue in Korea, 83–88; invasion of Joseon Korea, 73–76; investment in South Korea, 177, 183; relationship with Korea 10, 38, 53, 77–78, 177, 183, 215–16; takeover of Korea, 88–90
Japanese pirates, 63
Jeju, 52, 118
Jeon Dae-il, 187
Jeong Dojeon, 57
Jeong Jungbu, 48
Jeong, Mongju, 58
Jeongjo, 78–79
jesa, 67
Jinhan, 19
Jinseon, Queen, 41
Jinul, 50
Joseon (name for Korea), 17
Joseon dynasty, 17, 57–80; founding of, 54
juche, 141, 167
Jumong, 21
Jurchens, 45, 73

Kaesong, 43, 166–67
Kaesong Industrial Complex, 170
KCIA (Korean Central Intelligence Agency), 189

Keolchilbu, 29
Khitans, 45
Kim Chunchu, 29, 33
Kim Bushik, 46
Kim Dae Jung, 170, 188–89, 203–5, 210, 212
Kim Dubong, 111
Kim Gu, 104, 111
Kim Gyushik, 115–16
Kim Hongdo, 79
Kim Jaegyu, 194
Kim Jiha, 220
Kim Sung Kon, 184
Kim Il Sung, 105, 110–11, 118, 120, 122, 142–43, 153; consolidation of power, 124, 131–33; cult of, 111, 141–43
Kim Jeonghui, 80
Kim Jong Il, 143–44, 155, 161, 173, 174, 212; rise to power, 143–4, 161
Kim Jong Nam, 173, 222
Kim Jong Un, 173–74, 222–27; summits with President Trump, 227
Kim Okkyun, 86
Kim Seongsu, 95, 114
Kim Wonju, 96
Kim Woo-jung, 207–8
Kim Young Sam, 194, 203, 204–5
Kim Yushin, 30, 33
kisaeng, 68–69
Koo In-hwoi, 184
Koreagate, 194
Korean alphabet. See Hangul
Korean diaspora, 236
Korean language, 11
Korean People's Army (KPA), 113, 120, 122
Korean Provisional Government, 104
Korean War, 120–27; armistice, 127; impact, 127–29; origins, 119–20